MAHARAJA RANJIT SINGH
LORD OF THE FIVE RIVERS

JEAN-MARIE LAFONT

OXFORD
UNIVERSITY PRESS

Timeless Books

OXFORD
UNIVERSITY PRESS
YMCA Library Building, Jai Singh Road, New Delhi 110 001

Oxford University Press is a department of the University of Oxford. It furthers the University's objective of excellence in research, scholarship, and education by publishing worldwide in

Oxford New York

Auckland Bangkok Buenos Aires Cape Town Chennai
Dar es Salaam Delhi Hong Kong Istanbul Karachi Kolkata
Kuala Lumpur Madrid Melbourne Mexico City Mumbai Nairobi
São Paulo Shanghai Taipei Tokyo Toronto

Oxford is a registered trademark of Oxford University Press in the UK and in certain other countries

Published in India
By Oxford University Press, New Delhi

Timeless Books
46 Housing Society
South Extension – I
New Delhi – 110 049
as part of the
French Sources of Indian History Series

First published 2002
Second impression 2003

ISBN 019 566111 7

Sponsored by the Government of Punjab

Designed & Processed by Benchmark Graphic Pvt. Ltd.

Produced by Ariane Designs Pvt. Ltd.

Printed at Ajanta Offset and Packaging Limited
95-B, Wazirpur Industrial Area, Delhi 110 052

Published by Manzar Khan, Oxford University Press
YMCA Library Building, Jai Singh Road, New Delhi 110 001

Contents

[99] Maharaja Ranjit Singh Bahadur, King of Lahore

[8] Maharaja Ranjit Singh at Ropar in 1831
Oil on canvas. 31 x 36 cm. No date. No signature. Private collection

Parkash Singh Badal

CHIEF MINISTER, PUNJAB

On the occasion of the bicentenary celebrations of coronation of Maharaja Ranjit Singh, The Government of Punjab through the Department of Cultural Affairs, Archaeology and Museums and Archives, Punjab is organizing the exhibition, 'Life and times of Maharaja Ranjit Singh.' The superb collection of priceless artifacts would definitely highlight the political, social and economic history of Punjab during the reign of Maharaja Ranjit Singh. It is a great endeavor to provide the people of Punjab in particular and the country in general, a glimpse of rare paintings housed in museums all over the world through reproductions. I am sure it will leave an everlasting impression on the visitor.

Parkash Singh Badal

[40] The Fort of Lahore
The Sheesh Mahal
Built by Shah Jahan in 1631-32. Renovated by Maharaja Ranjit Singh
Courtesy: Director of Archaeology, Govt. of Pakistan

From the Director's desk

Very seldom do centenary celebrations leave any lasting impression on the generations that stand witness. To make this bicentenary celebration of Maharaja Ranjit Singh's coronation different, the Government of Punjab has taken the bold initiative to collect and display as many objects and reproductions as possible in order to capture the glory of that sovereign and create a memorable imagery of the life and times of Maharaja Ranjit Singh.

The Punjab - home of Sikhism founded by Guru Nanak who preached the almighty as one and indivisible – whose soil is blessed by the sacred blood of Guru Arjun Dev and Guru Teg Bahadur and whose people are infused with the indomitable spirit of Guru Gobind Singh to uphold human dignity, gave birth to a most remarkable man in the year 1780. This diminutive, scar-faced, illiterate chieftain led the destiny of Punjab for some forty years and put an end to the foreign invasions which had been the bane of the Punjab for over a thousand years.

There is no dearth of material on the history of the Punjab, more so, during the period of Maharaja Ranjit Singh in the 18th and the 19th century. Many contemporary accounts, both Indian and foreign, have given graphic descriptions of the political and cultural history of that time. But few in the present generation are aware of this splendid era since immediately after the annexation of the Punjab, its cultural treasures got scattered all over the world.

Dr. Jean-Marie Lafont, the French historian, was entrusted with the task of curating this exhibition and writing its catalogue. He has done a commendable work within a very short span of time. He composed the exhibition by collecting artifacts from sources which had not been tapped so far and presented them through brilliant reproductions, some of which will be on display (and in print) for the first time, supplemented by explanatory panels, maps and captions. The thoroughness of his research and the technical competence in selecting and presenting his material is likely to win him wide appreciation. The French connection of the Sikh Kingdom prominently projected in the exhibition is fascinating. Dr. Lafont has sought to cast a more intimate light on the relations of the Maharaja with the French which hitherto have remained little noticed. I am sure, the collection and display will enchant the visitor and leave a deep emotional impact.

On behalf of the Government of the Punjab and the Department of Cultural Affairs, I express gratitude to all those who have contributed and assisted to make the event a success.

Inderjit Singh Sandhu
Director, Cultural Affairs
Archaeology & Museums, Punjab

Preface

The Government of Punjab has decided to celebrate on a befitting scale the bicentenary coronation of Maharaja Ranjit Singh. One of the events is an Exhibition cum Catalogue on the life and times of Maharaja Ranjit Singh. The Exhibition is to open in the Rambagh Palace at Amritsar, renovated for this purpose, on 13 November 2001, two hundred years after Sahib Singh Bedi applied the saffron mark on Maharaja Ranjit Singh's forehead as a symbol of kingship.

I was formally requested on 24th April 2001 to prepare the exhibition and start writing the catalogue. The challenge was great, especially because of the acute shortage of time which eliminated any possibility to borrow items from abroad, where most of the masterpieces of the Punjab kingdom, such as the golden throne, the illuminated manuscripts and especially the Koh-i-noor and the other Jewels of the Crown from the *toshakhana* of the Lahore fort, were dispersed after the annexation of the country in 1849.

It was decided to exhibit the most of what is preserved in India, and to reproduce photographically whatever we could from museums and other institutions abroad. Mr. Inderjit Singh Sandhu, Director, Department of Culture, and I started composing lists of what could be used for the exhibition. A trip to France in the month of June and another one to Lahore in early July enabled me to photograph in person or to order photographic reproductions of documents kept there in public and private archives. Coming back from Lahore on 16th July I received in Amritsar the third and last list of items identified by the Director, Department of Culture, Government of Punjab. It was then possible to have a first exciting concept of what the exhibition could be.

The initial idea had been of about a hundred items presenting the life and times of Maharaja Ranjit Singh displayed on one floor of the Rambagh Palace. The documentation was so rich and expansive, however, that we considered the possibility of exhibiting nearly three hundred items and panels spread over the three levels of the Museum, and for this display to become the permanent exhibition on Maharaja Ranjit Singh. The Punjab Government subsequently decided to upgrade and embellish this catalogue in order to have a beautiful publication to accompany the exhibition.

There have recently been two major exhibitions on Sikh history and culture. The first, entitled *The Arts of the Sikh Kingdoms*, was held in the Victoria and Albert Museum in London for the tercentenary of the Khalsa, and it focused on the Sikh community and the Sikh states, both the Punjab Kingdom and the cis-Sutlej or Phulkian states. Its large panorama included much of Mughal, late Mughal and early British items, from arms to textiles to miniature paintings. Since that exhibition, which travelled to Canada and the USA, could not come to India, the Government of India asked Professor B.N. Goswamy to organize in the National Museum, New Delhi, an exhibition entitled *Piety and Splendour. Sikh Heritage in Art*, which also covered the whole span of Sikh history on both sides of the Sutlej. Its beautiful catalogue brings out a wealth of new documents from India.

The scope of the present exhibition is limited to the kingdom of the Punjab under Maharaja Ranjit Singh (1799-1839), and we did our best to limit ourselves to that period without covering the difficult decade (1839-1849) which saw the disintegration of the state and its absorption into the British Raj. The introduction, nevertheless, is an attempt to put the achievements of Maharaja Ranjit Singh in the perspective of a century-old, nay a millenary-old Punjabi culture and ethos whose origins can be traced in the first civilised settlements discovered in the Land of the Five (or the Seven...) Rivers. Of course, I am not expecting a consensus on this particular analysis. We are glad to present and illustrate splendid manifestations of artistic life in Maharaja Ranjit Singh's Punjab. We were not deterred from exhibiting and sometimes reproducing less flamboyant items, such as manuscripts without miniature paintings, miniature paintings less exquisite than the great masterpieces of the Punjab kingdom and lithographs like the ones coming from Honigberger's *Twenty-Five Years in the East*. It is important to know that simple copies of the *Bhagavat Puran* or the *Shiv Puran* were copied repetitively at Lahore for the spiritual welfare of the Hindu community.

The main focus of the exhibition is on Maharaja Ranjit Singh's dynamism in attempting to create a state within the limits of the five rivers, and then expand and modernize it to consolidate its structures and assure its survival in a particularly hostile environment. The history of the Indian states between the fall of the Mughal Empire and the paramountcy of the British Raj is too often considered as a static, uneventful period of Indian history, in spite of the turmoils and internecine feuds recorded in the chronicles – as if the destiny of millions of people had evolved in a kind of vacuum "between Empires", waiting for a new Imperial power to emerge and submerge them. Had it not been for the simultaneous growth of the British power, Maharaja Ranjit Singh might have changed the course of history in the subcontinent. Nevertheless he won his way to distinction and greatness.

Maharaja Ranjit Singh was the last great Indian ruler who modernized his state in an effort to create a place for it in the concert of nations. In an exceptional effort to unite all the people in his kingdom, he included members of the various ethnic, linguistic and religious communities in his *darbar*, administration and army. He looked for talent beyond his frontiers : in Afghanistan, whence his first great Finance Minister came, in an India whose map had almost entirely "turned red" and where natives could not expect much prominence under a foreign government, and in even more distant lands, other *wilayats*, recruiting the French and Italian officers he employed from 1822 onwards to systematically modernise his military forces.

The army and its commanders were the servants of the Maharaja in an all-encompassing policy of restorating peace and prosperity to a land regularly devastated by invasions from Iran and Afghanistan since 1738, a land where communal harmony had been severely impaired for almost two centuries. We wish to emphasize the dynamism of Ranjit Singh's policy in the fields of agriculture and trade as well, but also consider the energy he invested in the construction of monuments all over the kingdom, and the inspiration he gave to unknown, highly talented artists to decorate the palaces, residences, gardens and temples which flourished in the Punjab in the 1820's and 1830's. Several artistic schools developed under the kind patronage of the Maharaja and his courtiers, including the *farenghis*. Artists from abroad travelled to Amritsar and Lahore to see and put on canvas the grandeur of his *darbar* or the spectacle of Ranjit Singh listening to the *granthis* in the Golden Temple or the more intimate view of Fezli Azamjoo, General Court's wife, sitting in her Naulakha residence at Lahore, with their two eldest children.

In 1830 Ranjit Singh was amazed to learn that the tomb of Sikandar's horse may have been discovered in a small place called Manikyala, near Rawalpindi. I think it is important to note that the Maharaja's curiosity was aroused by archaeology as well –later he was elected an honorary member of the Asiatic Society of Paris. A full section of the exhibition is devoted to these archaeological activities in the Punjab kingdom, and the geological exploration of the Himalayas by Victor Jacquemont in 1831 which was possible only because Ranjit Singh aided him financially and gave him the necessary protection to travel in some of the remotest areas of his kingdom. Jacquemont's work on botany was echoed by the *Materia Medica* that Dr. Martin Honigberger, a Austro-Hungarian physician personally attached to Ranjit Singh since 1829, collected with the help of the Fakir brothers and prepared for publication.

To prepare this exhibition and catalogue in the span of a couple of months has been a real challenge. I could not obtain all I wanted, and in more than one case some information (size, number of pages of illustrations, sometimes even reference of items or English translations of Persian inscriptions on recently discovered arms) is missing in the captions. I apologize to the scholars, and I accept full responsibility for the shortcomings of the present volume. I invite you to look upon the charming visage of Fezli Azamjoo, reproduced here for the first time, and to enjoy the view of the beautiful butterflies which were flying in the meadows of her native Kashmir in the sunny summer of 1831.

Jean-Marie Lafont

October 2001

Acknowledgements

It is a pleasure to express my gratitude to Sardar Parkash Singh Badal, Chief Minister, and the Government of Punjab for the help they provided in preparing this exhibition.

I am especially indebted for this book and exhibition to the friendly and understanding help of Sardar Trilochan Singh. We have been discussing for years Maharaja Ranjit Singh and his achievements. This enlightened sovereign had an uncanny way to detect talent and use it for the benefit of his kingdom. Sardar Trilochan Singh was instrumental in forwarding the idea of this exhibition to the Bicentenary Committee and in helping to resolve the various problems which arose during its preparation.

Dr. Brajendra Singh, Principal Secretary, and Mr. Inderjit Sandhu, Director, Cultural Affairs, set up a Committee comprising of Mr. L.S. Sodhi, curator, Mr. Ranjit Singh, photographer, and Mr. Mohan Singh who helped in collecting and describing a number of items out of which we made a selection according to the themes of the exhibition. Many documents come from the Maharaja Ranjit Singh Museum, Amritsar, whose keeper Mr. Raman and staff have extended to us facilities for working there. The directors and staff of the Punjab State Archives at Patiala, the Government Museum and Art Gallery at Chandigarh, the Central Sikh Museum at Amritsar are among the institutions in Punjab whose contribution have made this exhibition possible. Mr. Devi Saran, Superintendent, Cultural Affairs, Punjab, and Mr. Jasbir Singh, Assistant, Department of Cultural Affairs, Punjab, have worked tirelessly for this project.

Dr. Sukumar Sarkar, Director General, National Archives of India, replied to our requests with his usual generosity and efficiency. Dr. R.D. Chowdhary, Director General, National Museum, New Delhi, as well as Dr. R.R.S. Chauhan, Assistant-Director, and Drs. A.K. Das, Naseem Akhtar and Daljeet, gave us all the required assistance. The Asiatic Society of Calcutta, through the kindness of Professor Aniruddha Ray, has kindly accepted to send us some photographs of the *Ain-i-Akbari* in their possession. The Shiromani Gurudwara Parbandhak Committee gave us the slides of four items from the *Toshakhana* and three from the Central Sikh Museum, Harmandir Sahib. Mrs. Jyoti Ray has kindly shared with us her deep knowledge of numismatics in Punjab under Maharaja Ranjit Singh, and wrote the captions of the coins shown or reproduced in the exhibition

Madame Colette Caillat is the person who introduced me to Sanskrit studies and Indian history. Mildred Archer, who spent a month with us in Delhi in early 1987, was the kindling spirit of my interest in painting in the subcontinent. Years later, after meeting with Barbara Schmitz, discussions focused more closely on Islamic painting and then Punjabi miniatures. Hopefully they will mature into some common publications in the near future.

In Pakistan, Fakir Syed Aijazuddin was most efficient in getting us permission to reproduce items from the Lahore Museum and in obtaining the ektachromes. The Department of Archaeology, Government of Pakistan, through Dr. Sarwat Beg kindly gave us the permission to reproduce the two paintings of August Schoefft in the Princess Bamba Collection as well as items of the *Fauj-i-khas* from the Sikh Gallery of the Lahore Fort. Dr. Muhammad Iqbal Bhutta helped us get the necessary permissions. Colin David, the well-known artist, as well as Rukhsana, Mark and Karen David have been most helpful at various stages for the preparation of the exhibition.

A few but significant reproductions come from England. I prefered to illustrate in this book the replica of the Koh-i-noor, since only the replica is now in India. But the British Library kindly allowed the reproduction of King Louis-Philippe's letter to Maharaja Ranjit Singh, and the Department of Coins and Medals sent me the ektachromes and slides of items discovered by Generals Ventura and Court at Manikyala. I am extremely grateful to Elizabeth Errington and Joe Cribb for their generosity, and to Rosie Llewellyn-Jones for rediscovering the letter of Louis-Philippe and personally bringing the ektachrome from London to Delhi.

This exhibition in Amritsar brings for the first time to Punjab the reproduction of paintings and items which belonged to the French officers who served in the Punjab army and are now kept in French private and public collections. As usual, the Musée d'arts asiatiques Guimet, Paris, gave me their consent for reproducing the miniature paintings of Imam Bakhsh Lahori and the frontispiece of the *Mémoires* of General Court. I express my deep gratitude to Jean-François Jarrige, Directeur Général, Pierre Cambon and Amina Okada, Conservateurs en Chef. The Bibliothèque nationale allowed the reproduction of the bronze mask of Shiva and Allard's collection of coins through the kindness of Michel Amandry, Conservateur Général, François Thierry, Conservateur en Chef, and Thierry Collin. Osmund Bopearachchi helped me in selecting the coins. The Museum d'histoire naturelle (Paris) gave me every facility to go again through the Jacquemont papers and select whatever we needed for the exhibition : Monique Ducreux, Conservateur Général, Pascale Heurtel, Librarian, and Véronique van de Ponseele did their very best to send me quickly the photographs of the selected documents. At Château-Thierry Christiane Sinnig-Haas, Conservateur en Chef, showed me again the miniature paintings of Imam Bakhsh Lahori for the La Fontaine *Fables*, and gave me permission to reproduce them. I thank her and the Museum staff for the warm welcome extended to me during my short stay at Château-Thierry.

It is my duty but also my pleasure to acknowledge the French authorities who allow me to stay and work in India on the history of Indo-French relations. The Ministry of Foreign Affairs of course, and H.E. M. Bernard de Montferrand, Ambassador of France in India. I am also indebted to Ambassadors Philippe Petit and Claude Blanchemaison as well as to Vincent Grimaud and Pierre Barroux for my stay here. I owe my gratitude to the DGRCST, Ambassador Serge Degallaix, Yves Saint Geours, Jean-Claude Jacq, Francine d'Orgeval, and to Dr. Frédéric Grare, Director of the Centre for Human Sciences, New Delhi. The Ministry of Education, especially Catherine Bizot and Christian Dupavillon, and INALCO, mainly Président André Bourgey, Président Gilles Delouche and Professor Eric Meyer, have every year taken the necessary steps to help me work on this almost forgotten, but most important aspect of Indo-French relations. I am grateful to all of them because they gave me the opportunity to reply positively to the request of the Punjab Government.

Many friends helped in some way or the other : H.H. Brigadier Sukhjit Singh (MVC), Maharaja of Kapurthala, for his stimulating exchange of views for the last twenty-five years. Colonel Henri Switzer intervened at a critical juncture to obtain some documents from France. Sardar Narinderjit Singh's hospitality in Amritsar made us feel at home there, while in France the Prévost-Allard family, Henri, Josiane and Frédéric, have always received us warmly and as members of their own family.

Mr. Inderjit Singh Sandhu has been following this project from the time it was proposed by the Punjab Government till the last item arrived in Amritsar and was installed in the renovated Maharaja Ranjit Singh Museum. He carefully read the manuscript and suggested several amendments which have improved the text. I am grateful for his help, kindness and perspicacity. It is obvious that any shortcoming, errors and mistakes are mine.

My wife Rehana incarnates for me the extraordinarily rich and diverse heritage of the subcontinent. She brought me from *wilayat* to her native Punjab and helped me to discover and appreciate the generosity and splendour of the Land of the Five Rivers, its culture and people. Without her, I would not have spent almost thirty years of my life working on the Punjab and Indo-French relations. This exhibition and book are a common endeavour : she read and transformed the first draft of this text into a readable volume which is now offered to the public.

To her and to our sons, Jean-François, Olivier and Xavier, this book is dedicated.

Jean-Marie Lafont

October 2001

Chronology of Punjab history

540-327 B.C.	Western Punjab part of the Persian empire
327-325 B.C.	Alexander of Macedonia/ Sikandar
325-303 B.C.	Western Punjab part of the Seleucid [Greek] empire
303- c. 180	B.C. Punjab part of the Mauryan empire Chandragupta Maurya, Ashoka Spread of Buddhism
180 B.C.-10 A.D.	Western Punjab under the Indo-Greeks Menander. Antialcidas
0	Foundation of Lahore by Lah, Lava, Loh or Low, son of Rama
30-385 A.D.	Punjab part of the Kushan empire
120-146	Huvishka, Kanishka
606-647	East Punjab under Harsha Visit of Hiuen Tsang, Chinese pilgrim
999-1195	Ghaznavid and Ghorid dynasties Mahmud Ghaznavi
1195-1526	Afghan and Turkish empires in North India
1469-1539	Guru Nanak
1526-1540	First phase of the Mughal empire with Babur, Kamran Mirza, Humayun
1540-1555	Suri dynasty. Fort of Rohtas
1555-1799	Punjab part of the Mughal Empire
1577	Foundation of Amritsar
1588	Foundation of the Harmandir
1799-1849	Kingdom of Punjab

Chronology of Maharaja Ranjit Singh's life

1780	13th November. Birth of Budh Singh, whose name is changed by his father to Ranjit Singh
1792	Death of Mahan Singh, Ranjit Singh's father. Accession of Ranjit Singh
1795	Ranjit Singh married Mahtab Kaur, daughter of Sada Kaur
1798	Last invasion of the Punjab by Shah Zaman of Kabul
1797	George Thomas, an Irish adventure, settles at Hansi, threatens Punjab
1799	Ranjit Singh takes Lahore. Contacts with French officers of Sindhia George Thomas invades the cis-Sutlej states
1801	Coronation of Ranjit Singh George Thomas threatens Ludhiana
1802	George Thomas surrenders to Bourquien Exchange of turbans between Ranjit Singh and Fateh Singh Ahluwalia Birth of Prince Kharak Singh Ranjit Singh takes Amritsar Ranjit Singh marries Moran Mission from Perron and Bourquien, French commanders, to Ranjit Singh
1805	British army on the Beas, pursuing Holkar Visit of Ranjit Singh to Lord Lake's camp
1806	Treaty of friendship between the English, Ranjit Singh and Fateh Singh Gurkha occupation of Kangra
1807	Ranjit Singh captures Kasur Birth of Princes Sher Singh and Tara Singh Treaty of Tilsit between Napoleon and Tsar Alexander I English fear of a Franco-Russian invasion of India
1808	Metcalfe's mission to Lahore for a defensive Anglo-Sikh alliance Capture of Pathankot
1809	British troops on the Sutlej, capture Ludhiana Treaty of Amritsar Protection of the Cis-Sutlej states by the British against Lahore Ranjit Singh acquires Kangra Conquest of Jammu Shah Shuja-ul-Mulk expelled from Afghanistan

1810	British Agency at Ludhiana Annexion of Wazirabad by Ranjit Singh
1812	Colonel Ochterlony at Lahore for the wedding of Prince Kharak Singh Sikh-Afghan invasion of Kashmir Shah Suja-ul-Mulk arrives at Lahore Ranjit Singh acquires Attock
1813	13 July. Victory over the Afghans at Chuch, near Attock
1813	Ranjit Singh gets the Koh-i-noor from Shah Shuja-ul-Mulk
1814	Shah Shuja-ul-Mulk settles at Ludhiana under British protection
1815-16	Conquest of Cis-Indus territories
1818	Ranjit Singh captures Multan
1819	Ranjit Singh captures Kashmir
1821	Ranjit Singh captures the Derajat, Rawalpindi and Mankera Birth of Prince Nau Nihal Singh
1822	Affair of Wadhni. Sikhs defeated by the British Allard and Ventura, French and Italian officers, arrive in Lahore Creation of the *Fauj-i-khas* Gulab Singh appointed Governor of Jammu
1823	Wade appointed Assistant Political Agent at Ludhiana 13 March. Victory of Naushera on the Afghans. Death of Phula Singh Akali
1826	Maharaja Ranjit Singh unwell. Dr. Murray's visit to Lahore
1827	*Jihad* of Syed Ahmed Barelvi against "the Sikhs". Repulsed at Akora Punjabi mission to Lord Amherst at Simla Captain Wade on a mission to Lahore Court and Avitabile, French and Italian officers, arrive in Lahore
1829	Dr. Martin Honigberger, Austro-Hungarian physician, arrives in Lahore
1830	Syed Ahmed Barelvi occupies Peshawar but defeated by Hari Singh Nalwa and Allard
1831	Syed Ahmed defeated and killed at Balakot by Prince Sher Singh 25 October : Meeting at Ropar between Ranjit Singh and W. Bentinck Alexander Burnes in Lahore Victor Jacquemont in Punjab for a geological survey of the Himalayas
1832	Treaty on the Navigation on the Indus between Lahore and Calcutta Ranjit Singh's designs on Shikarpur and Sindh thwarted by the English
1833	Secret treaty between Ranjit Singh and Shuja-ul-Mulk to restore him in Kabul
1834	Shuja-ul-Mulk defeated by Dost Mohammed Khan Capture and annexion of Peshawar by Ranjit Singh General Zorawar Singh starts the conquest of Ladakh for Raja Gulab Singh General Allard gets leave to go to France
1835	Aborted attempt by Dost Mohammed Khan to reconquer Peshawar Ranjit Singh marries Rani Jindan

1837 - March	Wedding of Prince Nau Nihal Singh General Fane, Commander-in-Chief, at Lahore General Allard returns to Lahore as Agent de France
1837 - April	Afghan attack on Jamrud and Peshawar. Death of Hari Singh Nalwa Vitkievitch Russian envoy to Kabul : Afghanistan under Russian protection Peshawar to be given back to Afghanistan
1838	Mission of Macnaghten to Lahore
1838 - June	Tripartite Treaty between Calcutta, Lahore and Shah Shuja-ul-Mulk Birth of Prince Dalip Singh
1838 - Dec	Ranjit Singh and Auckland meeting at Ferozepur
1839 - 27 June	Death of Maharaja Ranjit Singh

[36] Sword of Maharaja Ranjit Singh
Full length 32". Golden hilt studded with rubies and emeralds. Velvet scabbard with gold work
Entered in the *Toshakhana* register dated 3.10.97 at page 2, Sr. N° 24 under the title "Jalao Sri Harmandir Sahib"
Courtesy: Shiromani Gurudwara Parbandhak Committee

I

History of Punjab, Maharaja Ranjit Singh

Punjab

Punjab has been, as far as memory goes, a confluence of culture at the crossroad of civilisations, an area where people, acting under their own talented reflection and reacting to external impetus, have evolved original systems of thinking and created brilliant synthesis. A land open to passage and migration - geography is an unavoidable ingredient of history - but also a place from where people migrated, carrying with them their culture and know-how. Harrapan seals and potteries are found far away from present day Punjab and Sindh, while Shortugai in north-east Afghanistan is clearly an off-shoot of the capital city of Harappa. Much closer to our time - but going far back in history - the monastery of Jogis known as the Tilla Gorakh Nath, on the peak of Tilla (3200 feet high) twenty miles west of Jhelum, was one of the oldest religious institutions in northern India. Cunningham connected it to some story of Alexander the Great while Abul Fazl observed in the *Ain-i-Akbari* that it was held in veneration by all the *fakirs* of Hindustan. The 1904 edition of the District Gazetteer of Jhelum acknowledged the fact that the Jogis still kept up relations with branches in Nepal and Afghanistan. Moreover since time immemorial pilgrims from the Indian subcontinent crossed Punjab and Sindh on their way to Bakou to worship in the fire temple, and they are still mentioned going there in the 1830's. Mohan Lal Kashmiri has left us succinct but interesting information on the Indian and Punjabi diaspora in Afghanistan and Central Asia in the 1830's, of their involvement in trade and the eminent positions some of its members held in the local governments.

Religion and culture are rarely encompassed and constrained by political frontiers and natural boundaries. Yet their spread and evolution is often greatly enhanced by imperial structures facilitating the exchange of goods and the travel of people and ideas. These empires in fact rest on an elaborate network of civil administrators and military officers coming from all over the empire and serving in each corner of it. This is not the place to detail the history of Punjab under Persian, Greek, Mauryan, Indo-Greek, Indo-Scythian and Kushana rules, which form about a millenium (c. 540 BC-450 AD) of the collective memory of the populations. But the Persians definitely had precise geographical delimitations of their satrapies in northern India, even if it was only for collecting tribute and levying troops. After conquering the four doabs, it seems that Alexander the Great was ready to cross the Hyphasis (Beas) which formed the border of the Persian empire and move towards the Sutlej and the Jamuna, into less delimited and little-known terrritories, when his army refused to go further. The altars he erected and consecrated with grand festivities on the Beas confirmed a frontier well established for the last two centuries.

In 303 BC Seleucos ceded by treaty to Chandragupta Maurya precisely defined satrapies, from Kapisa to Arachosia, which the Indo-Greeks reoccupied in c. 180 BC. To describe the administration of the Mauryan empire, especially in the north-west areas, as similar, mutatis mutandis, to the administrative system in force under the British Raj is not driving us very far. We guess that the Indo-Greek kingdoms (c. 180 BC-10 AD), just

[252] **Bronze mask of Lord Shiva discovered by General Court at Peshawar**

like the Greek cities and states in the west, were more or less geographically defined entities economically united by one single standard of currency, yet distinguished by beautiful issues of coins struck with the portrait of each individual sovereign and carrying a bilingual inscription in Greek and Kharoshthi, giving the sovereign's name, his official titles and sometimes the place of the mint. Some day, no doubt, we shall be able to make a rather precise map of these Indo-Greek kingdoms which ruled over Kapisa, Gandhara and western Punjab for almost two centuries.

[249] Gold coin of Huvishka discovered in Punjab
Bibliothèque nationale. Cabinet des médailles. Acc. N° L 547

What became of these fairly precise administrative divisions under the Kushans we know not. Neither do we know the exact organisation of eastern Punjab under the rule of Harsha (606-647 AD). More important than the delimitation of frontiers and local policy are the intense intellectual and artistic activities which developed in these areas following the cultural encounter of a highly civilised Indian milieu with Central Asian, Iranian and Greek systems of thinking and aesthetic values. Punjab was the country of Panini, the celebrated author of the *Ashtadhyayi* and the father of Sanskrit grammar, who was born near Attock on the Indus river. As we have said, the Jogis of Tilla attracted pilgrims from all over the subcontinent. Under its various sects and denominations, Hinduism flourished and the cult of Krishna (and Balarama) was well developed in Taxila in the 2nd century BC. But Punjab was also the place - one of the places - where Buddhism spread at least from the time of Ashoka, where it attracted considerable attention from the rulers and the ruled alike and where it evolved into the Mahayana school under the influence of Greece, Iran and Turan through the meditation and reflection of vigorous and creative thinkers, who remain anonymous. The flamboyant development of Gandhara or Graeco-Buddhist art (whatever remains today of its architecture, sculpture and painting) is another proof of the artistic genius of the local people - devout donors like kings and merchants but also men and women from all walks of life - sponsoring artists and interacting with monks and high-profile metaphysicians living in the great monasteries around Taxila, Takht-i-bahi, Pushkalawati, Jellalabad or Hadda.

[250] Gold coin of Kanishka II discovered by Generals Allard and Ventura
Bibliothèque nationale.
Cabinet des médailles. Acc. N° AF (don Allard)

We do not lack evidence concerning the multi-ethnic, multi-cultural and multi-religious composition of the Punjab population from 6th century BC to the 7th century AD and we just have to turn to epigraphic evidence to have a rough idea of languages and scripts archaeologically attested in these areas from the 3rd century BC : the inscriptions of Ashoka in the doab (Meerut) and east Punjab (Topra, near Ambala) are in Brahmi script, those of Shahbazgarhi (Peshawar district) and Mansehra (Hazara) in northern Pakistan in Kharoshthi, the edicts of Kandahar (Afghanistan) in Greek and Aramaic. In an inscription of Kanishka discovered at Rabatak (Baghlan, Afghanistan) in 1993, the Emperor stated that in the year 1 of his reign (c. 120 AD) he first issued this edict in Greek and then turned it into "Aryan", which in that case is Bactrian, but still written with the Greek alphabet. The inscription of the bronze mask of Shiva (5th/6th century AD), discovered by General Court at Peshawar in 1834 [n° 252 and 253], remained undeciphered till 1990, when the study of the Gilgit and Bamyan manuscripts helped scholars decode this broken Sanskrit written in a broken Brahmi script.

[251] Silver coin of Antialcidas discovered by Generals Allard and Ventura
Bibliothèque nationale. Cabinet des médailles. Acc. N° OB 36

The question of whether Chandragupta Maurya, founder of the first Indian empire, was a "Punjabi" has been discussed from time to time. The posting of his grandson Ashoka

[244] The Stupa of Manikyala today

as viceroy at Taxila is attested by several sources: sometimes he is also credited with the construction of the first Grand Trunk Road running from Taxila to Pataliputra (Patna). Whatever it is, the Ashokan edicts are an interesting proof of the peculiar dynamism of the local Buddhist population in following Ashoka's instructions to sent missionaries to preach the Law of deliverance far beyond what we consider the geographical frontiers of the subcontinent. We shall not discuss here how the missions sent to five Greek kings of Occident, including Ptolemaueus of Egypt and Magas of Cyrene (Libya), reached their destinations and influenced Hellenistic philosophy and western civilization. But the expansion of Buddhism (Mahayana) in Central Asia, China and Japan is in itself an extraordinary religious and cultural adventure, with its specific architecture of stupas and monasteries spreading all over Central Asia and the Taklamakan desert, the gigantesque statues carved in the rocks and an extraordinary network of monastic cells and chapels linked with hair-raising flights of stairs carved in the cliffs.

The diffusion of Mahayana Buddhism - from Bamyan to Tun Huang and the Caves of the Thousand Buddhas on the Chinese border, and then through China to Korea, Japan and the Pacific ocean - had its first impulsion when the Buddhist communities of Kandahar, Taxila, Peshawar, Jellalabad and Begram carried out Ashoka's instructions. The results in the 21st century AD could hardly have been foreseen either by the emperor or by the first Buddhist missionaries who started their journey northward through the Gilgit, Khyber and Salang passes.

Centuries later, Chinese pilgrims started travelling to India on the traces of the Buddha. Fa-Hian in 400 AD, Sung Yun in 518 AD and Hiuen Tsang in 625 AD left China to visit the "western world" and they wrote descriptions of their travels and pilgimages to the cities and holy places of India. Hiuen Tsang, one of the most erudite and attaching personalities who ever travelled in the subcontinent, was also the most prolific. He visited Kapiça (Begram-Kabul), Laghman, Jellalabad, Gandhara (Peshawar), Taxila, Swat and Kashmir, recording the traditions of the Buddha's travels and miracles, describing the relics, recalling the gifts and foundations of Ashoka and Kanishka and the destructions of Mihirakula. After that, his journey brought him to the Punjab plains, and in his autobiography he explains that after leaving Sakala (630 AD) he crossed the frontier of the kingdom of Takka, where he reached a large Brahmanical town with thousands of inhabitants which Beal identifies with Lahore. He then proceeded to the capital of the Chinapati country which Cunningham situated eleven miles north of Amritsar, and Beal on the site of Kasur.

While Hiuen Tsang was describing the Buddhist monasteries and stupas with their glittering golden Buddhas and Boddhisatvas worshipped by thousands of monks and believers, Islam rose in Arabia. The expansion of Islam is a well-documented, well-known part of world history. Ibn Tariq crossed over the Gibraltar strait in 711 AD and the Muslim armies conquered Spain in a couple of years. Ibn Qasim took Dewal / Daibul in 712 and the conquest of Sindh was also completed in a couple of years. The maximal extension of the *Dar-ul-Islam* was in the 1680's, when the Ottoman armies besieged Vienna but failed to capture it in 1683, and when Aurangzeb started his Deccan campaign (1681) which failed in the face of the Maratha resistance. There is also, in the east and west, a striking similarity in the way the Muslim empires had to fall back on the core of their "Islamized" territories stretching in a long line from Central Asia to the Middle East and the Maghreb. The vast provinces which for a long time had been part of the *Dar-ul-Islam*, but whose populations had not been converted to Islam - Spain and eastern Europe in the west, India in the east - traced their own course with a more or less sizeable Muslim population scattered all over their territories. At the time Maharaja Ranjit Singh was fighting the *jihad* of Syed Ahmed Barelvi on the Indus and fearing renewed Iranian and Afghans invasions of Punjab, the Greeks had set up their government at Patras and were fighting the Ottoman armies for their own survival. But most contemporary historians do not like these general surveys because of their obvious simplifications.

[200] Shahnama of Firdausi
Scribe: Tavakal Beg
Copied in 1653
400 folios. 65 illustrations
Punjab State Archives. Acc. N° 363

To come back to Punjab, the Islamic conquest of northern India was a slow and difficult process. For more than two centuries the various Rajput principalities managed to contain the new power in Sindh. In his *Golden Meadows* Masudi wrote about the role of the Surya Temple of Multan in the bargain between the Muslim governors of Sindh and their Hindu neighbours. In 1001 Mahmud Ghaznavi defeated Jaipal near Peshawar, and the *Kitab-i-Yamini* of Utbi tells the tale of Mahmud's successive invasions of northern India. Lahore was taken in 1036, but the "Muslim" foundation of Lahore is attributed to Malik Ayaz in 1042. For a long time Lahore remained an outpost against the numerous Hindu principalities of the inner Punjab. In 1334 Ibn Battuta did not go through Lahore, but followed the usual and more secure road of Uchch, Multan and Dipalpur while on his way from Afghanistan to Delhi. It is not before the construction of the Rohtas fort by Sher Shah Suri in 1542 and the Attock fort by Akbar in 1581 that a direct line of communication was opened between Peshawar and Lahore. By that time, Lahore had become an important and beautiful city as a kind of royal resort for the Mughal dynasty.

This is not the place to study the architectural and artistic development of Lahore from 1530, when it came into the possession of Kamran Mirza, till 1799 when Ranjit Singh entered the city and settled into the fort. Still we must emphasize that like in Delhi and Agra, the *omrahs* built numerous gardens and *baradaris* on the banks of the Ravi which were swept away by the two floods during the reigns of Aurangzeb and Mohammad Shah. Fortunately the *baradari* of Kamran Mirza survived, and till 1849 one could still see one gate of another one of Mirza's gardens at Naulakha, embellished with superb enamelled work. But it is under Akbar that Lahore developed tremendously, with a new fort in baked bricks which was finished in 1566 and a complete rampart with twelve gates, which subsisted till the time of Maharaja Ranjit Singh. The one hundred and fourteen porticoes of the *Diwan-i-Aam* mentioned in the *Ain-i-Akbari* in 1579 are the same we can see on the "Kangra" map of Lahore in the 1810's [n° 184]. From 1584 to 1598 Akbar made Lahore his capital and he resided there, embellishing the fort with monuments and paintings, promoting a very active cultural life involving the wisest and most erudite members of the various ethnic and religious communities of the empire. A lot has been written of course on Akbar's miniature and manuscript workshops. The same artists were probably working on the same scale on the decoration of the imperial appartments and *zenana* at Lahore. The blending of Iranian, Central Asian and European artistic techniques and aesthetic canons which started in Agra was reinforced with the second and third Jesuit missions to the Mughal court. At Akbar's request, Father Jerome Xavier and Abdus Satar ibn Qasim worked together in Lahore for the translation of a number of Christian books into Persian. The result of this collaboration was, among other works, a *Dastan-i-Masih* (Life of Christ) by Father Jerome, a manuscript of which is preserved in the Lahore Museum. Dated 1602 AD and bearing Akbar's seal, it is illustrated with eleven pictures. As for Abdus Satar, he got the necessary documents to write a work entitled *Ahwal-i-Farangistan* (The History of Europe) which gave an account of Greece and Rome and described the lives of the "western" philosophers. In 1597 a terrible fire damaged most of the monuments in the fort of Lahore, and Akbar moved to Kashmir from May to November to allow the most urgent repairs to be undertaken. The year after the Emperor went back to Agra and never returned to Lahore.

[200 A] The Court of Sulaiman
Shahnama of Firdausi
Artist unknown. Lahore. c 1830
National Museum. New Delhi
Acc. N° L 532/8. 43 x 28 cm

Prince Salim, the future Jahangir, was very fond of Lahore. We know that his "auspicious palace" was completed in 1617-1618, inspected by Prince Khurram (future Shah Jahan) in 1619 and inaugurated in state by Jahangir in 1620. Within this chronological framework we must accomodate the very detailed description by William Finch of the paintings he saw inside the fort in 1611, the still existing glazed tile-work on the western and northern sides (a unique feature in Mughal architecture) and the mural paintings discovered in 1974 in the Kala Burj which Ebba Koch dates to 1605-1610. Nobody can say from Finch's descriptions which paintings survived the fire of 1597 or which ones were done after this fire, or which ones were commissioned by Jahangir himself for his new palace inaugurated in 1620. A few miniatures represent the *Diwan-i-Aam* of the Lahore fort during the time of Shah Jahan, with mural paintings in the background showing human representations which date back to the time of Jahangir. All this shows the unequivocal and constant presence of artists and painters in the Lahore fort, working under imperial patronage till the death of the emperor in 1627.

Jahangir did not limit himself to the embellishment of the fort. The *Wakaya-i-Jahangiri* tells us that he built a mosque in the Tripolia bazar of the city, with three bazars laid out to the east, north and south, each bazar containing two hundred and seventy shops furnished with upper storeys. In 1616 he built the Golan Wali Sarai on an extensive land, and in 1615 he had completed the tomb of young Anarkali. Many nobles followed the example of the emperor, starting with his own family. Maryam Zamani, Jahangir's mother, built a beautiful mosque with floral decorations, and Nur Jahan, the lovely Iranian lady he married in 1611, helped him in his architectural ambitions. Nur Jahan's father Itimad-ud-Daula and her brother Asaf Khan both built splendid residences in Lahore, gorgeously decorated with carpets and paintings. Nur Jahan herself lived in Lahore, where she built gardens and residences, including the Dilkusha Bagh at Shahdara where she erected the tomb of Jahangir after his death in 1627. We know of several other grand monuments built in Lahore under Jahangir, like the mosque of Dai Lado, a wet-nurse of the emperor, and the *mohalla* built by the same lady outside Lahore whose lofty and beautiful houses still existed in the time of Ranjit Singh. As in the case of Akbar, we must compare what we have just said of Jahangir's architectural activities in Lahore with what is widely known of his court artists illuminating manuscripts and making outstanding paintings for their imperial patron. By the end of Jahangir's reign there was a group of highly trained architects and artists in Lahore who had been working for the Mughal family for almost fifty years.

Prince Khurram was born in Lahore in 1592 and married Arjumand Banu Begum, daughter of Asaf Khan, in 1612. When he lost his wife in 1631, three years after assuming the throne, he started building her sumptuous mausoleum known as the Taj Mahal. That was the first and the most splendid of a series of buildings erected by that emperor in Agra, Delhi, Lahore and Kabul, for which according to his historians he paid two crores and fifty lakhs of rupees within a span of 20 years. In the absence of any mention in contemporary documents and epigraphical signature, the identity of the Taj Mahal's architect had always been a mystery. In a thesis defended at Paris in 1937, Abdullah Chaghatai claimed from documents kept in his family that this architect was Ustad Ahmed Lahori, a claim not many scholars were ready to acknowledge at that time. However, Begley and Desai, in their remarkable study on the Taj Mahal, upheld the theory of Ustad Ahmed Lahori as the chief architect of the Taj, and presented translations of documents supporting the identification. Lutf Ullah, second son of Ustad Ahmed, says in his *Diwan* that his father was first entrusted by Shah Jahan to built the Taj, and then with the building of the Red Fort in Delhi (well attested by the historians of Shah Jahan). Ustad Ahmed Lahori died in 1649, but his three sons continued to work for Aurangzeb and Dara Shikoh as architects and calligraphers. That a Lahori team of gifted architects worked for Shah Jahan on his major projects will not surprise us anymore. That one of these architects was probably the *maître d'oeuvre* of the Taj is indeed an achievement.

[180] Two complementary views of the fort and city of Lahore
Gulgashat-i-Punjab
Maharaja Ranjit Singh Museum. Amritsar
Acc. N° 38

The Lahore fort was transformed by Shah Jahan, under the guidance of his father-in-law Asaf Khan. Contrary to his father and grandfather, Shah Jahan did not like figurative paintings in his young years, although several miniature paintings show him in the Lahore fort where one can see these figurative paintings on the walls of the monuments. But many of these buildings were pulled down when he started his own programme of construction. The Shah Burj (Sheesh Mahal), the Diwan-i-khas and more intimately the small "bangla" (Naulakha) show a masterplan and workmanship which avoided the official and solemn aspects of the forts of Delhi and Agra. Under the guidance of the emperor, the architects and the artists, gave the Lahore fort a delicacy and a charm particularly evident in the details of the inlaid work of the Naulakha, with its 130 semi-precious stones scintillating on a few square inches to imitate the pleasures of the garden of paradise. The Moti Masjid, also in the Lahore fort, is the smallest but certainly the purest of the Moti Masjids built under the Mughals, while the Shalimar gardens brought to perfection the Central Asian nostalgic tradition of running water, cascading rivulets and fountains in an enchanting environment of flowers, sweet-smelling bushes and trees. According to Abdul-Hamid Lahori's *Padshanama*, Shah Jahan spent about fifty lakhs on the edifices and gardens of Lahore. This huge amount translates into a great number of outstanding, though anonymous, artists in the twenty years or so during which the emperor devoted part of his time to architecture and arts. The imperial family also invested in buildings and gardens which beautified the city and added to its glamour. During Shah Jahan's reign, Nur Jahan built the tomb of Jahangir at Shahdara with its unique design of a long building without a dome, and its four minarets of resplendant marble. The "Chinese" vases painted in the corridor leading to the cenotaph add to the aesthetic strangeness of this remarkable monument. Asaf Khan built his tomb in the same architectural complex, while Nur Jahan erected her mausoleum next to her brother's monument. According to the *Mirat-i-Waridat*, Asaf Khan's residence was built by Ustad Ahmed at a cost of twenty lakhs. The presence of Father Manrique at a banquet given in Lahore by Asaf Khan for Shah Jahan unexpectedly recreates the splendour of one festive day in the city.

[188] The Badshahi Masjid, or Imperial Mosque. Lahore
Gulgashat-i-Punjab
Maharaja Ranjit Singh Museum
Amritsar. Acc. N° 38

So many grandees built residences and public monuments at Lahore under Shah Jahan, and so many of them still exist today that it would be tiresome to list them. The Wazir Khan mosque and the Hamman, the Dai Anga tomb and the Gulabi Bagh, the Chauburji and the Nawankot monuments show the astounding mastery of the Lahore artisans in building majestic monuments and covering them with glazed tile-work (*kansi*) which in their pristine condition rivaled those of Persia and Central Asia. These are monuments that still exist today. Others have disappeared - partially or totally - such as the *haveli* of Mian Khan, "the highest house in the city, furnished with ten wells, numerous halls and arched chambers, reservoirs and fountains of water, underground chambers, balconies and upper storeys" (S.M. Latif). Or the Pari Mahal - "Palace of Fairies" - founded by Wazir Khan, the remains of which were described by Latif in 1892 as "substantial works of architectural beauty". But the most interesting monument built by an *omrah* of Shah Jahan and still existing in Lahore is probably the tomb of Ali Mardan Khan, the former governor of Kandahar and one of the most brilliant courtiers at the court of Shah Jahan. This monument is a model of proportion and harmony, and whatever remains today of its tile-work shows an interesting preference for brown, green and yellow colours which probably gave the Mughal monuments - and the Mughal school of architecture - of Lahore their peculiarity.

Prince Dara Shikoh, the eldest son of Shah Jahan, also liked Lahore where he was very popular and maintained a residence in the city. When Shah Jahan appointed him governor of the Punjab, he resumed Akbar's policy of meeting with the learned and wise men of every community and culture. His meetings and exchanges with the leading *sufis* and Hindu ascetics of the Punjab are recorded both in the literary works of the time and in contemporary miniature paintings. His contribution to Lahore architecture and culture was indeed considerable. Dara Shikoh built the tomb of Abul Ghani, a *khalifa* of Mian Mir, the tomb of Mian Mir himself on a grand scale and the tomb of Miskin Shah Amri, another disciple of Mian Mir. He also erected a beautiful tomb for Mulla Shah, his own spiritual master. Inside the ramparts, close to his private palace and the accommodations of his large establishment, Dara Shikoh had a great *chauk* erected with rows of shops, a thriving market called the Jowhari Bazar (Jewellers' market) and a *nakha* or horse market. Some of the beautiful gates with enamelled work subsisted till c. 1854. Dara Shikoh's wife erected a magnificent mosque - "a perfect triumph of architectural art" according to Latif - which still existed in 1849 and was destroyed after annexation. As we can see, Dara Shikoh's contribution to the architectural development of Lahore is well documented, even if today only two or three monuments survive. This architectural activity must be considered along with testimonies on Dara's involvement in the fields of arts and philosophy. Dara Shikoh's taste for refined paintings is attested in the Dara Shikoh's *Album*, which bears two Hijra dates corresponding to 1633, date of Dara's wedding with Nadira Begum, and 1641, when Dara offered the album to his wife. To that, we must add Dara's intellectual and mystical

[186] Panoramic view of Lahore in 1846
"Lahore during Sikh rule N° 1"
Lahore Museum, Lahore. Pakistan

[124] The Sonahri Masjid, Lahore
Detail

involvement at Lahore, with his friend Father Buzée, s.j. and the Punjabi *sufis* Mian Mir (died 1635) and Mulla Shah. The *Nadir al-nokat* contains some discussions between Dara and the ascetic Baba Lal Das in 1652-1653. Dara's own writings and publications, including the translations of Sanskrit texts he did himself or those he sponsored, are too well known to be detailed here. They extend from 1640 AD - he was then 25 years old - to 1657, when the war of succession between the emperor's sons started.

Aurangzeb's main contribution to Lahore's architecture is the magnificent Badshahi Masjid (1673-1674) which still dominates the urban landscape and whose colours and refined nuances make it so different from the other mosques in the subcontinent. But Emperor Aurangzeb never had the same emotional attachment for the city as his forefathers, whatever the reasons, one of them probably being Dara Shikoh's affectionate remembrance in many a Lahori heart. The political situation - with growing dissatisfaction in the province and the powerful rise of the Sikhs - did not attract him particularly to the Punjab. Yet the local nobility continued to built vast, richly decorated residences. First among them, Fidai Khan, foster-brother of Aurangzeb, governor of Punjab and builder of the Badshahi Masjid, built for himself a *haveli* which was one of the grand palaces of Lahore. Mausoleums and tombs remained an important part of the builders' activities, such as the tomb of Nawab Mian Khan built in black stone from Chiniot, his native place, or the mausoleum of Nusrat Khan, built by Aurangzeb himself and decorated inside with paintings [n° 197 and 209]. Mosques also continued to be erected in Lahore, some of them like the Chinianwala Masjid and the mosque of Abdullah Khan showing *kansi* or enamelled work still being done professionally in the city.

Such was Lahore, 180 years after Babur descended the Khyber Pass and fought his battle against Ibrahim Khan Lodi at Panipat: a *Dar-us-Sultanat* carefully looked after by the Mughal emperors and their close family who embellished it and sponsored artists and architects on a grand scale, a city which produced such "soft and delicate carpets that, compared with them, the carpets made in the manufactory of the king of Persia look like coarse canvas" (Abdul Hamid Lahori), but also a capital where great standards of education were achieved, books were published and men of letters flourished. Lahore was the city which gave to Shah Jahan some of his best architects for his imperial programmes and where some of the finest astrolabs were designed in the 17th century.

The period from 1707, when Aurangzeb died in the Deccan, to 1799 when young Raja Ranjit Singh captured Lahore was a difficult time for the city when after centuries of external peace it was threatened by foreign armies -the Iranians of Nadir Shah in 1738, the Afghans of Ahmed Shah Abdali between 1748 and 1767. There was a growing conflict between the capital and the countryside, which was gradually falling under the authority of the Sikhs. Nevertheless, till the 1750's Lahore more or less managed to keep its hold on the land: the area of Begumpura (Mughalpura) where the grand Muslim families resided and the newcomers settled down was extremely rich. Concerning

Begumpura, Latif says that "some conception of its magnificence may be formed from the fact that the Viceroy of Lahore [Zakaria Khan] had assumed the power of a satrap, and the whole wealth of the Punjab flowed into the palaces of Begumpura for the period of twenty-one years (1717-1738 AD)". Latif further says that in 1748, when Ahmad Shah Durrani first occupied the city, Begumpura was so wealthy that "he contented himself with its sack without being tempted to enter the city, as it brought him and his soldiers enormous wealth". Numerous buildings were erected in Lahore during that time. The ones surviving in the 1880's form an impressive list in Latif's *History of Lahore*. These buildings were the remains of intense construction and reconstruction work done in Lahore by the Mughal nobility between 1707 and 1757.

Begumpura was outside the ramparts of Lahore, but even within the city several impressive *havelis* were built in that period, some of them being later given by Maharaja Ranjit Singh to his senior officers. The Mubarak Haveli, near Mochi gate, is the place where Ranjit Singh secured the Koh-i-noor from Shah Shuja-ul-Mulk. The Kallo Bai haveli, built by Nawab Zakaria Khan for his mistress Kallo Bai, was given by Maharaja Ranjit Singh to Fateh Singh Ahluwalia. The Diwan Lakhpat Rai haveli was offered by the Maharaja to Nawab Sarfraz Khan of Multan, and the Haveli of Mir Javad to Ganga Ram and his son Ajudhia Prasad, the *bakhshi* of the *Fauj-i-khas*. The most elegant surviving edifice of that period is the small Sonheri Masjid, or Golden Mosque, built in 1753 by Bhikari Khan, a Turani general [nº 123-127]. The first desecration and destruction of the Harmandir Sahib, the holiest Sikh shrine at Amritsar, by Ahmed Shah Abdali in 1757 brought in retaliation the first, but brief, occupation of Lahore by the Sikhs. Repeating the process of 1757, Ahmed Shah attacked Amritsar again in 1762, at that time blowing up the temple with gun powder. He struck again at Amritsar in 1764, and then left Punjab after having appointed his own governor of Lahore. The Sikhs ejected the governor and took the city which they held under a triumvirate till 1799.

[103] Fort of Lahore
[Detail of Mughal tile-work]

Apparently there was a process of depopulation of Lahore during the second half of the 18th century for many high ranking Muslim families and landlords took refuge in Muslim lands. Many Hindu merchants, bankers and traders left Lahore, some of them settling down in Jammu. Most of the *mohallas* outside the walled city were depopulated at that time and those who wanted to remain in Lahore retreated within the walled city, where building activity went on since the famous Kashmiri brick-sellers had a tough time demolishing old monuments outside Lahore for extracting the bricks that they sold to build the new houses in the walled city. Latif just mentions a few important monuments erected during that time, but we do not know whether the families of artists and the educated elite (architects, painters, scholars) established and working in the capital till at least the 1750's stayed there or left the city. Delhi at that time was as bad as Lahore, having been plundered in the worst way by Nadir Shah, and then by Ahmed Shah Abdali. The Delhi artists had fled to Patna, Lucknow and Faizabad, while the Muslim nobility had taken refuge in Awadh and Hyderabad. It took some years after Ranjit Singh occupied Lahore in 1799 for the commercial, architectural and artistic activities to resume.

The question of the relations between Muslims and non-Muslims in India had been posed to the religious and political authorities of the Caliphate by the military officers and

[137] Jawalamukhi, with golden dome offered by Maharaja Ranjit Singh
From the *Gulgashat-i-Punjab*
Lahore, 1860
Maharaja Ranjit Singh Museum. Amritsar
Acc. N° 7

governors right from the time of the conquest of Sindh. Already in the 8th century AD, and still more in the 11th century, Islam had a well defined concept of the world, the *Dar-ul-Islam* and the *Dar-ul-harb*, with alternate rules (*jihad* and *aman*) concerning the relations between these two political entities. Resting on the Koran and the Hadiths, elaborated in the *sharia* and developed independently by each of the great legal "schools" of Islam, the relations between Muslims and non-Muslims inside the *Dar-ul-Islam* rested on the distinction between populations "of the Book" (*ahl-al-kitab*) and the *kafirs*. The former were considered as "protected" (*dhimmis*) population and were allowed to stay as they were if they accepted a code of conduct and norms embodied in the "Pact of Omar". Whether the Hindus, with their multiple gods and godesses and their absence of one single book should be considered as *ahl-al-kitab* (and offered the status of *dhimma*) or *kafirs* was hotly discussed by the *ulemas* of the different schools of Islam. The *dhimmis*, who cultivated the land and were the masters of trade, bore the bulk of taxations (*kharaj*, *jizya*) in the *Dar-ul-Islam* and had to submit to specific rules concerning their way of life, the maintenance of their churches and temples and the exercise of their religion. Any rebellion from the *dhimmis*, be it for refusing to pay the taxes or for setting up their own independent political states, was considered a rupture of the pact of *dhimma* and had to be answered by *jihad* inside the *Dar-ul-Islam*. Islam accepted conversion and offered the convert a kind of egalitarian position in the *umma* (community).

The manner in which the Muslim community developed in Punjab, and what was the proportion of converts compared to the incomers from Afghanistan, Iran and Turan is not a topic which can be treated in a few words. According to the time and changing circumstances, the Muslim historians themselves have at times emphasized the immigration factor, and at others the conversion factor. Whatever it is, till the mid-eighteenth century Punjab was on the passage of the immigration waves and the military reinforcements of *ghazis* crossing into India. But the impact of Islam in Punjab can by no ways be reduced to its military and economic "colonial" aspects. Punjab was the place where several large-hearted *sufis* developed original synthesis, sometimes at variance with the strict orthodoxy of Islam, which attracted a following much larger than the Muslim community of the time. Punjab was also the place where the justice of the *qazi* was sought long after the evanescence of the Mughal empire, even during the reign of Maharaja Ranjit Singh. The idea of a single god, of a single book containing the revelation or the doctrine of salvation, the concept of brotherhood among the believers whatever their origin, social background and caste, are some of the major contributions that almost eight centuries of Islamic rule brought to Punjabi culture and mentality.

[114] **Guru Arjun**
Military Manual of Maharaja Ranjit Singh
Probably the workshop of Imam Bakhsh Lahori
Lahore, 1822-1830
Maharaja Ranjit Singh Museum
Amritsar. Acc. N° 1035

Guru Nanak (1469-1539), the founder of Sikhism, had been in the service of Daulat Khan, the governor of Sultanpur, before embarking on his travels and then settling down at Kartarpur. As long as the Sikh community remained small it did not attract the attention of imperial authorities. There are traditions of Guru Nanak meeting Babur, and Guru Angad receiving Humayun. It is Akbar who is particularly present in the Sikh tradition for receiving and meeting Guru Amar Das and somehow helping him to acquire land in present-day Amritsar. Akbar definitely met Guru Arjun at Goindwal in November 1598, as attested by Badaoni. Considering the personality of Emperor Akbar and the deep mysticism of Guru Arjun, such a meeting was expected to take place. But the opposition to Akbar's religious policy, *Din-i-Ilahi*, and to his sympathetic stand towards Shias and non-Muslims had become intense among the *ulemas* and the traditional Islamic circles in the empire.

The rebellion of Prince Khusrau against his father emperor Jahangir in 1606, whatever the other political reasons involved, can also be seen as a contest between liberal and more orthodox Islam. Jahangir and his advisers were quick to see not only the political, but also the religious implication of Guru Arjun honoring Khusrau with the saffron mark on his forehead. The Guru was called to Lahore and executed there. He was not the only one to suffer from Khusraw's defeat: Jahangir had seven hundred followers of his son impaled alive in Lahore on a double rank of poles erected between the garden of Kamran Mirza and the city ramparts. In the first years of his reign, Jahangir kept an eye on any dissident power. The fact that Guru Har Gobind, after the death of his father, had taken the two swords as a symbol of *pir* and *mir* did not endear him to the intelligence network of the Mughal empire. Jahangir had him imprisoned in the fortress of Gwalior for more than ten years according to Sikh tradition. Although relations improved between the Guru and the Emperor in the last years of his reign, yet Guru Har Gobind instilled a strong martial spirit in the young Sikh community.

[116] **Guru Har Rai**
Military Manual of Maharaja Ranjit Singh
Probably the workshop of Imam Bakhsh Lahori
Lahore, 1822-1830
Maharaja Ranjit Singh Museum
Amritsar. Acc. N° 1035

When Shah Jahan succeeded his father in 1628, he proved to be a still more orthodox ruler on the throne of Delhi. The situation deteriorated quickly between the Sikhs and some of the Mughal governors of Lahore, although we can presume (no available information) that relations were cordial with Prince Dara Shikoh, who followed the Akbar tradition in the Mughal family and had been designated heir-apparent by Emperor Shah Jahan. Sikh tradition has it that the Guru cured the prince of an attempt to poison him. When the war of succession started again in 1658, young Guru Har Rai joined Dara Shikoh with a 2200 strong cavalry. Besides the usual rivalry of brothers to succeed their father, it was once again a conflict between an open enlightened Islam versus a rigid orthodox one. Whatever Aurangzeb's political genius and military superiority over his brother, the forces which supported him and assured his victory were clearly the ones asking for a stricter implementation of the *sharia* and a reassurance of Muslim domination over the non-Muslims. The reimposition of the *jizya* on the non-Muslims in 1679, the military operations in Rajasthan (Udaipur) and, soon, the Maratha wars were the follow-up of this politico-religious reassertion.

The situation in Punjab was not easy, since a great inflow of Afghan, Iranian and

Turanian *ghazis* came down the Khyber Pass to Lahore in order to participate in the *jihad* whose tremors were felt as far south as Pondicherry. Concerning the Sikhs, Aurangzeb took Ram Rai, the son of Guru Har Rai, as hostage to Delhi, and the Guru died heart broken at the age of 34 in 1661. Aurangzeb desired to meet the new Guru, Har Kishan, a five-year-old boy, in Delhi where the child died of smallpox at the age of eight (1664). Before dying, he appointed his grand-uncle Teg Bahadur as the ninth Guru of the Sikhs. One has to go back to the contemporary historians of Aurangzeb himself, the author of the *Masir-i-Alamgiri* or Khafi Khan, to judge what effect the orders issued by Aurangzeb concerning the Hindu and Sikh communities could have had in the minds and heart of the local populations. Aurangzeb's orders were particularly directed against the Hindus who looked towards the Sikhs to counter his oppressive policy. Espousing the cause of the brahmins, and specially the Kashmiri brahmins, Guru Teg Bahadur confronted the Mughal establishment. He was arrested in 1675 and publicly executed in Delhi, at the Chandni Chowk. Before his arrest, he had appointed his son Govind Singh as the tenth Guru of the Sikhs. His martyrdom in defense of religious tolerance and freedom of conscience was exemplary.

[118] Guru Tegh Bahadur
Military Manual of Maharaja Ranjit Singh
Probably the workshop of Imam Bakhsh Lahori
Lahore, 1822-1830
Maharaja Ranjit Singh Museum
Amritsar. Acc. N° 1035

At that time the Sikh community turned to arms, and not only the Sikhs, since they were joined by people of all creeds and castes in a kind of peasant revolt against the established authorities: the Mughals of course, with their governors and *faujdars* in Lahore and Sirhind, but also the Rajput hill states who had joined the standards of Delhi, due to their long-standing relations with the Mughal empire, fear of the Mughal armies and political expediency. For about thirty years Guru Govind Singh fought pitched battles, and in 1699 he created at Anandpur the militant order of Khalsa destined to fight persecution, injustice and uphold human dignity. On some occasions Guru Govind Singh barely escaped being captured, but his two eldest sons died valiantly in battle, and his two youngest sons were taken into custody by deceipt and executed in 1704 at Sirhind. Despite the warning of his entourage, in 1706 the Guru decided to move to the Deccan to meet Aurangzeb. He learnt of the Emperor's death on the way and, when Bahadur Shah was firmly established on the throne, went to meet him. That is where he was fatally wounded by a Pathan in 1708. Before dying, he declared that there would be no guru after him, and that the Granth Sahib would serve as guru for the Sikh community. He also sent Banda Bahadur to the Punjab, entrusting him to complete his work. He sent his bow, arrows and a *hukamnama* with Banda Bahadur ordering the Sikhs to follow him.

[42] Stand of traditional weapons
Maharaja Ranjit Singh Museum
Amritsar. Acc. N° 90-11

It is not possible to describe the spiraling of violence in Punjab from 1708 till 1764, when the Sikhs finally took Lahore and established their triumvirate. Banda Bahadur led an all-out attack on the Muslim positions, towns and big villages, which forced the Muslims to fall back on their main cities and particularly on Lahore where they camped outside the ramparts within the protection of the citadel and the Badshahi Masjid. The imperial army retaliated with flying columns all over the Punjab. There was no mercy on either side. Banda Bahadur was captured and executed in Delhi in 1716. From 1717 to 1738 Zakaria Khan, the governor of Lahore and satrap of Begampura, led a systematic hunt for Sikhs all over Punjab. The invasion of Nadir Shah (1739) brought the Sikh community a brief respite, but as soon as he left, Zakaria Khan resumed the "pacification" of the country.

This policy was pursued by his successors, Mir Moin-ul-Mulk, alias Mir Mannu, and then Morad Begum (Mughlani Begum), while the Sikhs organised themselves into fraternities, or "*misls*", which quickly came under the leadership of a few men of stature like Jessa Singh Ahluwalia. What increased the pressure on Punjab was the vital necessity for the Mughal authorities - whatever remained of the imperial power in Lahore and Delhi - to keep the Punjab plains open for the reinforcements coming through the passes of the Hindukush to fight the Marathas, now threatening the doab. The presence of these Iranian, Afghan and Central Asian troops in Aurangabad during the time of Aurangzeb, each having their separate quarter and their organised spiritual connections of *pirs* and *sufis* coming directly, as far as the Turanis were concerned, from Bukhara and Balkh to the Deccan, is indeed interesting. The foundation of the Rohilla power in Rohilkund is another result of such migrations, and the rivalry between the Iranis and the Turanis, as old as the first Muslim settlements in Hindustan, was part of the political process of the time. In Lahore itself the career of a Bhikari Khan illustrates this ongoing process, while the reading of Tahmas Khan Miskin's *Tazkirah* shows in very vivid terms the impact of the military campaigns of the imperial forces in the Punjab plains. The first invasion of Ahmad Shah Abdali was in 1747, the eighth and last one in 1767. In the meantime, in 1757 (or 1759-1761 according to H.R. Gupta), the Sikh briefly occupied Lahore - still *Dar-us-Sultanat* by any standards - where according to tradition Jessa Singh Ahluwalia struck coins, the very symbol of sovereignty. They did not stay long, and they were again pursued by flying columns all over the Punjab. The Afghans destroyed the Harmandir Sahib, the Sikh temple at Amritsar, twice and their greatest success was in 1762, which has passed in Sikh memory as the "Ghallu Ghara", or the great massacre. When in 1764 Ahmad Shah Abdali returned to Kabul, the government of Lahore was resumed by the Sikhs and the city was divided between three chiefs, hence the name of the triumvirate given to the period which immediately precedes the reign of Maharaja Ranjit Singh, from 1764 to 1799.

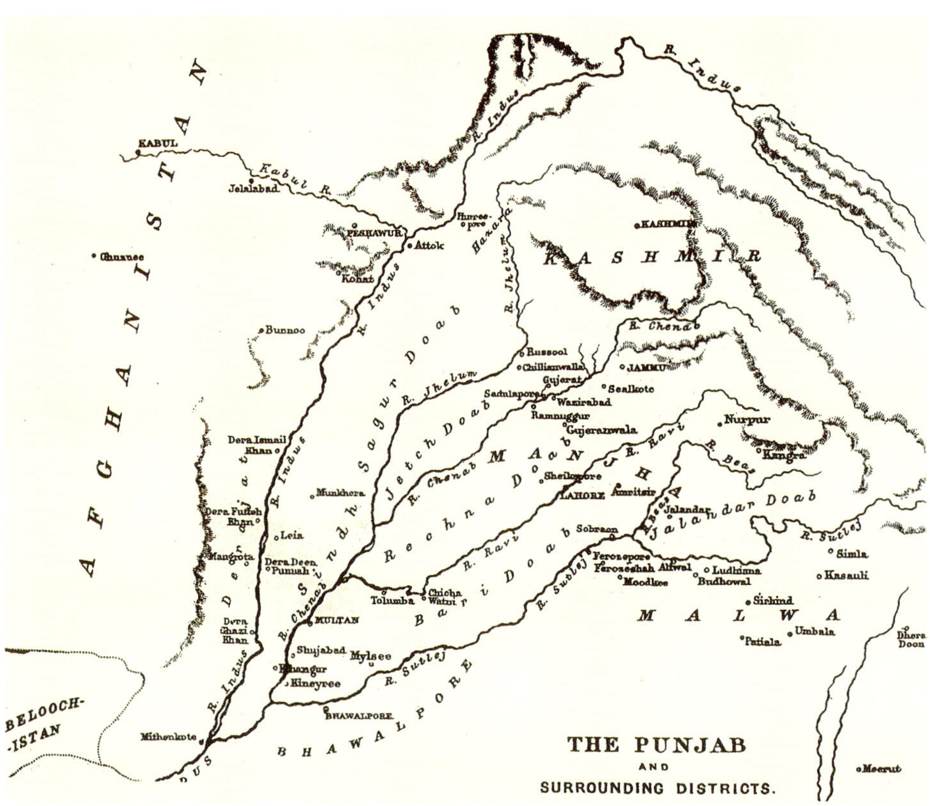

There is not much to say about this triumvirate which as we have seen witnessed a depopulation of the rich suburbs of Lahore and the relocation of the remaining population inside the ramparts of the city. An important section of the Muslim community remained, engaged in trade and liberal activities, while education survived, as is clear from the number of talented and educated Lahoris who lived under the reign of Ranjit Singh. According to Forster, who wrote in 1782-1783 and had already emphasized "the industrious skill of the Sikhs in the various branches of cultivation", trade also continued, or was resumed, since the Sikhs at that time maintained "an extensive and valuable commerce which had been extended to distant quarters of India, particularly to the provinces of Bengal and Bihar where many Sikh merchants of opulence at this time reside. [...] Merchants of every nation or sect who may introduce a traffick into their territories or are established under their government experience a full protection, and enjoy commercial privileges in common with their own subjets".

It is not easy to reconcile these two main histories of sixteenth to eighteenth century Punjab that we have been trying to resume uptil now : the history of Lahore and its Mughal elite with its resplendent aura of tile-glazed monuments and its artistic life (at least from the time of Kamran Mirza till the late 1750's), and the history of the people living in the *mohallas* as well as in near and distant villages, who in some way or the other had to interact with the capital of the *suba*. The eighteenth century looks like a nightmare to every community whose members heavily suffered during the almost permanent unrest in the country : the Muslim gentry of course, who lost their hold on the territory, their lands and the regular revenues some of them had been enjoying for generations. Most of the upper-caste Hindus, who were *diwans*, revenue-collectors, money-lenders or suppliers of the Muslim nobility stood by the Muslims against the Sikhs during this period. But it was a nightmare also for the rural population, mostly Hindu and Sikh, but poor Muslims as well, who were hunted down by the flying columns, their cattles and belongings stolen, their families captured and sold into slavery. In the meantime, the *Janamsakhi B-40*, whose wonderful illustrations are like a paradise of peace in a lovely landscape full of flowers and birds, was written and illustrated in 1733 AD, one of the darkest periods of conflict between the Sikhs and the Mughals. How to reconcile these different histories as a historian is an almost impossible task. How to built up these various legacies into one single political entity, the Kingdom of Punjab, was the life endeavour of Maharaja Ranjit Singh.

[2] **Sardar Fateh Singh Ahluwalia**
Courtesy : Brigadier Sukhjit Singh, MVC

The Sukerchakia *misl* was not the most powerful of the twelve *misls* which evolved in the second half of the eighteenth century. Budh Singh, the ancestor, was a disciple of Guru Govind Singh and a member of the Khalsa. His son, Naudh Singh, settled in the village of Sukerchak, hence the name of the *misl*. Chahar Singh, his son and successor, settled in Gujranwala and fortified the city. Maha Singh, third in line from Budh Singh, rounded up the possessions of the family upto Jammu, Sahiwal and Isakhel. When he died in 1792, he left these possessions to his only son, Ranjit Singh. The first marriage of Ranjit Singh, in 1795, was with Mahtab Kaur, the daughter of Sada Kaur, the head of the powerful Kanhaya *misl*. Ranjit Singh and Sada Kaur had a strange relationship, each using the other for help and self-aggrandisement. The capture of Lahore by Maharaja Ranjit Singh in 1799, where he was helped by Hindu, Sikh and Muslim followers of the remnants of the triumvirate, was a landmark in the history of Punjab since a son of the soil assumed the political direction of the state in the former capital of the *suba*, though the state did not include much of the former Mughal provinces. The coronation at Lahore in 1801 and the alliance in 1802 with Fateh Singh Ahluwalia, the heir of Jassa Singh and Raja of Kapurthala, greatly enhanced both his prestige and military possibilities.

[9] Family tree of Maharaja Ranjit Singh
Iqbalnama-i-Maharaja Ranjit Singh
Maharaja Ranjit Singh Museum. Amritsar
Acc. No nil

The most serious threat to the Sikh states, both cis- and trans-Sutlej, had come from George Thomas, an Irish adventurer settled in Haryana, who had dreamt of conquering Punjab for the East India Company. The threat was crushed in 1801 at the request of the Sikhs, by the prompt intervention of the 3rd brigade of Hindustan, detached by General Perron and commanded by Colonel Bourquien. That was the first recorded contact between the Maharaja and the representatives of some distant European powers, England and France. George Thomas returned home in 1802 : in a meeting with Lord Wellesley in Benares, Thomas put his hand on the Punjab in a map where the British provinces of India were coloured in red and declared : "Had I been left alone, I would have made all this red with this hand".

The following years were used by the Maharaja to strengthen his position and evaluate the situation in northern India. The Maratha power had crumbled down at Delhi in 1803, and in 1805 Holkar with a numerous army took refuge in Amritsar, pursued by the small military force of Lord Lake. Ranjit Singh visited the English camp in disguise, and it was there that he understood that modernisation was the key word for the survival and the development of his kingdom. For modernisation in the field of administration, he first employed highly trained Hindu finance specialists who had been working for the sovereigns of Afghanistan, and then Diwan Ganga Ram, from a Kashmiri family settled in Delhi, who had been the *diwan* of Bourquien. However, it took years to redress the economy and finances of the Punjab. The second aspect of modernisation was for his military forces, for which he enrolled officers and soldiers coming from the "French" Brigades of Hindustan and from the regular troops of the East India Company. The regular infantry quickly comprised of Sikh, Hindu and Muslim Punjabis, with units of *purbiahs* and *gurkhas*. The artillery, a key element in the modernisation of the force and in the overall industrialisation of the state, was mostly formed of Muslim officers and ranks. This modernizing drive did not happen without opposition from the traditional administrative and military hierarchy. One of the greatest achievements of the Maharaja was to sustain it day after day till the last months of his reign without antagonizing the bulk of his people.

To come back to 1805, Ranjit Singh tried for a while to test English resistance on his eastern frontier until political events in Europe - Napoleon's meeting with the Tsar Alexander at Tilsit in 1807 - and a flying British column coming to camp on the Sutlej river (1808) ended in a cat and mouse game with a series of treaties and proclamations between Lahore and Calcutta in 1809-1811. The border between the Punjab and the British territories was fixed on the Sutlej and remained there till 1846. In the meantime, Ranjit Singh had conquered Kasur (1807), Pathankot (1808), Kangra and Jammu (1809), Attock (1812). The same year he entered into an agreement with Shah Shuja-ul-Mulk, sovereign of Afghanistan, for a joint operation in Kashmir, then an Afghan province in rebellion against the Shah. The agreement was that the celebrated diamond Koh-i-noor would be given to Lahore in lieu of the Maharaja's military assistance. It was indeed ceded in 1813 despite the unsuccessful issue of the expedition. In 1813 also there was the first great battle between an Afghan army and the Punjab forces at Chuch, near Attock. The Punjabis won the day after a terrible fight. In 1815-1816 Ranjit Singh conquered the cis-Indus territories in the north-west, bringing under his authority the areas next to the river. Then, in a major operation in 1818, the Maharaja completed the conquest of the Punjab by the capture of Multan, the last great Afghan bastion in the Land of the Five Rivers. Kashmir was annexed in 1819, Dera Ismael Khan, Mankera and the Derajat in 1821.

By 1822 the kingdom of Punjab and its province of Kashmir formed a political unit of about thirteen million inhabitants. The integration of so many people of different races,

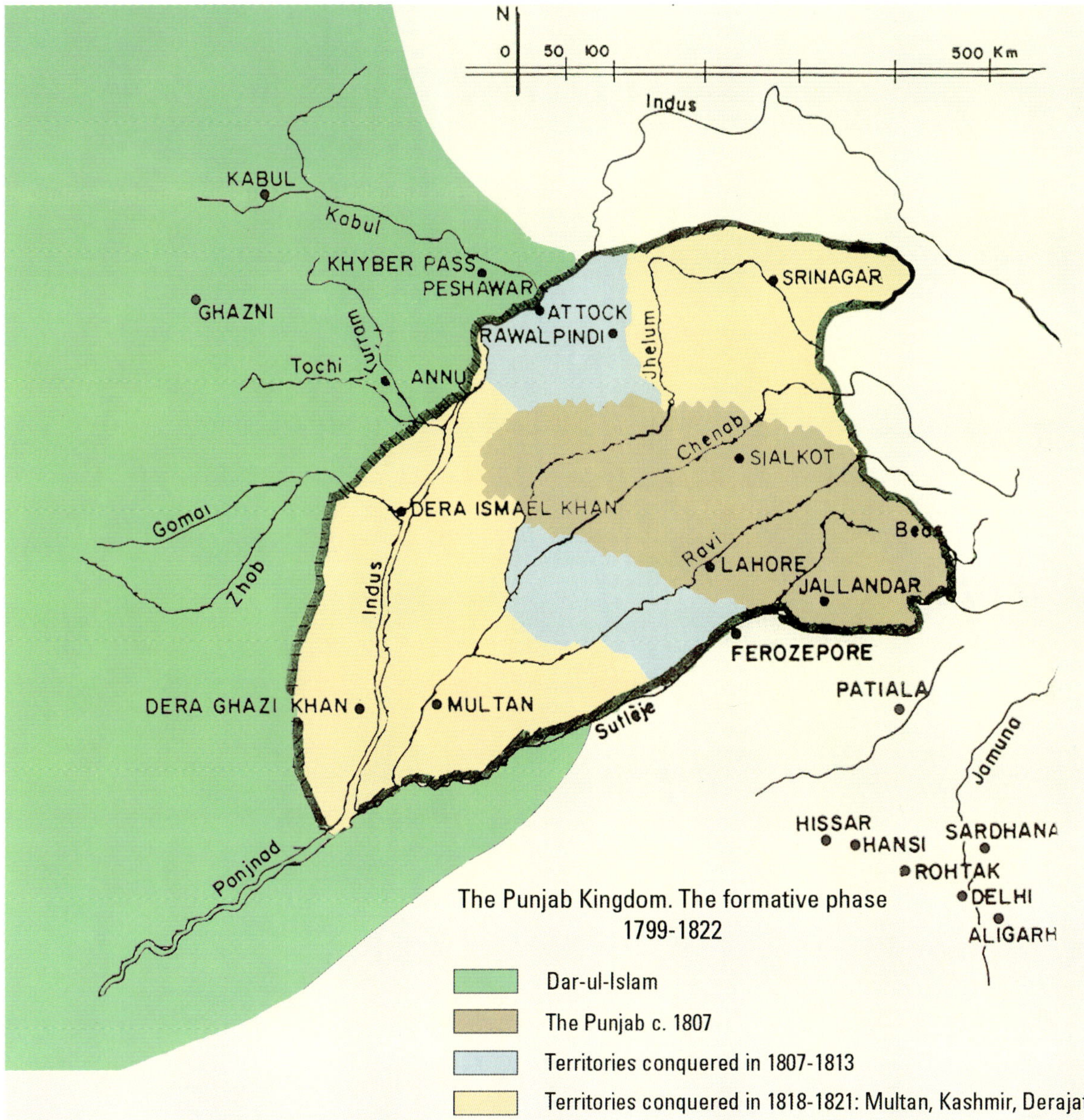

The Punjab Kingdom. The formative phase
1799-1822

creeds and former obediences into one political body was the main task of the Maharaja for the next seventeen years of his life. How he did it with perseverance, confronting so many odds and sometimes having more difficulties with his friends than with his enemies can be seen in the following pages. A sound agrarian policy and a balanced system of revenues was the backbone of his administration. The modernisation of his army, a must for the smooth development of the state, took an accelerated pace with the enrolment of French and Italian officers of Napoleon who joined him in 1822 and 1827. The economic and monetary restructuring of the Punjab was a much more difficult task than the conquest of so many cities and provinces : the Maharaja followed it patiently, in the wake of the modernisation of British India and the issue of the Company rupee in 1833-1836. His meeting with Lord William Bentinck, the second meeting of the "Camp of the Cloth of Gold" recorded in history, and the Treaty of the Navigation on the Indus in 1832 were partly due to the Punjab becoming part of a world economic system with navigation to all

[12] **Young Ranjit Singh**
Iqbalnama-i-Maharaja Ranjit Singh
Maharaja Ranjit Singh Museum
Amritsar. Acc. N° nil

[68] Military drill
Military Manual of Maharaja Ranjit Singh
Probably the workshop of Imam Bakhsh Lahori
Maharaja Ranjit Singh Museum
Amritsar. Acc. N° 1035

[17] Prince Sher Singh
"Maharaja Cheyr Singh" / "Maharaja Shair Sing"
Watercolour on European paper
By Imam Bakhsh Lahori. Lahore, 1841-1843
181 x 257 mm
Court collection, Musée Guimet. MG 78 III 39749

the continents. British authorities in India had taken great care to ensure that Ranjit Singh did not annex Sindh and get an outlet to the Indian ocean.

Along with his government policy, which of course concerned the welfare of his subjects at large and the place of his country in the concert of nations, Maharaja Ranjit Singh had a kind, personal approach to the people and as much as he could he tried to understand their feelings and always respected their beliefs. His personal leniency had been observed by many a curious visitor at his court. There was hardly any condemnation to death by the Maharaja during the forty-seven years of his reign, and he firmly opposed his French generals who wanted to introduce the death penalty in their brigades for high-treason and desertion. Leitner even discovered that "the famous mathematician and Arabic scholar Hashim Shah got a *jaghir* near Jagdeo in recognition of his literary eminence, and his Arabic scholarship secured his pardon from the ever-forgiving Ranjit Singh when he had once joined a revolution against the Sikhs". That was the general and courteous attitude of the Maharaja towards the public at large. But Ranjit Singh also took care on every occasion to celebrate the festivals of each community. He used to visit the Muslim shrines at Lahore, celebrated the Hindu festivals and, of course, was close to the members of his own community. What perhaps endeared him to the Muslim community is a very human feeling which cost him dearly : his love for Moran, a Muslim girl, for which he accepted a public punishment administered by Baba Phula Singh Akali at Amritsar. Moran was probably the only person who built a new mosque at Lahore under Ranjit Singh, and he still spoke affectionately of her twenty years after they had separated. The Badshahi Masjid had been taken over not by Ranjit Singh in 1799, but by the triumvirate in 1764, and already turned by them into a military building because of its strategic position. Ranjit Singh did not give back this symbolic monument to the Muslim community, but at the request of General Allard, he readily gave them back the beautiful Sonahri Masjid in the Kashmiri Bazar of Lahore.

After the containment of Syed Ahmad Barelvi's *jihad* on the Indus and the Himalayan foothills (1827-1831), and after the conquest and annexation of Peshawar in 1834, the frontier of the Punjab kingdom extended to the entrance of the Khyber Pass. The same year the governor of Jammu, Raja Gulab Singh, sent General Zorawar Singh to the conquest of Ladakh. The Maharaja was pleased with the conquest of Leh, but restrained Zorawar Singh to go further in fear of a clash with Chinese forces in the Himalayas : a wise step, considering what happened to Zorawar Singh there in 1841. Some years before, the Maharaja had toyed with the idea of restoring Shah Shuja-ul-Mulk on the throne of Kabul, and the British political agents on the Punjab border had taken up the idea. In 1837 Lord Fane, commander-in-chief, visited Lahore to attend the wedding of Prince Nao Nihal Singh, and he was deeply impressed by the review of the old regular troops who had beeen called back from Peshawar to Lahore for the same occasion. A few weeks later, the Afghans made a desperate attempt to recapture Peshawar and its province up to the Indus. It failed, because of the heroism of Hari Singh Nalwa and his men in holding Jamrud fort, but also because of the speedy movement of the same elite units of the army from Lahore to Peshawar. Lord Auckland, the new governor-general, found the idea of restoring the old Afghan monarch on his throne interesting, and in 1838 a Tripartite Treaty was signed according to which the English and Punjab governments were to join forces to reinstal Shah Shuja-ul-

[103] **Maharaja Ranjit Singh's fortifications of Lahore**
[Left section]

[102] **Maharaja Ranjit Singh's fortifications of Lahore**
[Front structure]

[169] Silver rupee
Amritsar mint. BS 1859 (1802 AD)
Punja (hand) and doted leaf
Private collection
Courtesy : Mrs Jyoti Ray

Mulk in Kabul. A summit meeting between Auckland and Ranjit Singh and a grand review of troops took place at Ferozpur in December 1838. In the follow up of the meeting, the Maharaja received Lord Auckland in Amritsar and Lahore in January 1839. But by that time Ranjit Singh was exhausted and ill. He died on 27 June 1839, after the British army had captured Kandahar, but before it captured Ghazni and entered Kabul, and also before his own Punjabi troops stormed the Khyber Pass, captured Ali Masjid and paraded under the Bala Hissar of Kabul.

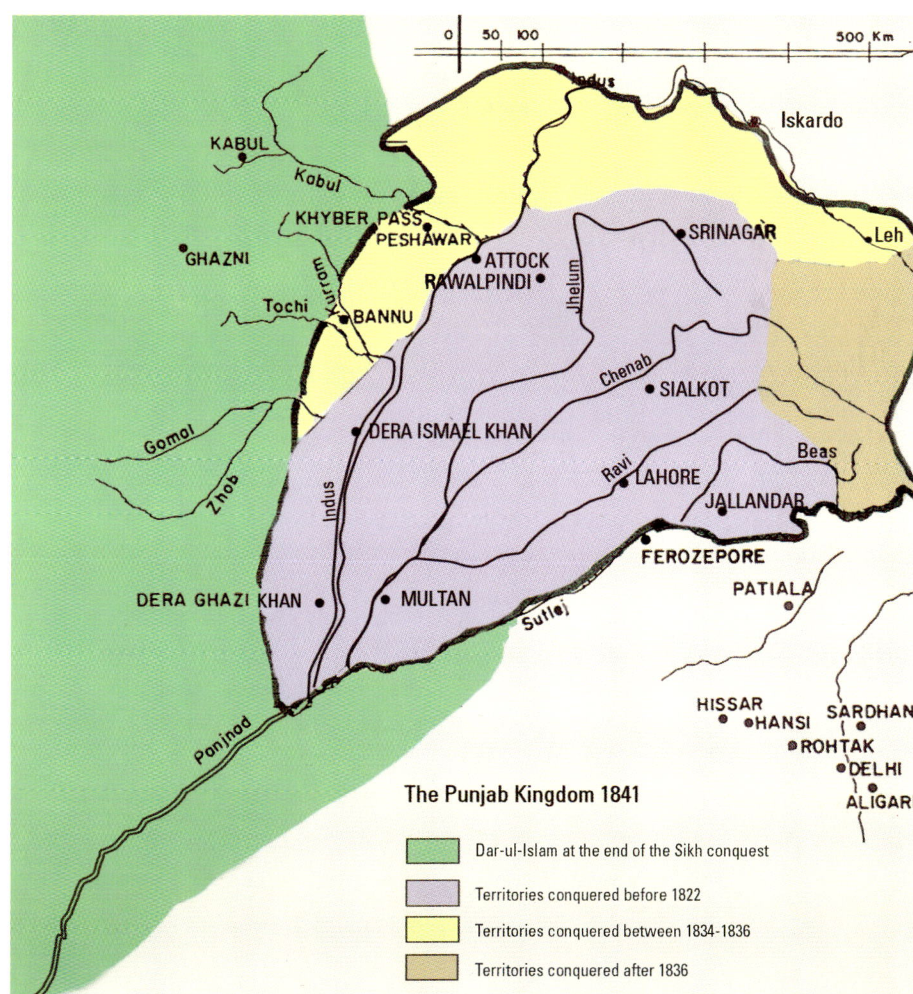

[33] The Darbar of Maharaja Ranjit Singh
Gouache on paper, stuck on wood panel. Artist unknown. c. 1850. 91.5 x 32 cm
Maharaja Ranjit Singh Museum. Amritsar. Acc. N° 110

II

The Court of Lahore

The free and direct approach of the Sikhs always surprised people accustomed to the more sophisticated manners of Hindustan and the Mughal *darbars* at Agra and Delhi. Mughal historians and European travellers have left us precise descriptions of ceremonies with sumptuous decorum and endless processions they witnessed at the court of Shah Jahan and Aurangzeb. One of the best evocations we have today of these splendid ceremonies is the "Court of Delhi on the birthday of the Great Mogol Aurangzeb", a magnificent piece created in Dresden by J. Dinglinger in 1700-1708 : a replica of Aurangzeb's court in a sumptuous decor on a trapezoidal platform (56 x 45 inches). The figures are of enamelled gold, and so are the palanquins, dais, arms and birthday gifts. The entire piece, including the elephants and the camels, is studded with 5223 diamonds, 169 rubies, 175 emeralds and a sprinkling of other precious stones. Indeed such were the Indian courts, and such they had to be according to Western imagination.

The Sikhs on the contrary did not have this court etiquette, and the first accounts of them frequently mention their republican and straightforward habits. Forster in 1782 said he found "an embarrassment in applying a distinct term to the form of the Sikh government, which on the first view bears an appearance of aristocracy. But a closer examination discovers a large vein of popular power branching through many of its parts. An equality of rank is maintained in their civil society, which no class of men, however wealthy or powerful, is suffered to break down". After he had crossed the Sutlej on his way to Lahore in 1831, Jacquemont was happy to walk freely on the river-banks without being followed by obsequious people as had been the case in British India. Ten years later Soltykoff was surprised to see, in a grand reception at the Sheesh Mahal in the Lahore fort, that "the Sikhs have little etiquette, even at court. What they have they offer frankly and without ceremony. Everything is patriarchal and warriorlike. The King [Sher Singh], in the midst of his courtiers, is on an equality with all the rest, a warrior like themselves, and they address him simply and without ceremony".

[16] Prince Nau Nihal Singh
"Le Prince Noh Néhal Singh. Kover Novn Nehal Sing"
Watercolour on European paper. 172 x 245 mm
By Imam Bakhsh Lahori. Lahore, 1837-1843
Court collection. Musée Guimet. MG 78 III 41826

The Sikh court at Lahore took some time before evolving its own etiquette and developing the grand *darbars*, although the Maharaja's coronation at Lahore was of a rare splendour. Ranjit Singh was consecrated Maharaja of the Punjab by Sahib Singh Bedi in Lahore on 12 April 1801 amidst great festivities. He immediately took mesures to reinforce the security of his capital and

[24] The Court of Lahore
Oil on canvas
by August Schoefft. Lahore 1841-Vienna 1855
120" x 192"
Princess Bamba Collection. Sikh gallery, Lahore Fort
Director of Archaeology
Government of Pakistan

[19] **Golden Throne of Maharaja Ranjit Singh**
Gold leaves on wood, with repoussé work. Height 93 cm
Victoria & Albert Museum, London, Acc. N° 2518 IS

[18] Maharaja Dalip Singh
"Maharajah Dhélip Singh" / "Maharajah Duleep Sing Bhadoor"
Watercolour on European paper
By Imam Bakhsh Lahori. Lahore, 1843
187 x 258 mm
Court collection, Musée Guimet
MG 78 III 39750

[210] Raja Hira Singh
"Rajah Hyra Singh" / "Rajah Heera Sing"
Gouache on European paper
By Imam Bakhsh Lahori. Lahore, 1827-1843
178 x 249 mm
Court collection, Musée Guimet. MG 78 III 41829

[34] Sozni of Maharaja Ranjit Singh
Gold embroidery on silk
Faqir Jalaluddin Collection
Lahore Museum, Lahore. Ref. Sr. N° 646 list 27

confirm the Muslim community in its privileges under their *qazis* and *muftis*. He appointed a Muslim, Imam Bakhsh, as *kotwal*, named *chaudries* all over the city and took the first general mesures of government in the land he controlled. The great *misls* who had helped the Sikh confederacy to emerge as the leading political force in Punjab in mid-eighteenth century - Ahluwalia (Jassa Singh, commander of all the *misls*), Bhangi (Hari Singh), Sukerchak (Naudh Singh, great-grandfather of Ranjit Singh), Kanhaya (Jai Singh), Ramgarhia (Nand Singh) - rallied around Maharaja Ranjit Singh when he consolidated the Punjab kingdom. Scions of these families and from other *misls* - such as Attariwala, Majithia and Sandhanwalia – played a great role in the court of Lahore. But Maharaja Ranjit Singh had kept his unassuming habits to transact business in private *darbars* where he called his most trusted advisers along with the concerned specialists, secretaries and the people involved. There are several surviving miniature paintings and European engravings of private *darbars*, and these miniature paintings were endlessly reproduced after 1849 till the end of the 19th century.

The Great Darbar was a display of might and magnificence, held on major political events, on state occasions like Prince Nao Nihal Singh's wedding at Lahore in 1837, and on religious festivals like Dussehra. We are fortunate to have two paintings representing a Great Darbar : one, undated [n° 33] by an anonymous Indian artist, in which the courtiers in gorgeous dress or uniforms are represented on rows right and left of the Maharaja. Persian inscriptions on each person identify the who's who of the Punjab Government. A total of forty-nine personalities including the Maharaja's family, his spiritual advisers, the actual and the former prime ministers and the actual finance minister, along with the most eminent members of the great families of the kingdom like the two Dogra brothers, the Sandhanwalias, the Attariwalas, two Fakir brothers, Lehna Singh Majithia and two members of the "Kabuli" family. The military establishment is represented by two legendary heros of the Khalsa army : Baba Phula Singh Akali (d. in 1823) and General Hari Singh Nalwa (d. 1837). The elite *Francisi* brigades of the kingdom are represented by five generals: Allard, Ventura, Avitabile, Ilahi Bakhsh (*topkhana*, artillery) and Diwan Ajudhya Prasad (bakhshi). The other regular brigades have two generals : Tej Singh and Dhunkal Singh.

The second painting [n° 24] is *The Court of Lahore* ("Der Hoft von Lahor") by August Schoefft, an Austro-Hungarian artist who came to Lahore in 1841. The painting was completed in Europe in 1852 and exhibited in Vienna in 1855. Its size (192 x 100 inches) makes it close to the paintings ordered by the

[35] Golden Gates of the Harmandir Sahib (Golden Temple)
Offered by Maharaja Ranjit Singh.
c. 1830. Length 6' 3". Breadth 4' 6"
Entered in the *Toshakhana* register dated 3.10.97 at page 2, Sr. N° 17 under the title "Jalao Sri Harmandir Sahib"
Courtesy : Shiromani Gurudwara Parbandhak Committee

[37 A] **Jarau sehra of Kanwar Nau Nihal Singh**
Length 1' 3". Breadth 2'
Studded with uncut diamonds and pearls
Entered in the *Toshakhana* register dated 3.10.97 at page 2, Sr. N° 9 under the title "Jalao Sri Harmandir Sahib"
Courtesy : Shiromani Gurudwara Parbandhak Committee

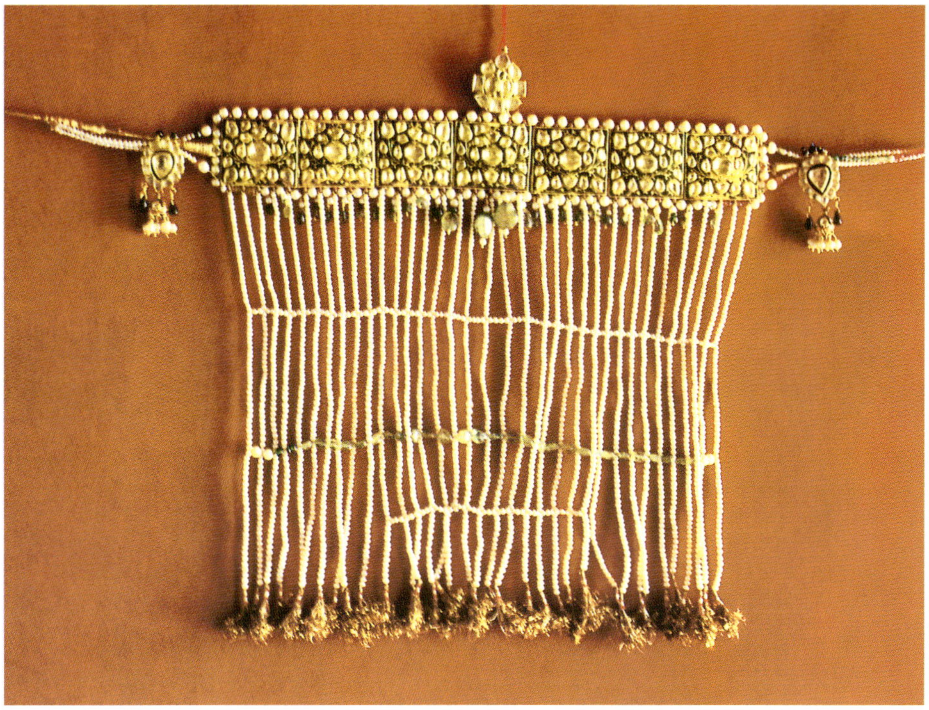

[37] **Gold Chhatar studded with emeralds and neelam (blue saphire) peacock on the top.**
Diameter with the string of pearls 2' 6"
Length with peacock 1' 7"
Entered in the *Toshakhana* register dated 3.10.97 at page 1, Sr. N° 1 and 2 under the title "Jalao Sri Harmandir Sahib"
Courtesy : Shiromani Gurudwara Parbandhak Committee

French Government for the new Galerie de l'histoire de France at the Versailles palace in the 1840's. There is also a key giving the names of the main figures (62 according to Fakir Syed Aijazuddin's remarkable publication), most of them being the same as on the precedent *darbar*. But there are some new figures here : members of Afghan families who ruled over Multan and Peshawar before their conquest by the Punjab army, or Fakir Haridas, the "burying fakir". Schoefft also gives more portraits of the Europeans in the Lahore service, English (van Cortland and Foulkes), Prussian (Steinbach), Austro-Hungarian (Honigberger), and French (General Court, colonels Mouton, de Laroche, Lafont). F.S. Aijazuddin has pointed out the many symbolic associations in his analysis of the painting.

These Great Darbars gave opportunity to the courtiers to wear their most resplendent costumes and exhibit their most precious jewellery, while the military officers of the regular brigades put on their uniforms inspired by the Hussar units of old Europe and Napoleon's army. If the simplicity of the *sardars* and the highest officers of the state was noticed by most of the travellers, they also described the splendour of the court of Lahore. Maharaja Ranjit Singh was the most amiable host and the least pretentious sovereign, but on state occasions he wore on his arm India's most prestigious diamond, the Koh-i-noor.

[29] The Koh-i-Noor on the English crown (Replica)
Maharahja Ranjit Singh Museum. Amritsar
Acc. N° nil

The story of the Koh-i-Noor
The Toshakhana at Lahore

The anonymous Punjabi artist of the "Darbar of Maharaja Ranjit Singh" and August Schoefft in his "Court of Lahore" have each represented Maharaja Ranjit Singh wearing the Koh-i-noor on his right arm, and Schoefft has insisted in his painting on the sumptuous jewellery and strings of pearls worn by the princes, displayed on horses or carried in trays by young servants of the household.

A millenary tradition in India connects diamonds with high spirituality and power, be it the Syamantaka jewel of the *Vishnu Purana*, Asvattham's jewel in the *Mahabharata*, the Triratna of the Buddhist canons or the "Seven jewels" - the last one a real one - which were the attributes of a king Chakrawartin in the Buddhist tradition.

The origin of the Koh-i-noor is far from clear. In his *Memoirs* Babur described a great diamond "said to be worth half the daily expenditure of the whole world", which Humayun had seized as booty at Agra in 1526. It supposedly came from Gujrat, and its weight had been estimated at c. 180 carats. A second diamond, much bigger and more recently discovered, was offered to Shah Jahan by Mir Jumla in 1652: it weighed 787 carats. In 1665 the French jeweller Tavernier was allowed by Aurangzeb to see and draw the imperial jewels in Delhi. He did not see the former diamond, but in the plates of his *Travels* there is a drawing of the "Great Mogul", a 280 carat diamond. The unresolved question is : which of these three diamonds, if any, is the ancestor of the Koh-i-noor?

The Koh-i-noor of today belonged to Emperor Muhammed Shah. It was taken by Nadir Shah to Persia in 1739 after the sack of Delhi. On Nadir Shah's death, it was taken by Ahmad Shah Abdali and remained with the Durrani family of Kandahar and Kabul. In 1812 Shah Shuja-ul-Mulk, then sovereign of Kabul and owner of the Koh-i-noor, requested Maharaja Ranjit Singh for help to reconquer Kashmir from his rebellious subjects. The Maharaja agreed against the promise of the Koh-i-noor. After the unsuccessful expedition

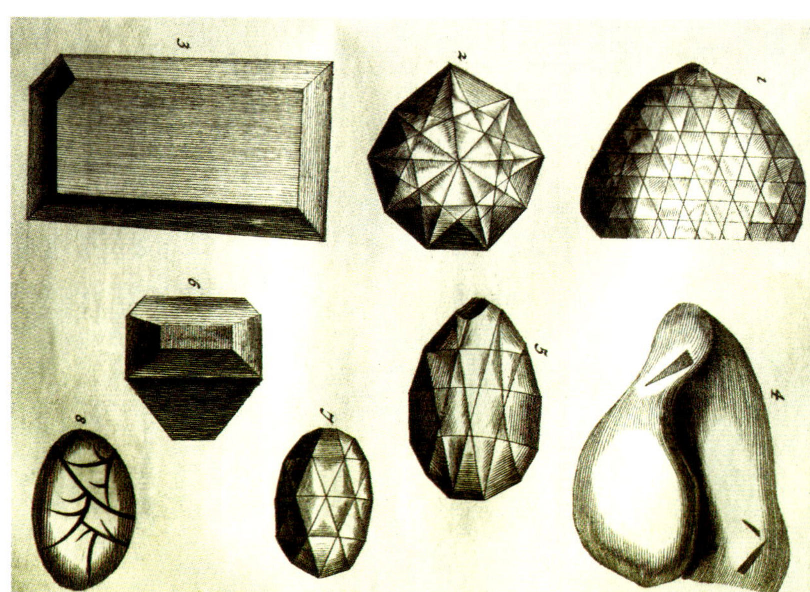

25] Tavernier : The "Great Mughal" in the Delhi Red Fort, c. 1660
(top right)
From Tavernier's *Travels in India*,
"Figures of large diamonds"

[39] Jewellery
Lahore. 1825-1841
Private collections

to Kashmir, Shah Shuja-ul-Mulk was reluctant to part with the famous diamond, and Ranjit Singh had to put some pressure on him and his family, then residing in Lahore, to get the price of his intervention. The Koh-i-noor was then kept in the *Toshakhana* (treasury) of the Lahore fort, worn by Ranjit Singh on special occasions and shown to distinguished visitors.

After the annexation of the Punjab in 1849 the British took it immediately and, at Queen Victoria's request, sent it to England. Since 1850 it has been there, first presented to the public in the Great Exhibition in Hyde Park in 1851. Today it is in the Tower of London along with the other crown jewels. On several occasions it has been claimed by India as well as Pakistan.

In the *Toshakhana* of Lahore there was an incredible collection of diamonds and precious stones, mounted or in pouches, which were the crown jewels of the Punjab kingdom. In April 1849, just after annexation, Henry Lawrence appointed Dr Login as the Director of the Fort, guardian of little Maharaja Dalip Singh and responsible for making the list of the royal household : arms, carpets, shawls and diamonds. Login appointed some other officers for the first three items. "I myself take the jewel department in the *Toshakhana*. The extraordinary way in which jewels of the greatest values are packed Avay would amuse you. I cannot arrive at a valuation of the jewels (exclusive of the Koh-i-noor), but I don't think it will be far short of a million! and the other valuable property as much more". The list was sent by Login to the "Government" in mid-July and in 1850 many items from the *Toshakhana* of Lahore sailed to England. Some of the jewels, like the emerald belt of Maharaja Sher Singh, were also presented in the Great Exhibition of 1851. Most of them were subsequently offered to Queen Victoria and are now part of the Queen's collection in England.

[47] **"Three Akalis"**
From an original drawing of
Emily Eden, Lahore, 1838
c. 38 x 25 cm
Private collection

III

The Army of the Punjab

Phase I. Tradition and early modernization 1799-1822

The martial tradition in the Sikh community goes back to Guru Har Govind (1606-1644) and Guru Govind Singh (1675-1708). As attested by all accounts, both Indian and European, the Khalsa army before 1799 consisted chiefly of cavalry equipped with traditional arms, although some matchlocks had been introduced in the 1770's, but practically no artillery. Each unit fought under its local chief. The basic tactic was to strike and run. Forster, who got an interesting account of the Sikhs written in Delhi par Colonel Polier in 1777, wrote this description of the Sikh army in 1782 : "Their military forces may be said to consist essentially of cavalry; for though some artillery is maintained, it is awkardly managed, and its uses ill understood. And their infantry, held in low estimation, usually garrison the forts and are employed in the meaner duties of the service. A Sikh horseman is armed with a matchlock and sabre in excellent metal, and his horse is strong and well formed. The predilection of the Sikhs for the matchlock musket, and the constant use they make of it, causes a difference in their manner of attack from that of any other Indian cavalry. A party from forty to fifty advances in a quick pace to the distance of a carbine shot from the enemy, and then, that the fire may be given with greater certainty, the horses are drawn up, and their pieces discharged. When, speedily retiring about one hundred paces, they load and repeat the same mode of annoying the enemy".

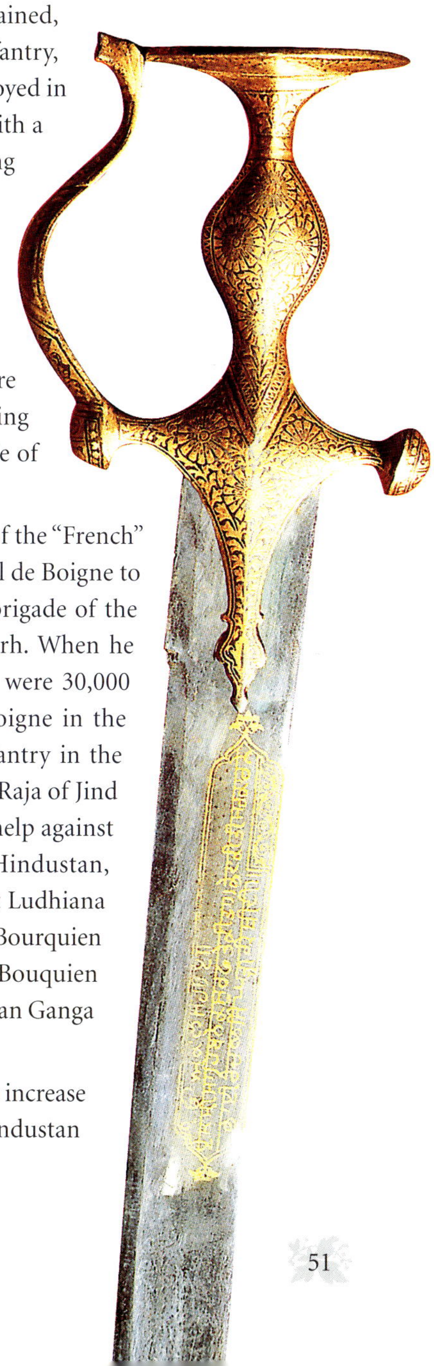

[20] Inscribed sword of Maharaja Ranjit Singh
Used during the conquest of Kasur in 1807
Central Sikh Museum, Amritsar
Courtesy : Shiromani Gurudwara Parbandhak Committee

Born in 1780, Maharaja Ranjit Singh knew of the power of the "French" brigades of Hindustan. In 1784 Madhoji Sindhia asked General de Boigne to raise the first regular units of his army. Trained in the Irish brigade of the French army, de Boigne established his headquarter at Aligarh. When he returned to Europe in 1796 the three brigades he had raised were 30,000 strong. From 1796 to 1803 General Perron succeeded de Boigne in the command of these troops, raising the number of regular infantry in the doab to 45,000. In 1799 the cis-Sutlej states led by Bagh Singh, Raja of Jind and maternal uncle of Ranjit Singh, asked General Perron for help against the Irish adventurer George Thomas. The 3rd Brigade of Hindustan, commanded by Louis Bourquien, crushed Thomas, camped at Ludhiana and Pinjaure and operated in these areas till 1803. Like Thomas, Bourquien had fixed his headquarters at Hansi. The political adviser of Bouquien during his operations on the cis-Sutlej areas of Punjab was Diwan Ganga Ram.

[46] "Nahang, or Akalee (Immortal, fanatic Sikh)"
From Honigberger, *Thirty-Five Years in the East ...*, plate V, p. 121
Probably from an original painting by Imam Bakhsh Lahori
Punjab State Archives. Acc. N° 279

Three events were instrumental in Ranjit Singh's decision to increase the strength of his regular troops. In 1803 the Brigades of Hindustan

[49] Irregular infantry
19 x 24 cm
Middle 19th century
National Museum. New Delhi. Sr.n 79.332

were destroyed by the East India Company, whose territories therefore extended to an undefined border between the Sutlej and the Jamuna. In 1805 Holkar, pursued by Lord Lake, took refuge in Amritsar, where Ranjit Singh was amazed to see a big Maratha army pursued by such a small body of regular troops. In 1809 the Metcalfe "incident", when a party of Akalis was repulsed at Amritsar by the small infantry escort of Metcalfe, aggrieved Ranjit Singh. The Maharaja decided to develop regular units in his army.

The first regular regiments of the Punjab army came mainly from the remains of the Brigades of Hindustan. Hence the title of *kumedan*, from the French "commandant". They also incorporated Indian officers and deserters of the East India Company. Ranjit Singh also started developing a regular artillery which was cast and manned by specialists originally coming from Aligarh, and then recruited from Delhi. In 1809 the total strength of the army was about 24,000 men, out of which only 1,500 were regular troops called the "foreign corps" by British observers.

[53] General Perron
Engraving from an oil painting by
Robert Lefèvre, 1822
Private collection

[54] General Lake
Engraving by R. Cooper published in London
in 1807, after a painting by George Place,
Lucknow, c. 1804. 52.1 x 37.5 cm
Victoria Memorial, Calcutta. Acc. N° C 347

In 1813 Ranjit Singh employed Ganga Ram, the former *diwan* of Bourquien, to take charge of his regular units and his artillery. A year later Ganga Ram called his son Ajudhya Prasad to Lahore, and his nephew Dina Nath in 1815. Ajudhya Prasad became the *bakhshi* of the regular army in 1819. These three men from the same family played a major role in the modernisation of the civil and military administration of the Punjab Kingdom. In 1821 the army was 50,000 strong, 10,000 of whom were serving in regular regiments. This small core of regular units, as Ranjit Singh himself acknowledged, were no match for the regular troops of the East India Company. However, a modernization process had begun, which was to be accelerated from 1822 onwards. In the meantime the irregular units of the Punjab army also existed in 1839. They lasted till 1849 and numerically speaking remained superior to the regular troops, although they took no real part in the fighting during the two Anglo-Sikh wars of 1846 and 1849.

[45] **Phula Singh Akali**
"Poullah Singh Naheng. Général des Akalis, fanatiques sikhs"
Gouache on European paper
by Imam Bakhsh Lahori, Lahore, 1827-1843
163 x 242 mm
Court collection. Musée Guimet
MG 78 III 39748

[44] **Stand of traditional weapons**
Maharaja Ranjit Singh Museum. Amritsar

[65] Maharaja Ranjit Singh with Generals Allard and Ventura
Military Manual of Maharaja Ranjit Singh
Probably the workshop of Imam Bakhsh Lahori
Lahore, 1822-1830
Maharaja Ranjit Singh Museum. Amritsar
Acc. N° 1035

IV

The Army of the Punjab

Phase II. 1822-1839
Modernisation drive

[100] **General Sham Singh Attariwala**
[Sitting/ front]
Oil on canvas
Detail from A. Schoefft's 'The Court of Lahore'
Lahore 1841-Vienna 1855
Princess Bamba Collection
Sikh gallery, Lahore Fort. Director of Archaeology
Government of Pakistan

From 1815 onwards, the English officers and regiments coming from England to India had been through twenty years of revolutionary and Napoleonic wars in Europe. They had acquired new military technologies and extensive strategic experiences which they were not ready to share with any of their Indian subjects or allies.

Arthur Wellesley had played a prominent part in the destruction of the sultanate of Mysore in 1799 and the annihilation of the Maratha power in the doab and central India in 1803-1805. Back in Europe, he had spear-headed the guerilla war in Portugal and Spain against the French. Created Duke of Wellington in 1814, his unflinching resistance and the timely arrival of the army of Blücher assured the victory of the allies at Waterloo and the crumbling of the French empire. However interested he was in European affairs, Wellington never ceased to follow the affairs of India: after the battle of Chillianwala in 1849, when Gough had been recalled and Napier did not want to go back, the 80-year-old Wellington offered to return to India as commander-in-chief.

The difficult task for the Maharaja was to modernise his regular troops without inducting English or "country-born" (of mixed parentage) officers. In 1803 the massive desertion of these "Anglo-Indian" officers of the Brigades of Hindustan had been the decisive factor of the English victories of Aligarh, Laswari, Assaye and Delhi (Patparganj). Ganga Ram, at that time Colonel Bourquien's *diwan*, had witnessed the disastrous result of these desertions. He was now in charge of the regular units of Maharaja Ranjit Singh, and there was no question of entrusting the overall command of these elite units to English or "Anglo-Indian" officers.

In 1822 two former French officers of Napoleon, Allard and Ventura, arrived in Lahore. After a systematic enquiry to discover whether they were British officers in disguise, the Maharaja asked them to raise the *Fauj-i-khas*, or Special (Royal) Brigade, called *Francisi Campu* by the common folk and the "French Legion" by English intelligence. The corps, with five regiments of infantry, three regiments of cavalry and the *topkhana*, was c. 10,000 to 15,000 strong according to the period considered.

As soon as Calcutta was informed that French officers of Napoleon had been enrolled by Maharaja Ranjit Singh to raise a new corps, the British authority appointed Lieutenant Claude Martine Wade as assistant political officer at Ludhiana. Wade's godfather was Major-General Claude Martin of Lucknow fame and he spoke French and Persian fluently. His first detailed report to Delhi (11 September 1823) gives precise information on the creation of the *Fauj-i-khas*:

"The disposition of the battalions is this : There were 1200 men formerly raised by these gentlemen [Allard and Ventura in 1822]. In this number some diminution afterwards occurred, but when the Raja came from Deena Nagar about three months ago, he put a battalion of *Gurkhas* under their command, the corps being without a head, its former commandant Palhordal Singh having been killed in battle at Peshawar.

The *Gurkhas* battalions used to practice the English mode of exercise, but it is now trained to the French. 200 men were drafted from the original 1200 and incorporated with the *Gurkhas* battalion, so that there are altogether under the personal orders of M. Chevalier Ventura about 2000 regular infantry. The disposition of the regiments of horse is as follows: M. Chevalier Allard, the senior, originally raised 1200 men whom he has brought to a state of discipline, and to them 300 fine well mounted men have since been added. They are taken from the force commanded by Kour Kharak Singh (the Raja's son) who oppresses his men and witholds their just demands. In addition to their number, the French officers have been ordered to raise 500 more horsemen. They are accordingly being enlisted everyday and by Dusserah there will be altogether under the immediate command of M. Chevalier Allard about 2000 effective horses. The artillery consists of the following divisions : Misr Dewan Chand has the charge of a division of 40 pieces. Ilahi Bakhsh, formerly a personal attendant of the Maharaja, another division of 40 pieces. Ameer Chand, also once a personal servant of the Raja, a division of 12 pieces of different calibres. These three divisions are composed of foot-artillery. Of horse-artillery there are two divisions : Mirza Muezzin Ali has one of 15 guns, Sultan Muhammed another of 15 guns.

M. Ventura receives the reports of the battalions every morning in the European manner, M. Allard those of the regiments of horse in like manner".

In 1827 three other French officers arrived from Persia: Oms, who quickly commanded a full brigade of five regiments of infantry and one of cavalry (c. 6000 men), Court and

[57] General Allard
Oil on canvas
Copy of an original painting signed "Court. 1837"
By Joseph-Désiré Court, Paris 1837
127 x 97 cm. Private collection

[58] General Ventura
Oil on canvas
Artist unknown. 1838 ?
Size not recorded. Private collection

[60] General Avitabile
Detail from "The Darbar of Maharaja Ranjit Singh" [N° 33]
Gouache on paper, stuck on wood panel
Artist unknown. c. 1850
Maharaja Ranjit Singh Museum. Amritsar
Acc. N° 110

Avitabile who each formed his own brigade (5700 men in all). Though Oms died mysteriously in 1828, these French brigades rapidly became the spearhead of the Punjab army. General Court, a former cadet of the military academy of Saint-Cyr (1813), was entrusted by the Maharaja with the reorganisation of the artillery. He did it in a very superior way, in collaboration with his Punjabi colleagues like Lehna Singh Majithia. His success was acknowledged by the Maharaja as well as by every European specialist who visited Lahore and recorded his opinion on the subject.

Highly satisfied with the discipline and the efficiency of his "French" brigades, Maharaja Ranjit Singh decided in 1833 to reorganize the *Campu-i-mualla* (all his other regular units) in brigades on the pattern of the *Fauj-i-khas*. In 1835, the whole regular army was divided into divisions, with the creation by Maharaja Ranjit Singh of eight posts of general.

Size of the Punjab army. 1830 and 1839

It is rather difficult to have an accurate idea of the size of the Punjab army according to contemporary intelligence, and since the *Khalsa Darbar Records* are incomplete, the best source is the cautious and certainly conservative estimates of Fauja Singh Bajwa in his *Military System of the Sikhs* :

	1830	1839
Regular infantry	c. 20,000	c. 30,000
Regular cavalry	c. 4 to 4,500	c. 4,700
Irregular infantry	c. 24,000	c. 25,000
Irregular cavalry	c. 10,000	c. 11,000
Guns	c. 300	c. 300 of the new types and calibres.
Swivels	c. 300	Estimates vary from 150 to 500
Jaghirdari Fauj	c 27,000	No estimate
Total strength :	c. 90,000	c. 80,000*

*(F.S. Bajwa, who also quotes Van Orlich's estimate of 150,000)

[75] Cuirass of Allard's cavalry
Lahore Museum, Lahore. Pakistan

[61] Dr. Martin Honigberger
(Austro-Hungarian), Colonels Mouton, de La Roche, Lafont. Oil on canvas
Detail from A. Schoefft's The Court of Lahore
Lahore 1841-Vienna 1855
Princess Bamba Collection. Sikh gallery
Lahore Fort. Director of Archaeology
Government of Pakistan

[59] General Court
Detail from Schoefft's The Court of Lahore
August Schoefft,
Vienna, 1850-1855
From drawings made in Lahore in 1841-42
Princess Bamba Collection, Sikh Gallery
Lahore Fort. Director of Archaeology
Government of Pakistan

[227] Honigberger's Thirty Five Years ...
Plate VI [Detail] "Mooselman, or, Mussulman
Sipahee (Mahommedan Sepoy)"
Probably from original paintings by
Imam Bakhsh Lahori, 1829-1849
Punjab State Archives
Acc. N° 279

[78] Fauj-i-khas: Sikh infantry, Gurkha [Purbiah]
"Soldat Sikh. Soldat Pourpié"
Watercolour on European paper
By Imam Bakhsh Lahori. Lahore, 1827-1843
198 x 270 mm
Court collection, Musée Guimet. MG 78 III 39746

[62] **General Ilahi Bakhsh commanding the topkhana**
Detail from [33]

[63] **Diwan Ajudhya Prasad bakhshi of the Fauj-i-khas**
Detail from [33]

The important increase in the regular infantry between 1830 and 1839 comes from Maharaja Ranjit Singh's decision to transform the bulk of his regular infantry (*Campu-i-mualla*) on the pattern of the *Fauj-i-khas* from 1833 onwards.

The Fauj-i-khas and the other French brigades

The *Fauj-i-khas*, the elite unit of the Punjab army, was created in 1822 for Maharaja Ranjit Singh by his two French officers, Allard and Ventura, out of existing regiments, but with immediate fresh enrolments both of infantry and cavalry. Some of the first Punjabi, Purbiah and Nepalese officers who joined it in 1822 served till they retired or till 1849 : Sheikh Bassvan, Ajudhya Prasad, Colonel Chet Singh, Kahn Singh Rosa, and of course Ilahi Bakhsh, the officer in charge of the *topkhana*.

Although we have more information on the *Fauj-i-khas* and the two other "French" brigades of Court and Avitabile than on the rest of the army, still it is not easy to have a clear view of their evolution till 1846, not to speak of 1849. We give hereunder the most precise information we have for each brigade, although it is not taken in the same year:

Fauj-i-khas

Generals Allard and Ventura
Bakhshi Diwan Ajudhya Prasad
Brigadier Sheikh Basawan
Headquarters: Anarkali, Lahore

Infantry (1837-9) :	Cavalry (1823)
Paltan-i-khas	Rajman khas Lansia (Lancers)
Paltan Dewa Singh	Rajman Sheikh Qamar-ud-Din
Paltan Sham Sota	Rajman Daragun Anwal (First Dragoon)
Paltan Gurkhas	Rajman Daragun Dugan (Second Dragoon)
Artillery (1823)	Topkhana Ilahi Bakhsh (40 guns)

Court's brigade

General Court
Headquarters : Naulakha, Lahore

Infantry (1837-9)	Paltan Baj Singh
	Paltan Buddh Singh
	Paltan Dewan Singh
Artillery	Derah Jodh Singh (7 guns)

Avitabile's brigade

General Avitabile
Headquarter : Budhu-ka-Ava, Lahore. From 1838-39 at Peshawar

Infantry (1838-9)	Paltan Bhup Singh
	Paltan Captain Ford
	Paltan Captain Lafont
Artillery	topkhana Ford Sahib (2 guns)

[72] **A "French" brigade on the battle front**
From the lithoprint 'The Battle of Moodkee',
18th December 1845
Engraved by J. Harris
from a painting by H. Martens
Published in 1849
Maharaja Ranjit Singh Museum. Amritsar
Acc. N° 10

The cantonments of the regular troops at Lahore

Lahore, capital of the kingdom, was well protected by troops distributed all around the city. The "French" troops, just outside the ramparts, formed the last line of defense: Avitabile's brigade was stationed at Budhu-ka-awa, midway between Shalimar Gardens and the Lahore Fort. Court's brigade was at Naulakha, the *Fauj-i-khas* at Anarkali and Oms' brigade at Shahdara on the northern side of the River Ravi. The *Fauj-i-khas* cantonments at Anarkali were a model of order and cleanliness. Built around a *champ de mars* or parade ground they had residences for the officers and barracks for the troops. The banks of the Ravi were beautified into a "Jardin du Soldat" (The soldier's garden), and soon a fashionable bazar (now "old" Anarkali) developed between the cantonment and the city. Allard and Ventura had their own residence cum headquarters in the garden of Anarkali. These cantonments were so comfortable that in 1846 the British occupying forces settled there, and Henry Lawrence occupied the residence of generals Allard and Ventura.

The other regular troops, called the *Campu-i-mualla*, were distributed in a wider circle extending from Nawankot (on the road to Multan) to Mian Mir, where the British later established their own cantonments, putting the strategic railway track between themselves and the city.

[73] **Allard's Lancer**
Water colour on paper
Artist unknown
24 x 18 cm
National Museum, New Delhi. Acc. N° 79.326

The missions of the Fauj-i-khas

The *Fauj-i-khas* was kept by the Maharaja as a reserve force to be engaged only in case of emergency, as in 1827 when Syed Ahmed Barelvi declared a *jihad* against Lahore, or in 1837 when Punjabi troops were encircled and besieged at Jamrud. They were also used as a deterrent against potential enemies, like in 1831 when Ventura was appointed governor of Dera Ghazi Khan and his troops were deployed both against the Baluchi tribes and the

[76] Carbines of Allard's cavalry
Sikh Gallery, Lahore Fort. Lahore
Director of Archaeology
Government of Pakistan

Nawab of Bahawalpur. The *Fauj-i-khas* was ultimately positioned at Peshawar after the battle of Jamrud and the death of Hari Singh Nalwa in 1837, and its units remained there till 1839.

The *Fauj-i-khas* was also used against powerful feudal chiefs against whom no other Punjabi commander dared to move, for example in 1828-9 Maharaja Ranjit Singh imposed a fine of rupees two lakhs on General Hari Singh Nalwa. Nobody dared to move against Hari Singh and Ranjit Singh had to entrust the task to General Allard and the *Fauj-i-khas*. Because of the excellent relations between the two men the matter was of course amiably settled.

The Anglo-Sikh frontier on the Sutlej was particularly sensitive, and between 1822 and 1824 the situation deteriorated because of the more than thirty Sikh enclaves in cis-Sutlej British protected territories. In 1825 Ranjit Singh entrusted the whole frontier to the *Fauj-i-khas*. Allard's cavalry was deployed along the Sutlej. Four hundred lancers occupied the fort of Phillaur under Colonel Chet Singh and piquets of cavalry were established on every ford and in the most volatile Sikh enclaves dispersed in British Protected Territories. Colonel Chet Singh remained in charge of the frontier from 1825 to practically 1846, reporting directly to General Allard's headquarters at Anarkali, while Jamadar Hafiz Ibrahim commanded the units on the left side of the river. A detachment of Allard's cavalry was permanently posted at Ludhiana to protect Maharaja Ranjit Singh's *vakil* appointed to the British Political Agent.

[82] Fauj-i-khas
Two bombs for mortar
and Honigberger's instrument for testing powder
Sikh Gallery. Lahore Fort. Lahore
Director of Archaeology. Government of Pakistan

[74] Allard's Cuirassier
"Chairana Sowar (a Cuirassier)"
Lahore, 1837-1843
From Honigberger's *Thirty Five Years in the East ...*, plate V, p. 121
Probably from an original painting by Imam Bakhsh Lahori
Punjab State Archives. Patiala
Acc. N° 279

The Jamrud Campaign. 1837

On 7 March 1837 Maharaja Ranjit Singh celebrated the wedding of Prince Nau Nihal Singh at Lahore. General Fane, commander-in-chief of the British army, attended it. In order to impress the British delegation, the Maharaja called back all his elite troops, including the *Fauj-i-khas*, from Peshawar to Lahore. Fane was deeply impressed by the review of the regular troops of the Punjab army.

Dost Mohammed Khan seized this opportunity to launch an all-out offensive to recapture Peshawar and its province. The Punjabi garrison of Jamrud shut itself inside the fort and resisted till Hari Singh Nalwa, having secured Peshawar, made a dash against the Afghans and surprised the besiegers whom he managed to draw into the open plain. Then his artillery opened a well-directed fire against the enemy, followed by a massive attack by columns of infantry. The Nalwa had won the day when his *gorcharas*, against his orders, pursued the enemy and therefore disturbed the line of battle. The Afghans rallied and made a counter-attack which the Punjabi troops could not sustain. Hari Singh then led the charge against the incoming enemies and repelled them, but he was mortally wounded and had to retire from the battlefield. He died a few days later. The Punjabi army fell back on the fort and dug up trenches, waiting for reinforcement.

Maharaja Ranjit Singh, then at Sheikupura, did not believe the first reports of Hari Singh Nalwa asking for the immediate return of the French brigades to Peshawar. When on 27 April he realised his mistake, he ordered General Allard to march at once with the *Fauj-i-khas*. Allard said there was no time to loose in going back to Anarkali (Lahore) to take the heavy equipment of the *Fauj*. Ranjit Singh gave him permission to take whatever he needed at Rohtas and Attock. The *Fauj-i-khas* and the other brigades made forced marches from Sheikupura to Jamrud, three hundred miles in eleven days with their artillery,

[96] The Fauj-i-khas Headquarters at Anarkali, Lahore
From a photograph in a private collection

[106] The fort of Jamrud
"Dgémrod à l'entrée du Kheïber" /
Forteresse construite par les Sikhs
"Attaque du Kheïber"
Watercolour on European paper
By Imam Bakhsh Lahori. Lahore, 1827-1843
285 x 193 mm
Court collection. Musée Guimet
MG 78 III 39733

taking at Rohtas and Attock the arms and ammunitions they needed. When they approached Jamrud on 9th May, the Afghans retired to the foothills. During the night General Court set up his batteries of howitzers, mortars and heavy guns. In the morning, he opened such a terrible fire on the enemy that they ran away to Ali Masjid and Jalalabad. After reviewing the situation, Maharaja Ranjit Singh appointed General Allard as military governor of the province, with General Court as his assistant-commander. They kept with them the French brigades and other crack regular units. General Avitabile was appointed civil governor of Peshawar. This situation lasted till 1843, when the French generals left the service and retired to Europe.

[51] General Hari Singh Nalwa
Detail from "The Darbar of Maharaja Ranjit Singh"
Gouache on paper, stuck on wood panel
Artist unknown. c. 1850
Maharaja Ranjit Singh Museum. Amritsar
Acc. N° 110

[105] The fort of Attock with boat bridge
"Forteresse d'Attok sur l'Indus"
Watercolour on European paper
By Imam Bakhsh Lahori. Lahore, 1827-1843
291 x 183 mm
Court collection, Musée Guimet
MG 78 III 39731

Creation of a mountaineering division. The conquest of Ladakh. General Zorawar Singh

Maharaja Ranjit Singh received the submission of the Raja of Jammu in 1800-1801. A Sikh army was sent there in 1809 to quell a rebellion, and in 1812 Prince Kharak Singh was given Jammu as *jaghir*. These are also the years (1810-1812) when Gulab Singh arrived in Lahore and joined the Punjab army. Ranjit Singh noticed him, acknowledged his ability and gave him important commands. According to W. Archer the Maharaja appointed him governor of Jammu in 1820, which position he held till 1846. General Court and Raja Gulab Singh of Jammu were close friends. Court was one of the instructors of Udham Singh, eldest son of Gulab Singh. According to Court's unpublished *Mémoires*, the Raja asked him to raise and train a mountaineering division.

In 1834 Gulab Singh ordered General Zorawar Singh, his Governor of Kishtwar, to conquer Ladakh. Leh was taken, but Ranjit Singh imposed caution and restraint in order not to antagonize the Chinese authorities. The situation came to a standstill till 1840, when after the Maharaja's death, Zorawar Singh was ordered to move again. The conflict in the Himalayas lasted till 1842, when a treaty fixed the frontier between the various belligerents.

Many reasons might explain this Punjabi / Dogra move into the Himalayas, the most potent being the fact that the British had just closed for Ranjit Singh the conquest of Sindh and an opening to the sea. Besides, an extension in the mountains might help coordinate an alliance with Nepal and balance the overwhelming East India Company. Last but not least there was also an attempt to reconnect directly with the supply of pashmina wool which the British had diverted to their profit after they built a road to Bussahir in the 1820's.

The Campu-i-mualla

The greatest number of regular infantry was till 1826 under the orders of Diwan Ganga Ram. They comprised of various units, some of them with their artillery. When Ganga Ram died in 1826, Ranjit Singh offered the command of the *Campu* to his son Diwan Ajudhya Prasad, bakhshi of the *Fauj-i-khas*, who

[79] Fauj-i-khas : A Muslim Gunner
"Canonnier Mahométan"
By Imam Bakhsh Lahori. Lahore, 1827-1843
186 x 278 mm
Court collection, Musée Guimet
MG 78 III 39745

[93] **Medal of the Kaukab-i-Iqbal-i-Punjab or Auspicious Star of the Punjab**
Gold and enamelled, set with diamonds and emeralds
Sheesh Mahal Museum, Patiala
Acc. N° P 73-111-1

refused, declaring that he prefered to serve in the "French Legion". He then offered it to Tej Singh, who kept it till 1846. According to British intelligence, Tej Singh commanded 22 regular regiments in 1831.

J.S. Grewal and I. Banga, in their *Civil and Military affairs of Maharaja Ranjit Singh*, have translated 462 orders issued in Persian by Ranjit Singh to Raja Tej Singh from 14 November 1833 to 21 December 1834. This is the best documentation we have of the care taken by the Maharaja in military affairs.

The striking observation coming out from these documents is that the *Campu-i-mualla* was not an easily identifiable entity, since in some cases units of the *Fauj-i-khas* like the *sawaran-i-lansia* and some "Regiments of the French officers" are mentioned, as well

[80] **Arms and artillery. Punjab army**
Miniature painting from *Ain-i-Akbari*
Artist unknown. Lahore, 1838
Asiatic Society, Calcutta. Acc. N° P 128

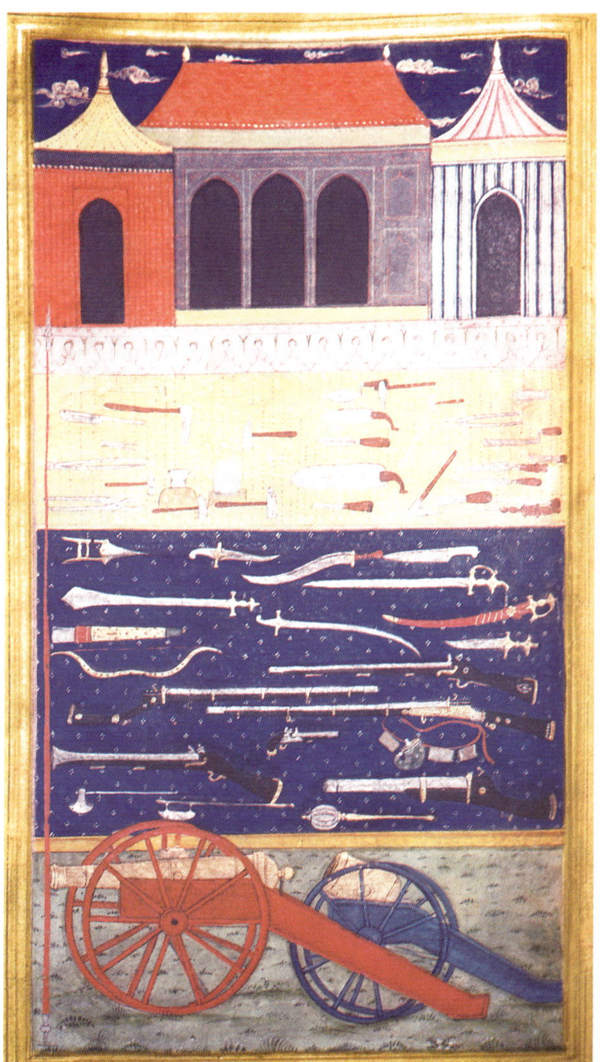

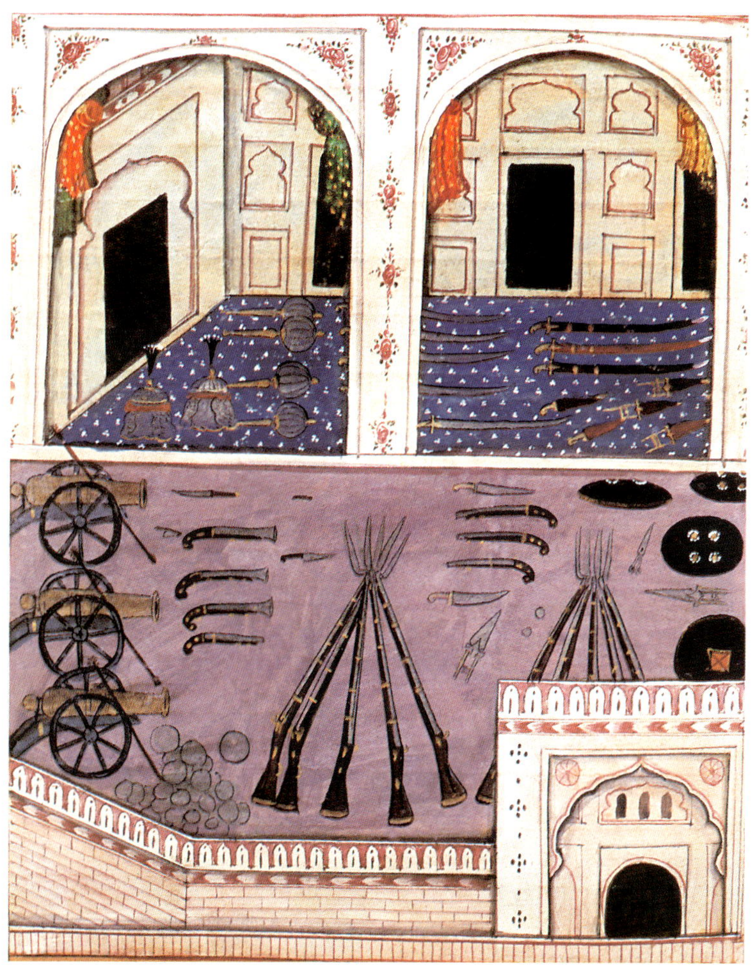

[131a] **Ain-i-Akbari**
by Abul Fazl
copied at Lahore under Maharaja Ranjit Singh. Illustrated. Artist unknown
Punjab State Archives. Patiala. Acc. N° M 658

as batallions of najibs (Avitabile), *gurkhas* (Ventura) etc. In these documents even some *nihang* and *jaghirdari* units are included in the Campu.

From 1833 to 1835 the *Campu* was reorganised on the pattern of the *Fauj-i-khas*. The greatest difficulty was to find enough staff, senior and subaltern officers, to train the new units on the latest European system of warfare. This anomaly was easily detected by the British military delegation at Ferozpur in 1838, and it was confirmed in the battlefield during the First Anglo-Sikh War. The Government of Punjab appointed Raja Tej Singh commander-in-chief of the army, with Raja Lal Singh (of the *gorcharas*) as field commander. In the battles of the First Anglo-Sikh War, the brunt of the fighting was borne by the old regular units while the new ones were the first to disband and retire under fire or when hand to hand fighting started with the enemy. As far as the conduct of the war was concerned, the turning of victory into defeat at Ferozeshah and the disaster at Sobraon were due to the treachery and incompetence of these two officers.

[94] Khilat awarded by Maharaja Ranjit Singh to General Allard
Gold embroidery on pashmina
Private collection

Conclusion

During the formative phase of the Punjab kingdom (1799-1822) the irregular units of the army were instrumental in the conquest and aggrandisement of the state.

With the setting up of an administration and the task of building up a modern state, Maharaja Ranjit Singh needed a unifying tool in his hands alone : he created for that purpose the *Fauj-i-khas* and the other regular brigades of the Punjab army. That was also necessary because of the growing military power of the East India Company on the east, the renewed Iranian threat on the west (siege of Herat) and the possible unification of Afghanistan under Amir Dost Mohammed Khan.

[92] General Allard's medal of Commander of the Order of Guru Govind Singh
Private collection

The recruiting of the army, including the

French units, was open to all, Punjabi and non-Punjabi (*Purbiahs*, *Gurkhas*, Pathans, Afghans, "country-born" Europeans and continental Europeans). This in turn allowed the Maharaja to assure to all his subjects, despite the sporadic difficulties and the bitter memories of the past, a certain freedom of religion and culture which he always emphasised at Court and did his best to implement in the land.

[83] **Miniature French gun**
Faqir Jalaluddin Collection. Ref. 666 / List n° 38
Lahore Museum. Lahore, Pakistan

[95] **Khilat awarded by Maharaja Ranjit Singh to General Allard**
Gold emboidery on pashmina
Private collection

[85] **Fauj-i-khas. Musique**
Sikh Gallery. Lahore Fort. Lahore
Director of Archaeology
Government of Pakistan

[108] "Maharaja Ranjit Singh listening to the Granth being recited near the Golden Temple, Amritsar"
Oil on canvas by A. Schoefft
Amritsar 1841-Vienna 1855. 4' 8" 1/2 x 3' 7"
Princess Bamba Collection. Sikh gallery, Lahore Fort
Director of Archaeology. Government of Pakistan

V

Religion and Education

Religious Freedom in the Punjab under Maharaja Ranjit Singh

In 1799, most of the territories under Ranjit Singh's command had a predominantly Hindu and Sikh population, including Lahore though it had been for so long the capital of the Mughal *suba*. After the conquests of Attock, Multan, Kashmir and the first inroads towards Peshawar and the Derajat, a substantial part of the kingdom's population in the early 1820's included Muslims.

Maharaja Ranjit Singh, no doubt, was a strong believer and a devout Sikh, following the principles of his religion. In the meantime, as Maharaja of the Punjab and head of a state with so much ethnic and religious diversity, he showed a remarkable interest in preserving the religious and cultural freedom of his subjects, showing a respect, a curiosity of mind and a sympathetic approach to the feelings and beliefs of others. The care he took for protecting and developing the various vernacular education systems in his country is a clear indication of this constant policy.

Ranjit Singh took care that the places of worship of the Muslim community be preserved, although a few prestigious, symbolic monuments that are also strategically situated like the Badshahi Masjid at Lahore, had been attached by the triumvirate as state property in 1764. In the meantime, he allowed Hindu and Sikh temples to be erected freely, especially at Lahore, which was a total departure from the policy of the former governments of the land.

Every religious institution had a teaching unit. The number of indigenous educational institutions recensed by Leitner in the Punjab in 1882 shows that there was great care, under Maharaja Ranjit Singh, to allow these various institutions, Hindu, Sikh or Muslim, to function properly, disseminating knowledge and transmitting culture, both religious and profane, with the help of the state (grants, *jaghirs*) and the freedom guaranteed by the power of the government.

Leitner estimated at 330,000 the number of pupils studying in the various religious schools before the annexation of the Punjab (as against 190,000 pupils in 1882). These children were acquainted at the elementary level by their teachers- *maulvis*, *pandit* or *gurus*- with reading, writing, and some method of computation.

Maharaja Ranjit Singh and Sikhism

It is well-known that Ranjit Singh had a strong attachment to Sikhism. Bhai Ram Singh, his most trusted spiritual adviser, was always in attendance on him, having the privilege to be seated in his presence, and Bhai Gurmukh Singh was his family priest. Both of them are represented on the grand painting of Schoefft. Listening to the Granth Sahib was a regular feature of the Maharaja's life, and he regularly visited the Harmandir and

[110] Guru Nanak
from the *Military Manual of Maharaja Ranjit Singh*
Probably the workshop of Imam Bakhsh Lahori
1822-1830. Maharaja Ranjit Singh Museum
Amritsar. Acc. N° 1035

other Sikh shrines in the Punjab. In Lahore he built the gurudwara of Guru Ram Das, on the model of the Golden Temple of Amritsar, and the mausoleum of Guru Arjun with its gold cupola next to the fort.

As soon as he captured Amritsar in 1802, Ranjit Singh appointed a committee to look after the affairs of the temple, and Sardar Lehna Singh Majithia was put in charge of the Harmandir. The octroi income from Amritsar and land in the form of *jaghir*s were given to the temple for the expenses of the community. Many *bungas* were built to accomodate pilgrims and visitors, and Ranjit Singh built his own *bunga* in the north-west corner of the temple, where he stayed whenever he visited the Harmandir. The beautification of the Harmandir was a major religious and artistic contribution of the Maharaja to his community and to the Punjab as well. The temple was covered with marble and gold at a total cost of sixty-four lakhs, of which the Maharaja contributed sixteen lakhs. All over Punjab (including in the cis-Sutlej States which were not under Ranjit Singh's authority) the Sikh community decorated their gurudwaras and other buildings attached to them with splendid frescoes. Most of these decorations have disappeared in Amritsar, but beautiful paintings of that time can still be seen today at Guru Harsahai, near Ferozepore.

[111] **Guru Angad**
from the *Military Manual of Maharaja Ranjit Singh*
Probably the workshop of Imam Bakhsh Lahori
1822-1830. Maharaja Ranjit Singh Museum
Amritsar Acc. N° 1035

[117] **Guru Har Krishan**
from the *Military Manual of Maharaja Ranjit Singh*
Probably the workshop of Imam Bakhsh Lahori
1822-1830 Maharaja Ranjit Singh Museum
Amritsar. Acc. N° 1035

[115] **Guru Har Gobind**
from the *Military Manual of Maharaja Ranjit Singh*
Probably the workshop of Imam Bakhsh Lahori
1822-1830 Maharaja Ranjit Singh Museum
Amritsar. Acc. N° 1035

Ranjit Singh gave splendid offerings to the Harmandir: they include two of the four gold portals of the temple showing the life of Guru Nanak in repoussé, the famous canopy embedded with gold and studded with diamonds, emeralds, rubies and pearls. Among many other precious gifts was the *jarau sehra* or bejewelled gold-pearl headband which the Maharaja had given to Prince Nau Nihal Singh on his wedding in 1837. Before he died, Ranjit Singh ordered his horses to be given to the Harmandir. Maharaja Ranjit Singh's authority concerning the Harmandir was never questioned. Two years after his death, when August Schoefft came to Amritsar and Lahore, Maharaja Sher Singh commissioned the beautiful painting "Maharaja Ranjit Singh listening to the Granth being recited near the Golden Temple at Amritsar", a befitting tribute to the care Ranjit Singh had taken of the Harmandir all his life.

Sikh educational institutions in Punjab

Maharaja Ranjit Singh made a special effort to give landed endowment for Gurmukhi schools, since they had not been so favoured by the former governments of the land, and he recommanded all who came near him to learn how to read Gurmukhi. Leitner observed in 1882 : "The number of Gurmukhi manuscripts on various subjects connected with science and religion scattered all over the province, in the possession of bhais and shrines, is very considerable". He adds that Bhai Budh Singh was one of the foremost translators of Sanskrit works into Punjabi, and that Sardar Lehna Singh Majithia, engineer and mathematician, was said to have translated Euclid from Arabic into Punjabi. Leitner even gave some details on the syllabus, from elementary to higher education like medicine, astrology and rhetoric, precising that all the text books were in Gurmukhi. Using a litote, since he was already fighting against a disinformation campaign of colonial

[119] **Guru Govind Singh**
from the *Military Manual of Maharaja Ranjit Singh*
Probably the workshop of Imam Bakhsh Lahori
Lahore, 1822-1830
Maharaja Ranjit Singh Museum. Amritsar
Acc. N° 1035

propaganda, Leitner felt obliged to affirm that "nor were the Sikh Sirdars, as is generally alleged, illiterate. Sirdar Lehna Singh Majithia was no mean mathematician and engineer. Kanwar Nau Nihal Singh, Ajit Singh and Lehna Singh Majithia studied the higher branches of mathematics and astronomy under the famous Akhwand Ali Ahmad who was specially called from the frontier to Lahore".

Maharaja Ranjit Singh and Islam The historical connection from Babur to Akbar to Aurangzeb

Sikhism was born and grew at a time when the great established religions, Hinduism and Islam, were both strengthening their othodoxies and evolving under the influence of original thinkers and reformers, *bhagats* and *sufis*. The *Adi Granth* contains hymns of Namdev, Kabir, Rav Das and other *bhagats* as well as *shlokas* of Sheikh Farid of Pakpattan.

On the political side, according to Punjabi memories and traditions, there were no

[130] Ain-i-Akbari
by Abul Fazl
copied at Lahore in 1838
Illustrated. Artist unknown
Asiatic Society of Calcutta. Inv. N° P.128

major problems with Babur and Humayun. With Akbar, both traditions and information attest the consideration this emperor had for Guru Amar Das and Guru Arjun.

Orthodox Islam had more influence on Jahangir, Shah Jahan and Aurangzeb. Among the many plausible reasons are their personal beliefs and education of course, but also the growing feeling of the Muslim community at large against the *dhimmis* and the *kafirs*. Moreover, *ghazis* continued to come in large numbers from Central Asia, Iran and Afghanistan, getting *jaghirs* and grants in the Punjab, thus increasing the fiscal pressure on the *ryots* and non-Muslim population. And ultimately, it was necessary for the Mughal power to keep open the Punjab plains at any cost in order to get constant reinforcements from the *Dar-ul-Islam* during the Mughal conquests of the Deccan and the wars against the Marathas.

This context explains the deteriorating relations between the Sikhs and the Mughal or Afghan powers in the Punjab, from the execution of Guru Arjun at Lahore in 1606 till the capture of Lahore by Ranjit Singh in 1799.

Maharaja Ranjit Singh and Akbar

In restructuring Lahore as the capital of a state much bigger than the former *suba* of the Mughal empire, Ranjit Singh renewed with an imperial tradition which can easily be traced to Akbar. His own policy of religious tolerance and sympathetic curiosity towards the diversity of human nature was another connection with the real founder of the Mughal dynasty.

For fourteen years (1584 to 1598) Akbar resided at Lahore, which was the *de facto* capital of the Mughal empire. He continued his liberal policy towards the non-Muslims, entertaining liberal discussions on religion, philosophy and science. Akbar erected three buildings on the outskirts of Lahore for receiving and feeding poor people : a *dharmpura* for the Hindus, a *khyrpura* for the Muslims, Jews and Parsis, and a *jogipura* for the Yogis. In 1591-98 the second and third Jesuit missions to the Mughals were sent to Lahore.

Whatever the various versions concerning the purchase of land at Amritsar by Guru Amar Das, they all point to the goodwill and reverence of Akbar for the head of the Sikh community, and there is a tradition of Akbar's visit to Guru Amar Das at Goindwal. Another Sikh tradition remembers two visits of Akbar to Guru Arjun, the second one (November 1598) attested by Badaoni. No surprise therefore that Prince Khusrau was well received by the Guru : he was known, just like Akbar, for his liberal views and sympathy for the Hindus, contrary to his opponent Prince Salim (Jahangir) who had Guru Arjun executed for applying the saffron mark on Khusrau's forehead.

There are few interesting references to Akbar and Abul Fazl in Maharaja Ranjit Singh's entourage, as reported for example in the

[127] The Holy Koran
Copied in Lahore under Maharaja Ranjit Singh
offered by Maharaja Ranjit Singh
to Fakir Nuruddin (sic). 47 x 69 cm
Lahore Museum. Lahore

Umdat-ut-Tawarikh, including Kalanaur, where Akbar had been enthroned. But several copies of the *Akbar Nama* and the *Ain-i-Akbari* from Lahore in Maharaja Ranjit Singh's period are glaring examples of Akbar's living memory in the Punjab. The illustrations showing "Akbar and his Court" at Lahore, and "Maharaja Ranjit Singh and his Court" establish the parallel and the comparison between two great men fascinated by the diversity of human nature and respectful of others' opinions.

The history of the Sonahri Masjid

Under Maharaja Ranjit Singh, the Muslim community of Lahore, continued to enjoy the possession of most of its mosques and sacred monuments. S.M. Latif mentions a few occasions when Muslim monuments were destroyed, like the tomb and mosque of Shah Sharaf (died in 1692) in order to make the ditch of Lahore. According to Latif, the remains of the saint were buried again at Ranjit Singh's request. The tomb of Shah Bilawal, whom Shah Jahan used to visit, was not destroyed by Ranjit Singh, but threatened by the Ravi. The Maharaja requested Fakir Syed Aziz-ud-Din to transfer the remains of the saint at their present place, and built a garden on the site.

The story of the small, and elegant Sonahri Masjid, or Golden Mosque, in the Kashmiri bazar of Lahore, is an interesting illustration of Ranjit Singh's attitude towards his non-Sikh subjects. Guru Arjun had dug up a *baoli* (well) in that area in commemoration of his father. After the Guru's execution in 1606, the *baoli* was confiscated by the state. In 1753 Nawab Bhikari Khan, an officer of Turkish origin, built a mosque near this *baoli* "by seizing money from the living and bricks from the dead", as an irreverent poet scribbled in verse on the gate of the mosque. He also built several shops just next to the baoli, the whole area being now attached to the mosque. When Ranjit Singh captured Lahore in 1799, the *baoli* was reoccupied by the Akalis, and the mosque turned into a *gurudwara*, with the *Adi Granth* installed in it.

[123] The Sonahri Masjid, Lahore
Built in 1753. Domes regilded in c. 1827
General view

In the late 1820's the Muslim officers of the *Fauj-i-khas* asked General Allard to intercede with the Maharaja so that the mosque be returned to the Muslim community. Allard did it in coordination with the Fakir brothers and, probably, with the backing of his personal friends, both Hindu and Sikhs, in the *darbar*. The Maharaja complied, and General Allard paid from his purse for the regilding of the three domes of the Sonahri Masjid.

[132] **Ain-i-Akbari**
by Abul Fazl
copied at Lahore under Maharaja Ranjit Singh
Illustrated. Artist unknown
Lahore Fort Museum Library, Lahore
Director of Archaeology. Government of Pakistan

This little known manuscript has two opening illustrations: one showing Akbar in court the other Ranjit Singh in court

[129] Maharaja Ranjit Singh
From an *Ain-i-Akbari*
copied at Lahore in 1838
Artist unknown
National Museum. New Delhi
Acc. N° 59.587, fol. 540v -541r

Muslim education in Punjab

Education was one of the main functions of the mosques in the *Dar-ul-Islam*. And Muslim education continued to flourish in the kingdom of Ranjit Singh. No contemporary information has survived on this topic, and we are in some way obliged to work "backwards" from Leitner's remarkable report on the *Indigenous Education in Punjab*. After reminding his readers that "Urdu, which we [the English] imported, did not boast of a single school on our avent", Leitner gives an interesting description of the Persian, Koranic and Arabic schools in Punjab as they still existed thirty years after annexation. Under Maharaja Ranjit Singh, both Hindus and Muslims who aimed for employment under the state studied Persian. Leitner has no figure concerning the number of *maktabs* and students since, with the disappearing support of the British administration, these schools were either absorbed in the new government schools or conducted in the teachers' residences. But he gives the syllabus : a fascinating list including the *Sikandarnama* of Nizami and the *Letters of Abul Fazl*. Concerning the Koran schools, the 1857 report gave their number at 1785. But Leitner has no doubt that there were "innumerable Koran schools in the private houses of *moulvis* and religious patrons", and that the widows used to teach the Koran to young boys and girls.

Leitner recalls that "The Punjab has ever been proverbial for the thoroughness with which Arabic grammar (etymology) was studied in it. These schools taught from the most elementary knowledge of reading Arabic up to the highest standard of Arabic law and literature, and the sciences contained in that literature, such as medicine". One anecdote reported by Leitner concerns "the famous mathematician and Arabic scholar Hashim Shah [who] got a *jaghir* near Jagdeo in recognition of his literary eminence. His Arabic scholarship secured his pardon from the ever-forgiving Ranjit Singh, when he had once joined in a revolution against the Sikh *sirkar*". This might have been Ahmad Shah Barelvi's *jihad*. Whatever it is, it shows the consideration the Maharaja had for knowledge irrespective of political or communal differences.

Maharaja Ranjit Singh and Hinduism
Hindu temples in Lahore before and under Maharaja Ranjit Singh

The *sharia* has very precise and stringent restrictions concerning the maintenance, and still more the construction, of non-Muslim religious buildings in the *Dar-ul-Islam*. Lahore being termed *Dar-us-Sultanat* during the Muslim rule on Punjab, it is not surprising that there were no architecturally great Hindu temples or Sikh gurudwaras in the city in 1799.

In his *Lahore* (1892), Syed Muhammad Latif, lists the thirty-one most important "*shivalas* or Hindu temples" then existing in the city: thirteen date from Ranjit Singh, two from 1839-1849, seven from the English period and the remaining have no specific datation,

[139] The Temple of Jawalamukhi today
Gold was offered by Maharaja Ranjit Singh
Courtesy: Government of Punjab

[140] Maharaja Ranjit Singh worshipping Devi
Gouache and gold on paper
Artist unknown. 1838 AD
26.5 x 21 cm
National Museum, New Delhi. Acc. N° 72.313

[138] Silver gates of the temple of Jawalamukhi
Courtesy: Government of Punjab

although some very small ones are identified as "very ancient". This mere fact, more than anything else, shows the freedom which suddenly induced the Hindu community to express its faiths and mark its presence through architecture in the capital of the Punjab.

Raja Dina Nath was particularly active in enlarging old temples and building new ones in Lahore. The *shivala* Tibbi Wala, "perhaps the most ancient Hindu temple of Lahore" (Latif) had in the 1820's the dome of the mandir on a level with the ground: Dina Nath built the high dome with which it was then covered. The *shivala* of Bawa Thakurgir, a small temple built by the Bawa during the triumvirate, was also enlarged and rebuilt by Raja Dina Nath and adorned with a domed roof surmounted by a golden pinnacle. The *shivala* of Raja Dina Nath was also a "handsome edifice. The walls fronting the streets are tastefully decorated with paintings of *devatas* and *avatars*. The inside walls are decorated with paintings of deities and gods. The shining golden pinnacle on the top of the dome contributes much to the attraction and the gate of this most popular place of Hindu worship. The floor inside the mandir is of pure marble" (Latif).

Many other *shivala*s were built, by Golab Rai, a *jamadar* in Ranjit Singh's *darbar*,

[139] The Temple of Jawalamukhi
Courtesy: Government of Punjab

[133] **"Om" with Vishnu, Lakshmi, Brahma and Shiva**
from the *Military Manual of Maharaja Ranjit Singh*
Probably from the workshop of Imam Bakhsh Lahori
Lahore, 1822-1830
Maharaja Ranjit Singh Museum
Amritsar. Acc. N° 1035

with a large gild dome, or by Dilbagh Rai, the *diwan* of Raja Dhyan Singh. The *thakurdwara* of Chor-Mor, profusely decorated with paintings and mirrors, was regularly visited by the Maharaja. Another imposing *shivala* was built in 1818 by Pandit Radha Kishan, with the upper portion of the tower covered with copper gild plates and a golden image of Hanuman on top of the tower. The *thakurdwara* built in 1834 by Pandit Radha Krishna, son of Madusudan, the family priest of Ranjit Singh had "the walls inside and the roofs ornamented with paintings of gold and silver" (Latif).

These are but the main temples as they subsisted in the late 1870's when Syed Muhammad Latif was compiling his *Lahore* with information from Kanhaya Lal and others. Many more smaller temples could be seen in the streets, corners and lanes of Lahore. This intense architectural activity was accompanied by a full fledged programme of paintings, frescoes and gilding, giving an incredible impetus to the art workshops of the capital of the Punjab kingdom.

Hindu education under Maharaja Ranjit Singh

The upper caste Hindus have a long tradition of learning and oral transmission of knowledge. From the time when Hiuen Tsang described Lahore as a brahmanical town down to 1799, when Ranjit Singh took Lahore, this scholarly tradition remained, although under Mughal rule we know more about Islamic teaching in sciences and art in the Lahore *suba*. Leitner has a lot to say on the Hindu schools which existed in the 1860's-1880's in Punjab. He dwells at length on the "Chatsalas : Mahajani and Lande Schools", explaining that "what gives the Lande school its special character is its arithmetic, both mental and oral". That is, "the rules of *gurs* by which chiefly business calculation of the most intricate kind, especially as reflects the fluctuations of the grain market, can be carried on with ease mentally". The school also taught how to conduct business correspondence in various scripts (shorthand) and keep the *bahi-katas* (ledger and index) in the account keeping books.

[134] Temple north of the Lahore Fort (present state, detail)

Concerning Sanskrit teaching, it started with the learning of Nagri characters, then went on to Sanskrit grammar, poetry, rhetoric, the *puranas* and *itihas* (ancient history), *jotish* (astrology and astronomy), the *vedant* and *nyaya* (philosophy and logic), *mantra, tantra, puja path* (religious books) and it may also finish with vaidik or the Hindu system of medicine. It was rare to find the whole system taught in one place by one teacher, though Leitner still found some eminent scholars at Ludhiana, Amritsar, Kangra, Rainika Raipur, Gujranwala, Sujanpur etc. who taught "all the shastras". Leitner added to his analysis a list of Sanskrit books used in Punjab for these teachings.

Leitner concluded this section of his report on the specific higher schools of Sanskrit studies, similar to the ones in Bengal, giving information on the age of the students and the time spent in these schools : schools of general literature, Hindu law, schools of logic, puranic schools. One chapter deals with "Female indigenous education" in which it is stated that this policy "requires less development than revival".

Maharaja Ranjit Singh and Christianity

A small European community, mostly military officers and merchants, lived in the Punjab kingdom and enjoyed complete freedom of religion. In 1830 a Roman Catholic priest came from Sardhana to Lahore to celebrate General Ventura's wedding with Anne-Marguerite. It was a splendid ceremony and the Maharaja and the court offered a timbol of Rs. 10,000. In 1834, Ranjit Singh agreed to give General Allard's two years leave to bring his four children to France in order to give them a Christian education. The Maharaja's reply is quoted in the French press (1835) as follows : "Since you mention religion, I can say nothing more to oppose your wish. It is a matter of conscience. Every person should be free to follow the religion he chooses, and it is his duty to obey its commandments. You can go".

In the 1830's Maharaja Ranjit Singh started to understand that behind the growing power of the West, and behind its terrifying military technology lay a system of knowledge and education which he tried to penetrate. In 1834 Captain Wade, the British political agent in charge of "Sikh" affairs, opened a school at Ludhiana which he quickly entrusted to an American missionary society. In 1835 Ranjit Singh invited the director, Lowrie, to Lahore to discuss the possibility of expanding western education in Punjab. It seems that Lowrie insisted on including the Holy Bible as a scientific topic of the syllabus, while the English press at Calcutta revealed that Lowrie was planning "a religious campaign against the Sikhs"! Lowrie was very politely sent back to Ludhiana, carrying shawls and other magnificent gifts from the Maharaja.

Conclusion
State and Religion in the Punjab kingdom under Maharaja Ranjit Singh
The Indian Concept of Secularism

Being questioned as to why he spent Rs. 10,000 for a book (the Holy Koran) for which he, being a Sikh, had no use, the Maharaja is believed to have replied : "God intended me to look at all religions with one eye. That is why he took away the light from the other".

Maharaja Ranjit Singh kept a constant watch on each extremist – today we would say fundamentalist - element which could disturb the peaceful life of the common folk in the kingdom. Considering the checkered Punjab history from. c. 1670 till 1799, that was not an easy task. The creation of the *Fauj-i-khas* and the other regular brigades of the Punjab army, trained on the pattern of European discipline and under his direct command, was the best tool the Maharaja devised to keep the kingdom unified and peaceful.

Each and every community of the kingdom was represented at court by its most eminent members, and the administrative and military structure of the state reflected the multi-ethnic and multi-cultural diversity of the 14 to 15 millions inhabitants of the Punjab. This in turn gave a feeling of belonging to the people, which might, or might not, be called Punjabi ethos or culture, at least between Indus and Sutlej, from the Himalayan foothills to the frontiers of Sindh.

[122] **The Harmandir Sahib**
Photograph from a private collection

[218] Frontispiece of the
***Fables* of La Fontaine**
Gouache and gold on paper
Imam Bakhsh Lahori. Attock/Peshawar, 1837
Musée Jean de La Fontaine, Château-Thierry

VI

The Punjab
A Flourishing Country

A Flourishing Country
A Prosperous Punjab

The kingdom of Punjab under Maharaja Ranjt Singh comprised of several *subas* of the Mughal empire : Lahore, Multan, Kashmir and part of the *suba* of Kabul. The unification process took a little more than twenty years of wars and political skill in dealing with the former authorities of these states, most of them being in possession of petty Afghan potentates (Multan, Kashmir, the Derajat, Peshawar) following the invasions of Nadir Shah and Ahmad Shah Abdali.

The political integration of these different units into one single kingdom or empire could be done only through a long, patient and systematic effort of establishing peace, favouring economic development and assuring a kind of uniform justice from the Khyber Pass to Philaur, from the Himalayas to the frontiers of Sindh. That could not be achieved through the irregular military forces which indeed the empire had already built up. The creation of the *Fauj-i-khas* and the other "French" and regular brigades of the Maharaja gave him the strength he needed for a balanced secular policy allowing each separate unit to live according to its own pace, and still participate in the overall economic development of the kingdom of the Punjab.

Administration

One of the first steps taken by Maharaja Ranjit Singh after his occupation of Lahore was to reorganise the administration of his kingdom in different ministries ("*daftar*") and assure regular revenues to the state. The *daftar* called *Sarishta-i-hazar* dates from 1800, the *daftar* of Devi Das from 1803. In 1808 Bhawani Das, brother of Devi Das, was appointed by Ranjit Singh (*Daftar-i-Bhawani Das*) with orders to clean up the financial mess of the kingdom. This the two brothers were able to do in a couple of years.

[148] Raja Dhyan Singh
Prime Minister of Maharaja Ranjit Singh
"Raja Dhyan Singh Ministre" / "Rajah Dhian Sing"
Watercolour on European paper
By Imam Bakhsh Lahori. Lahore, 1827-1843
176 x 263 mm
Court collection, Musée Guimet. MG 78 III 39751

In 1813 Ranjit Singh called to Lahore Ganga Ram, the former *diwan* of Louis Bourquien. Ganga Ram first assisted Bhawani Das for the military accounts. He then started his own *daftar* in 1817. At his death in 1826 he was succeeded by his nephew Dina Nath as keeper of the seals and in charge of military expenses. When

Bhawani Das died in 1834, Dina Nath took charge of the Finance ministry which he kept till 1846, becoming one of the most important persons in the kingdom.

For several years Maharaja Ranjit Singh did not have a Prime minister. Then, in 1811, he appointed *as deorhidar* (chamberlain) *Jamadar* Khushal Singh, a Hindu from Sardhana (Meerut) who had joined his army in 1807. In 1817 Khushal Singh was replaced by Dhyan Singh, one of the three Dogra brothers, who held the post almost without interruption till his death in 1843.

On international relations, Ranjit Singh had his own personal formation and information concerning the political situation in his area. Sohan Lal Suri, the chronicler, knew a lot about the historical and diplomatic relations of the Sukerchakia *misl* with the local powers. Ranjit's maternal uncle Bagh Singh of Jind gave him sound advice concerning the French and the English, the two international powers who could play a political game in the subcontinent. And in 1813 he engaged Ganga Ram, the former political assistant of Bourquien (and later of Ochterlony) on the Anglo-Sikh border. But right from the time of the acquisition of Lahore Maharaja Ranjit Singh trusted Fakir Syed Azizuddin, both as a physician and as a confidant on external affairs. From 1822 onwards Azizuddin was helped in this field by General Allard who was receiving the Russian gazetteers (published in French at that time).

[153] Lehna Singh Majithia
Artist unknown. Middle 19th century
11.8 x 9 cm
Chandigarh Museum. Acc. N° D-35

These long appointments of trusted and qualified people at the helm of affairs gave the government of Lahore a stability which never degenerated into routine because of the quality of the men in charge and the Maharaja's energy.

Agriculture

During the forty seven years of his reign Maharaja Ranjit Singh took systematic care of the peasants who formed 66 percent of the population, most

[150] Raja Dina Nath
"Daftri Dina Nath" in Devanagari
Finance Minister of Maharaja Ranjit Singh
Artist unknown. Early 19th century
[post 1826]. 18.2 x 15.4 cm
Chandigarh Museum. Acc. N° D-28

[154] Punjab countryside and folk
La Fontaine, "Les souhaits" ["The Wishes"]
Gouache and gold on paper
Imam Bakhsh Lahori. Attock, 1837-1841
Musée Jean de La Fontaine, Château-Thierry

of them living in some 31,000 villages (*mooza*).

Ranjit Singh removed the *zamindars* of the former Mughal administration and gave the land to the people who cultivated it. By 1839 about 40 percent of the cultivators owned their land, and a systematic policy of resumption of wasted lands and rehabilitation of devastated areas was implemented by the Maharaja (*taqawi*, tax exemptions etc.). He also promoted the restoration of old canals and the digging of new ones, and the surface of artificially irrigated areas increased from 400,000 acres in 1820 to 1,000,000 in 1839. Ranjit Singh himself used to tour the countryside wherever he went and inquired from the peasants about their problems and the conduct and efficiency of the state officers.

The cultivated area in the kingdom in 1839 can be estimated at 13 million acres, which is the whole area which could be cultivated with the technology of the time. In 1831 the Punjab was self-sufficient in food, had silos in its main cities and could dispatch in an emergency fifty thousand maunds of grain to Kashmir in 1833. The first British surveys in 1847 attested the very high level of agricultural production in the state, as good as in the best provinces of British India.

[161] Dress of the son of General and Mrs Allard
Lahore. c. 1834
Private collection

Kashmir and the Shawl trade

It is a fallacy to maintain that Kashmir "under the Sikhs" was at the lowest ebb of its prosperity, between an *akmé* under the great Mughals and a kind of renaissance under the Dogras. This vision rests on the Moorcroft papers, a series of documents written in 1821, two years after the conquest of Kashmir and before Maharaja Ranjit Singh's policy could bring some relief to a province which since 1739 had officially passed under Iranian and Afghan rule.

Kashmiri migrant workers and shawl weavers are attested in Hindustan at least since mid-17th century. Fresh and massive waves of migration started after Kashmir came under Iranian rule (1739) followed by massive Afghan colonisation of the valley and the *Chach (or Chahar) Mahals* in the piémont. In 1819 Ranjit Singh conquered and annexed Kashmir. How to put Kashmir back to its former, almost mythical prosperity was the foremost concern of the Maharaja. To deal with a population whose Muslim section was hostile to "Sikh" rule required a strong hand, while dealing with day-to-day life and restoring the shawl trade needed soft governance and an amiable policy. Ranjit Singh was not satisfied with the first governors he sent to Srinagar. He toyed with the idea to entrust it to one of his French generals, and ultimately sent Meifredy to Prince Sher Singh in 1833 with the request that he prepare a general report on the condition of thc vallcy.

No senior French officer was appointed governor of Kashmir, but they all had an interest in shawl manufacturing, since according to the laws of the kingdom they were allowed, like any high ranking servant of the state, to conduct commercial activities through their own agents. In spite of the French prohibition on import of Kashmiri shawls, there was a strong demand for original items, and French experts travelled to Kashmir with their portfolios of drawings adapted to the Parisian fashion. Monsieur Leboeuf who came there in 1838 was one of them, and Frank Ames's book *The Kashmiri Shawl* gives a lot of information.

Frank Ames's contribution to the study of Kashmir shawls was to underline the important artistic changes introduced both in the technique and design of

[156] Tarikh -i-Kala Kashmir
By Mir Ahmed Jalalawad
Artists unknown
Maharaja Ranjit Singh Museum, Amritsar
Acc. N° M 829

[159] **Shawl of Bannu Pan Dei, wife of General Allard**
Detail: parrots in a field of flowers
Kashmir. C. 1826-1841
Private collection

[208] **Bannu Pan Deï, wife of General Allard**
Oil on canvas
Artist unknown
No place, no date [Lahore, 1837-1839?]
72 x 58 cm
Private collection. Stolen in 1977

shawls during the reign of Ranjit Singh by breaking "the sacred shawl-design rules". Struck by the expression of its "genuine Indian heritage" Ames delineated the "rich variety of abstract images from all walk of oriental culture" incorporated by "the eclectic Sikh influence" in the artistic production of the valley. Although Ames has been criticised for the stress he put on the new trends which evolved in the Kashmiri shawl production (the "tapestry shawl") between 1820 and 1840, the dynamism and the originality he was able to discern in this production must be acknowledged as a significant contribution to a major artistic expression in the subcontinent.

Shawl production resumed and prospered again from 1825 onwards, and great care was taken that the workers get their fair share of the price. Shawls were part of the tribute paid by Kashmir to the government. Colonel Mian (Mohan) Singh (governor from 1834 to 1841) did his best to improve the situation. But in the long run European production of "Kashmiri" shawls destabilised Ranjit Singh's efforts.

The famine of 1833 in the Valley was not caused by misrule or abuse, but by a succession of natural calamities : earthquake and cholera in 1828, frost and cholera in 1833. We know that Ranjit Singh immediately sent 50,000 maunds of grain in 1833 along with money to be distributed among the poors, and he abolished all tax on the circulation of grains to the valley.

Price of weaving a shawl in Kashmir in 1832

So much has been written on the desperate plight of the Kashmiri weavers under Punjabi rule, exploited by brokers and

[167] **Patka (sash)**
Kashmir. c. 1820-40
316 x 50 cm
National Museum. New Delhi
Acc. N° 62.2351

burdened by extravagant taxes levied by the state, that it is necessary to correct it. We have to go to C.M. Wade's detailed report of 1832 to assess the conditions in the province since its conquest by Maharaja Ranjit Singh in 1819 :

"In order to shew the process of the manufacture, I annex an estimate of the actual charges which a pair of red shawls valued at F[arukaba]d Rs. 500 incurs from its origin till it comes from the loom :

- 4 F[arukabad]d seers weight of wool	Fd.Rs.	12.8
- Duties on importations & sale of d.		3.14
- Expense of cleaning and spinning		50
- Duty after it has been spun into thread		8
- Dyeing		11
- Weavers wages		264.6
- 25% exacted by government while the fabric is in loom		125
- 5 % fees paid to chowdries, brokers, assessers, etc.		25
Prime cost of article		**500**"

This document clearly shows that the weavers were getting 53% of the cost-value of the product, and the brokers 5% only.

[160] **Shawl of Bannu Pan Dei, wife of General Allard**
Detail
Kashmir. c. 1826-1841
Private collection

[145] Diwan Bhawani Das
"Peshoria Bhuni Dass" in Devanagari
First great administrator of Maharaja Ranjit Singh
15.1 x 11.6 cm
Chandigarh Museum
Acc. N° D-27

Economy Punjab commercial exchanges in 1832

The kingdom of Punjab was never an autarkist state. It exported its own productions and imported foreign goods according to the needs of the state and the population. It is interesting to draw here a list of imports and exports showing the state of the economy in 1832

Exports from Kashmir : shawls, saffron and fruits.

From Lahore : salt, arms (matchlocks, swords, bows and arrows), several kinds of cotton and silk cloth, mules and horses, kut [*Saussurea*] upto Calcutta and China, salt from the Salt Range.

From Multan : silk scarfs, indigo, chintz and carpets. Salt by radiation.

Imports from British India : woollens, velvets, satins and silks, *kimkhabs*, cochineals, chintz, calicoes and muslins; raw silk, wool, cotton, indigo, gold and silver, copper and iron in sheets, tin lead, pewter, quick silver, cinnabar, sulphur and arsenic ; glasswares, pearls and precious stones, hardwares, shields, spices, drugs, sandal and ivory. These articles are all brought from Hindustan. The wool is that of the shawl goat, purchased at Rampoor in Besahir. The spices, copper, woollens, velvets, satins, silks and muslins which come from Hindustan are in greatest request.

From Afghanistan : horses, green and dried fruits, asafetidae, meneghinite, some precious stones and drugs.

From Persia : Chintz and cochineal, gold in Venetian ducats and copper in square flat pieces or made into vessels, nankeens, needles, gold and silver laces from Bokhara which are derived originally from the Russian market.

From Yarkend, Tibet and the Chinese frontier : ingots of silver, shawl-wool, skins, musks, silk, and tea of an inferior quality. The wool from Tibet is in the greatest request.

[149] Raja Gulab Singh
"Rajah Goulab Singh"
"Maharaja Golab Sing Bhadoor.
Now he is doing Khizab"
Watercolour on European paper
By Imam Bakhsh Lahori. Lahore, 1827-1843
198 x 272 mm
Court collection, Musée Guimet. MG 78 III 41835

Marwari / Lohani trading networks in Punjab in 1832

An important part of the Indian trade since the 1770s was in the hands of the Marwari houses, based in Shekawati and Calcutta. Most of the caravans plying between north-west India and Central Asia were in the hands of the Lohani houses based at Shikarpur (Sindh).

The two networks were connected along a line crossing the Punjab. In 1832, the volume of import from British India to Amritsar was estimated at Rs. 14 lakhs. And the whole volume of exports beyond the Sutlej (Punjab) and the Indus (Afghanistan,

Central Asia) by the Marwaris was estimated at Rs. 49 lakhs. That is why in 1828, Ranjit Singh had 15 shops and a stable built in Lahore for Seth Mirza Mal of Chooroo, head of the Marwari houses, to whom he accorded a discount of 25% on the octrois of the city.

Gold and Silver in the Punjab Kingdom

The prosperity of the Punjab came from silver and gold earned from exports as well as from duties of goods transiting through the kingdom. The effect was a growing monetarization of the economy (circulation of coins) and some splendid artistic realizations like the gilding of the Harmandir Sahib at Amritsar, of the temple of Jawalamukhi and the regilding of the Sonahri Masjid at Lahore.

[168] Twelve coins of Maharaja Ranjit Singh
Private collection
Courtesy: Mrs Jyoti Ray

The circulation of gold and silver in north-west India in the 1830's was as follows:

"In Bombay the return of opium sent to China is principally in dollars, and bullion to the amount of 30 or 40 lakhs of rupees is annually imported from Persia in return for the goods sent to this country.

Considerably upwards of a crore of rupees worth of silver is annually sent from Bombay to Gwalior, Jeypore, Patiala, Amritsar and other principal places in Hindustan, where the greatest part is coined in the mints and the rest is sold in the bazars. The silver is mostly in dollar and is sent via Bawnaggur and Pali. None comes from Calcutta. A few lakhs of rupees worth of gold ingots are imported annually by the same road, but it seldom finds its way further than Jaipur.

The transport is done by camels, and each camel carries about 4000 dollars. The despatch of silver are said to reach Amritsar from Bombay in 40 days" (1834)

Coins of the Sikh Kingdom

The Sikhs rapidly evolved a complete monetary system of their own. Banda Bahadur struck the first Sikh coin in 1710 AD. During the *Misl* period, coins were struck at Lahore in 1765 and 1772, and in Amritsar in 1775. The Amritsari issue had a Persian inscription in the name of Guru Nanak, hence the name *Nanakshahi* which was ultimately given to the Sikh coins.

Maharaja Ranjit Singh extended this currency system all over his kingdom. Like the Sikh *misls* before him, he believed that he was but the servant of the Gurus and did not put his name on the coins, a significant difference from the coinage current in Punjab under the Muslim dynasties. The couplets on the coins are as follows:

Sikka Zad Bar Har Do Alam Fazl Sachcha

Sahib Ast Fath-i-Gur Gobind Singh

Shah-i-Shahan Tegh-i-Nanak Wahib Ast

[Translation : "Coin struck in the two worlds (spiritual and secular) by the grace of the true Lord. Nanak is the provider of the sword (power) by which Guru Gobind Singh is victorious"]

The other couplets on the coins is patterned after the seal of Guru Gobind Singh :

Deg Teg o Fateh Nusrat Be-dirang

Yaft Az Nanak Guru Gobind Singh

[Translation : "Abundance, the sword, victory and help without delay Guru Gobind Singh obtained from Nanak"]

[172] **Tak Shal Mint**
Artist unknown
27.5 x 21.5 cm
National Museum. New Delhi
Acc. N° 88.342

The currency system developed by the Maharaja comprised of gold mohurs and silver coins in denominations of one, half and quarter rupees, inscribed in the Persian script. The silver rupees had a high content of silver with a value of sixteen annas to the rupee and generally weighed 10.7g – 11.1g. The main mints were at Lahore and Amritsar. As the Sikh dominions increased, mints were established at Multan (1818 AD), Kashmir (1819), Derajat (1821) and Peshawar (1834). These coins exhibit a refinement in terms of calligraphy, style, artistry and workmanship. They are adorned with dots and flowers, moons and stars, and encircled with beaded or chevron borders. A leaf is a common symbol of most of these coins, while a hand (*punja*), royal umbrella, *kartar* appear on some. At times, people became linked with a particular symbol on a coin or a certain legend connected with it. The *Nanakshahis* of Kashmir were called *Hari Singhji* after Hari Singh Nalwa, one of the governors of Kashmir. The *Morashahi* and *Arsiwallashahi* from the Amritsar mint were associated with Bibi Moran. Coins minted in Peshawar were known as *Peshawari Naunihal Singhji* rupees after Kanwar Nau Nihal Singh, grandson of Maharaja Ranjit Singh and Governor of Peshawar [Jyoti Ray].

The political fragmentation of Punjab and northern India in 18th century led to the development of local taxations, octrois and duties levied on goods by each and every petty *zamindar*, *nawab* and *raja*. In 1830, in the British protected territories between Ludhiana and Jagadhree, about 15 states levied duties on the goods transiting between Sutlej and Jamuna.

The development of trade in Punjab and northern India in the 1820's, although impeded by the shortage of silver in 1829-1831, led to a reorganisation of financial and taxation structures of these areas with the introduction of the Company rupee in British India in 1833-1836 and the unification of transit duties in the Punjab kingdom in 1833. The consequence was the integration of northern India and Punjab in an increasing world trade extending from Europe to China and the Americas.

Rumours grew very soon concerning the metallic reserves of the Punjab kingdom : 10 million pounds according to Murray in the early 1830's, but 30 million according to hearsay. What is sure is that after ten years of anarchy (1839-1849) and two Anglo-Sikh wars which exhausted the Punjab treasury, the British could write in 1851 : "The financial result of Annexation during the first two years was a surplus of 52 plus 64 lakhs, or one million and one hundred and sixty thousand pounds sterling". The Jhalandar doab and the cis-Sutlej territories, annexed in 1846, had yielded 84 lakhs : all this money was "consigned to the general Treasury for Imperial purposes".

[107] **The fort of Govindgarh**
Watercolour on paper
Artist unknown. Middle 19th century
20.5 x 34.5 cm
National Museum. New Delhi. Acc. N° 85.26

VII

Urbanization: Amritsar. Lahore. Other Punjab towns

The census of 31 december 1854, taken five years after annexation, gives an impressive description of the urban distribution in the former Punjab kingdom. 2124 small towns had 1000 to 5000 inhabitants ; 72 cities had 5000 to 10,000 souls ; 30 cities had 10,000 to 50,000, and four main cities had a bigger population : Amritsar (122,000), Srinagar (120,000), Lahore (94,000) and Peshawar (53,000). In these towns were concentrated the industrial, business, intellectual and artistic activities of the kingdom. The *Char Bagh-i-Punjab* of Ganesh Das presents the general condition of the country doab after doab and describes some of these cities, big and small, with their old and new features. This document reveals an extraordinary renaissance of the urban tissue. With peace and prosperity returning to the country after more than a century of turmoil and disorder, people again started building residences and gardens outside the ramparts. Following Kanhaya Lal, Syed Muhammed Latif is extremely useful in giving us a description of Lahore as it was in 1882, with details of the beautiful Mughal monuments he saw being destroyed after annexation. The Murray's *Handbook of Punjab* (1883) also gives information on where to find food for your horse, and the earliest *District Gazetteers* provide a glimpse into the beautiful small cities of Punjab, from Chiniot to Gujranwala, with their gaily painted facades and their picturesque decorations.

Two main cities dominated the heart of the Punjab Kingdom : Lahore, the former capital of the *suba*, and Amritsar, the quickly developing religious capital of the Sikhs. Both of them were flourishing markets with commercial networks extending from Russia to China.

Amritsar

Amritsar was a new city, organised around the Harmandir and lately protected by Govindgarh fort. As soon as Ranjit Singh captured it in 1802, he unified its administration and started constructing the walls of the city for which Fateh Singh Ahluwalia sent 1000 masons and many other chiefs contributed in money and work force. To give it water, Ranjit Singh extended a branch of the Hansli canal from Madhopur to Amritsar. New localities developed, and numerous gardens were built outside the ramparts. The most important was Rambagh, built by Maharaja Ranjit Singh as his residence. Amritsar was perhaps a greater trading place than Lahore in the 1830's. And though Jacquemont saw many shawl-makers already established there in 1831, the famine of 1833 in Kashmir brought in many more Kashmiri families who started a good quality shawl industry on a large scale.

What we said concerning the great programme of Maharaja Ranjit Singh for beautifying the Harmandir applies to the city as a whole. All the grandees of the kingdom, to whatever community they belonged, including the French officers, had residences in the city which were decorated and embellished with paintings and gold inlay. The *haveli* of *Jamadar* Khushal Singh, former *deorhidar* (prime minister) of Ranjit Singh, had lovely paintings in the *darbar* room, showing architectural landscapes, and mirrors in the ceiling.

[183] **Map of the Darbar Sahib and environs**
Watercolour and gold on paper
c. 1840
Central Sikh Museum, Amritsar
Shiromani Gurudwara Parbandakh Committee

Kanwarjit Kang, writing in 1977 on "Survival of wall paintings in Amritsar", said that at least fifty buildings in the city still had such paintings, and he identified a number of painters, Hindus and Sikhs, who worked in Amritsar from the time of Ranjit Singh till the early 20th century

There are some descriptions of Amritsar by European travellers, one of the less known being by Victor Jacquemont in 1831, which is as follows:

[182] **Rambagh Palace, Amritsar**
Gulgashat-i-Punjab
Maharaja Ranjit Singh Museum. Amritsar
Acc. N° 38

[191] **Nau Nihal Singh Haveli**
Lahore. c. 1835-1837
Detail

"Amritsar is the largest city in the Punjab. It is said by the natives to be nine kos in circumference. I put the population at 100,000 to 200,000. There is more movement and life in Amritsar than in any other town in British India, and it is the first city I have seen showing obvious signs of expansion. The bazars are very numerous. The rich bankers and merchants have houses three to four storeys high, the front being whitened and covered with coarse mythological figures. The rock salt of Lahore, which passes through Amritsar in enormous quantities to be exported to India, has its own quarter. Timber and firewood have another quarter. The wool spinners, the cotton weavers, the Kashmiris usually occupy distinct quarters. There are a large number of Kashmiris and Afghans. The former weave or spin, the latter speculate. The greater part of the Kashmiris are occupied in cleaning the shawls brought from Kashmir and destined to the Indian market"

Victor Jacquemont, 8 March 1831

Lahore

Right from1799, Ranjit Singh started a programme of renovation and embellishment of Lahore, with renewed building activity, which started with the complete renovation of the Lahore fort and its water-works. The Sheesh Mahal was repaired, and a new *baradari* was erected by Ranjit Singh, which August Schoefft used as the setting for his grand painting "*The Court of Lahore*". Some old residences of ministers were also renovated, and new building erected on top of former Mughal structures. In 1818 Ranjit Singh built the Hazuri Bagh, in the midst of the former Aurangzeb *sarai*. He also built the shrine of Guru Arjun with its pretty golden dome next to the Roshnai Darwaza. To keep on with former Mughal splendor, the Maharaja also entirely restored the Shalimar Gardens after cleaning and repairing the Hansli (Ali Mardan Khan's) canal. But an enquiry among the most learned people of the kingdom could not give him the etymology of the name "Shalimar".

The Punjab nobility - Sikh, Hindu and Moslem - did the same in their *haveli*s and gardens. In the city around the fort, the new nobility occupied many a residence which had been built by the Mughal grandees. But after the difficult period of 1750 to 1799 all these

[192] **Nau Nihal Singh Haveli**
Lahore. c. 1835-1837
Detail

[185] A three-dimensional model of Lahore city and fort with ramparts
Lahore, 1847. Destroyed 1949
From a photograph in a private collection

big palaces and *haveli*s had to be restored. Others were built anew. The *havelis* of *Jamadar* Khushal Singh, Raja Dhyan Singh and Raja Dina Nath rivaled in splendour and beauty. The *haveli* of Nawab Imam-ud-Din Khan, governor of Kashmir at the end of the Sikh rule, had all its paintings intact in the 1880's.

None of these splendidly decorated residences exist today, except the *haveli* of Nau Nihal Singh, completed in 1837 for the marriage of the prince. This is a remarkable piece of architecture, with elegant balconies overlooking two squares and embossed with external decorations of elephants and birds which still have part of their original painting. The internal decoration was no less sumptuous : "The roofs are decorated with paintings and mirrors and are worked in gold. The walls are richly and tastefully ornamented with glasses and artificial flowers" (Latif), to which must be added scenes of Hindu mythology. This is certainly one of the most outstanding "private" residence of a grandee remaining from the time of Maharaja Ranjit Singh.

The French officers were few, but their military and political influence was great and they had their main residence in Lahore near the headquarters of their brigades. The common residence of General Allard and Ventura still exists today, but without the sumptuous paintings and gilded mirrors which adorned it in the 1830's. An oil painting and its miniature copy show it as it was in 1834-1838: a European classical building with columns. The residence of General Court has disappeared, but a recently discovered miniature painting shows that it was a typical Punjabi "farm-house" of the time, and an oil painting by Schoefft [N° 209 published here for the first time] shows its rich and tastefully decorated interior. As far as Avitabile is concerned, nothing remains of his splendid house built at the top of Budhu-ka-Ava, and apparently no painting has survived. We have to rely on the following complimentary appreciation : "The Maharaja happily proceeded to the Kiln-mound of Budhoo. He told the Raja Kalan [Dhyan Singh] that Avitabile had built a very good house. The Raja Kalan replied that the glorious sahibs were very fond of good buildings". An amusing detail of these French residences were the persiennes of Provence which one can find on the miniature paintings of the Imam Bakhsh Lahori school.

We have already noticed the frantic construction of Hindu temples and Sikh gurudwaras at Lahore under Ranjit Singh, and how much they changed the very sky-scape of the city, up till now reserved for the marble and glazed tiles of the domes of the mosques and tombs. This was one of the major irritants – according to the *sharia* - to orthodox Muslims and *ulemas* living for generations in the *Dar-us-Sultanat*, and one major, but unstated, cause of the biased description of Lahore under "the Sikhs" by Muslim historians after annexation.

Lahore was also a city of gardens, Mughal gardens renovated under Ranjit Singh, and

[197] L'Ermitage. Residence of General Court at Lahore
"L'Ermitage. Habitation du général Court à Lahore"
Watercolour on European paper
By Imam Bakhsh Lahori. Lahore, 1827-1843
325 x 593 mm
Court collection, Musée Guimet. MG 64836

[220] **La Fontaine, "Le petit poisson et le pêcheur"**
"The Little Fish and the Fisherman"
Gouache and gold on paper
Imam Bakhsh Lahori. Attock/Peshawar, 1837-1839
Musée Jean de La Fontaine, Château-Thierry

new ones built by the nobility of the time. Ganesh Das gives a list, and Latif mentions the ones still existing in the 1870's. Raja Dina Nath had a garden which "was once unrivalled for its beauty, fertility and elegance. It was the old place for Hindus and Mahomedan garden parties. It is furnished with reservoirs, tanks, splendid summer houses and buildings for the accommodation of visitors..."(Latif). The garden of Bhai Maha Singh was "the most luxuriant of its kind in the time of the Sikhs" (Latif). In the 1970's the Fatehgarh garden, not noticed by Latif, but mentioned by Ganesh Das as a Sikh garden, still existed : the walls of the *baradari* stood more or less intact, along with the gateway adorned with beautiful paintings (cypresses and floral decoration). That garden disappeared as late as July 2001.

Two interesting documents, presented here together for the first time, are the great map of Lahore by a Pahari artist in c. 1810-1820, and the photograph of the three-dimensional model of Lahore ordered by Henry Lawrence in 1847. On both of them one can see the density of the buildings inside the city. Some of the old gardens and shrines (Data Ganj Bakhsh) can be identified on the painting, and the powerful ramparts built by Ranjit Singh are strikingly visible on the model.

Lahore was the political capital of the kingdom. The government offices (*daftar*s), the Crown Jewels (*toshakhana*) and the state archives were located in the fort. There were also intense banking, trading and manufacturing activities in the city, and the military industries were also established there, like the gun-foundries at Idgah. The cantonments were all around the city, with the

[194] **Hazuri Bagh**
Lahore. 1818

[173] A Punjabi provincial town
La Fontaine, "Le meunier, son fils et l'âne"
["The Miller, his Son and the Ass"]
Gouache and gold on paper
Imam Bakhsh Lahori. Attock, 1837-1839
Musée Jean de La Fontaine, Château-Thierry

new fashionable bazar of Anarkali and the "Garden of the Soldier" on the Ravi bank near Anarkali. The European accounts that we have of the walled city of Lahore describe an overpopulated city with narrow lanes where huge elephants squeezed through with amazing agility, and beautiful women with charming smiles, more attractive than anywhere else in India, appeared on the terraces and the balconies...

Wazirabad

We do not have many descriptions of the smaller towns of Punjab, because the European travellers often did not say much beyond uttering repetitive accounts. Gujranwala had been taken care of by Maharaja Ranjit Singh as his native place and the capital of his *misl*. It was also the residence of Hari Singh Nalwa, one of the most famous generals of the Punjab army : in his splendid *haveli* he kept his collection of paintings. We know that Chiniot was extremely picturesque, with rich houses that were beautifully painted and decorated. So were probably most of the medium size towns of the Punjab. There are a few precise descriptions of the city of Wazirabad, which commanded a strategic ford on the Chenab, because of the modernizing and beautifying drive decided and implemented by General Avitabile when he was governor of the city. An unpublished letter of General Court to Jacquemont, dated 1831, says that Avitabile had pulled down a great part of the crumbling buildings of Wazirabad and was erecting a "big and spacious bazar". Ganesh Das confirms the building of a new trading center, but he also mentions a new sector, Ram Katra, built inside the city, and a huge octogonal tower erected in the same bazar. Hügel, who saw the city in 1836, said that Avitabile "almost rebuilt the town in the European style, and pulled down the old bazar, making the streets wide enough to admit a carriage and four horses. The people are enraptured with the present beauty of the bazar of Wazirabad, and its charms were boastingly represented to me long before I saw it". Barr is still more precise concerning this large street, almost one mile long, with regular buildings erected on both sides. Since Barr was there in 1839, the wall paintings were completed and he mentions them, noticing the large size of the human figures. Maharaja Ranjit Singh paid a visit to Avitabile at Wazirabad in June 1833. He was received there with an artillery salute and, as Sohan Lal Suri says, "the Maharaja felt very happy to inspect a map of the town which had been prepared very carefully and precisely".

CONCLUSION

Two provisional observations can be made at the end of this brief presentation. The first concerns the oft-repeated affirmation that "the Sikhs", and Ranjit Singh, indiscriminately pulled down a great number of Mughal monuments at Lahore. Even if we acknowledge the fact that there was not yet any concept of "protected monuments" in Punjab - nor in British India or Europe for that matter - at that time, this lingering accusation is somewhat disturbing. How such rumours took root deserves to be briefly analysed. We have seen that the tomb and mosque of Shah Sharaf (died in 1692) were destroyed for making the ditch of Lahore, and that the remains of the saint were reinterred at Ranjit Singh's sollicitation. This fact has taken incredible proportions in later and even modern

[174] A Punjabi provincial town
La Fontaine, "Les deux aventuriers et le talisman"
["The two Adventurers and the Talisman"]
Gouache and gold on paper
Imam Bakhsh Lahori. Attock, 1837-1839
Musée Jean de La Fontaine, Château-Thierry

[199] Inside a Punjabi residence
La Fontaine, "Le mari, la femme et le voleur"
"The Husband, the Wife and the Robber"
Gouache and gold on paper
Imam Bakhsh Lahori. Attock, 1837-1839
Musée Jean de La Fontaine, Château-Thierry

historical writings. Latif for instance insists that in 1841 General Allard was ordered to clear up Lahore of its old Muslim monuments, which he did without paying attention to the grief of the Muslim community. The fact that Allard died in January 1839 did not prevent some more seasoned scholars like A. Chaghatai and even Annemarie Schimmel to repeat that statement without a squalm of hesitation.

As a matter of fact all European travellers from 1809 to 1849 mentioned the magnificent ruins that they could admire all around the city of Lahore. Von Orlich for instance, who was staying in Ventura's residence at Anarkali in 1842, climbed up to the terrace: "We had a fine view of the city and its environs from the platform of general Ventura's house, outside the city, on an arm of the Ravi. The minarets, the winter palace, and the glittering domes of some mosques of the time of the Emperor Jahangir were particularly striking. To the south of the city are hills of débris formed of the ruins of the ancient Lahore, and these again are joined by a town lying in ruins, interspersed with decayed caravanserai, sepulchral towers and mosques, of which I counted no less than forty. These once splendid mosques call to mind a wealthy and religious age, fond of arts!". The fact is that we know, through Syed Muhammed Latif himself, of more beautiful and significant Mughal monuments pulled down in Lahore between 1849 (annexation) and 1882 (publication of his book) than during the whole reign of Maharaja Ranjit Singh.

The second observation concerns the tremendous renewal of architectural and artistic activities under Maharaja Ranjit Singh. In Lahore and Amritsar this happened right from the beginning of his reign, but in the second half of his reign it took place in almost each and every corner of the country, in the hundreds of medium-size cities where the local nobility still lived when they returned from the capital or from the army.

These activities are a clear indication of the growing prosperity of the kingdom. They also point to a strong artistic feeling in the populations of the Punjab, and a staggering pool of artists for decorating the temples and the gurudwaras, the forts and the palaces, the private residences and chapels of the great and common men. Ganesh Das has mentioned some of the most famous calligraphists in these small cities and bigger towns. Obviously

[178] The Fort of Kangra
Gulgashat-i-Punjab
Maharaja Ranjit Singh Museum. Amritsar.
Acc. N° 38

most of them came from old families who did not migrate during the darkest periods of the 18th century. They stayed where they were and resumed their trade as soon as peace returned in the land of the five rivers. B.N. Goswamy in 1981 mentioned the great number of buildings with paintings from the Sikh period all over the Punjab, from Lahore and Amritsar down to the smallest villages having a *haveli*, a Hindu temple or a gurudwara. And he observed that 700 gurudwaras were identified in East Punjab alone. Such a large distribution over the whole country shows that prosperity was not confined to the capital or to the narrow political elite of the land.

A few monuments still have traces of these beautiful decorations and must be urgently preserved. The destruction of the *Jamadar Haveli* at Amritsar after 1985 and the Fategarh Bagh at Lahore in 2001 are sad testimonies of a quickly disappearing heritage which rightly belongs to the present generation of Punjabis and to the art-lovers of the world.

[175] A Punjabi countryside
La Fontaine, "Le milan, le roi et le chasseur"
["The Hawk, the King and the Falcon"]
Gouache and gold on paper
Imam Bakhsh Lahori. Attock, 1837-1839
Musée Jean de La Fontaine, Château-Thierry

[177] Fort of Kamlagarh
Gulgashat-i-Punjab
Maharaja Ranjit Singh Museum.
Amritsar. Acc. N° 38

VIII

Illuminated Manuscripts and Miniature paintings

Book illustrations and Miniature paintings

In a much more cultured Punjab than described by British imperial propaganda after annexation, the art of the book flourished, with an impressive production of manuscripts in the various languages and scripts used by the population. Most of them were of utilitarian use : treatises for education of the children and students, religious books and pamphlets, copies of classical and more contemporary literature, medical writings, military manuals for the instruction of the army staff etc.

But some of the manuscripts were admirably illustrated by the various artistic workshops which flourished in the kingdom. The *Char Bagh-i-Punjab* gives the name of famous calligraphists who lived in the big and small towns of the five doabs. But it is in Lahore that the great traditions converged : the Pahari school of course, so well illustrated by the sons and grandsons of Pandit Seu and other Pahari masters, and so well studied by B.N. and K. Goswamy. The Kashmiri school, also studied by K. Goswamy, which perhaps deserves more attention today: many scribes of Persian manuscripts came to Lahore from Kashmir, and many Persian manuscripts were copied in Srinagar to be kept in Punjab libraries. But we should not forget the old Lahori school, dating back at least to Kamran Mirza and which continued, almost forgotten, till the early 19th century. It is a workshop of that school which blended Indian and Punjabi traditions with French influence and gave us the extraordinary masterpieces of Imam Bakhsh Lahori.

Several beautiful manuscripts illustrated during the reign of Maharaja Ranjit Singh help us discern these various schools and trends in the Punjab kingdom. The *Ain-i-Akbari* of course and the *Akbarnama* confirm the classical connection between the "Sikh" kingdom and the great production of Akbar's workshops. We know in several cases that the 19th century artists in Punjab got inspiration from 16th and 17th century miniature paintings kept in the libraries of the time, and the illuminated correspondence of Akbar's portrait and Ranjit Singh's portrait as frontispiece or illustrations of some *Ain-i-Akbari* illustrate this spiritual filiation. The interesting point is that the plates showing arms have been up-dated since some of them include the carbines of the *Fauj-i-khas* and the artillery of the *topkhana*.

The splendid *Shahnama* of Firdausi copied by Kifayat-ud-Din Qadiri and illustrated "during the reign of Maharaja Ranjit Singh" at "*Dar-us-Sultanat*" Lahore is today in the National Museum, New Delhi (Acc.N° L 532/8). The celestial creatures in the illustrations around Suleiman and Bilqis are partly inspired by classical miniature paintings in the 16th and 17th century, but partly also from the glazed-tile frieze on the north and west sides of the Lahore fort (Jahangir) : the *peris* (fairies) for instance. The cherubs are not dissimilar to the ones discovered in the 1970s in a tower of the Lahore fort dating from the same period. But along with the century-old traditional trumpets these celestial beings are blowing into more modern clarions of 19th century cavalry : General Allard used them to direct his Lancer and Dragoon regiments when they crossed the Indus to take on the Afghans

[209] **Fezli Azam Joo, wife of General Court**
Oil on canvas
by August Schoefft
Signed "Schoefft 1841 Lahor"
114 x 95 cm (with frame)
89.5 x 70.5 cm (within frame)
Private collection

[224] La Fontaine, "L'huître et les plaideurs"
"The Oyster and its Claimants"
Gouache and gold on paper
Imam Bakhsh Lahori. Attock / Peshawar, 1837-1839
Musée Jean de La Fontaine, Château-Thierry

and Yusufzais on the right bank of the river. Although these miniature paintings have the marks of the Kashmiri style, the strange creatures and horned demons, the wild and domesticated animals under the throne of Suleiman and the blue carpets under Suleiman and Bilqis are not dissimilar to the ones found in the La Fontaine *Fables* illustrated at that time by Imam Bakhsh Lahori.

Other popular stories repetitively copied at Lahore were the *Qissa*, or fairy tales, in some cases sumptuously illustrated to stimulate the imagination of the readers. In a forthcoming study on Imam Bakhsh Lahori, Barbara Schmitz and I will call attention to the *Qissa-i Kamrup va Kamlata* in the Bibliothèque nationale, Paris (Supl. Pers. 929) which had been offered to the library by a French orientalist in 1838. It might have been one of the Lahori manuscripts brought to France by General Allard or Ventura in 1835-1837, and its eighty-nine miniatures were certainly illustrated by Imam Bakhsh Lahori and his team.

The *Qissa-i-Chahar-Darwesh* of the Punjabi University, Chandigarh, studied by K. Goswamy, is another splendid manuscript illustrated in Lahore, most probably also by Imam Bakhsh Lahori since its illustrations have a striking resemblance to the Fables of La Fontaine. There is a signature of the scribe, Abdulla-al-Azim, but no signature of the artist. However the fact that it was illustrated for *Diwan* Ajudhya Prasad in 1838-1839 is significant : as *bakhshi* of the *Fauj-i-khas* and a personal friend of generals Allard and Ventura, Ajudhya was in constant contact with the artists working for the French officers at Lahore, and in his rich library there might

[223] La Fontaine, "Le singe et le léopard"
"The Ape and the Leopard"
Gouache and gold on paper
Imam Bakhsh Lahori. Attock/Peshawar
1837-1839

have been other classical and more modern Persian texts illustrated by this remarkable artist.

This brings us to the sponsorship of artists by the French officers at Lahore. These officers, Allard, Ventura, Court, Avitabile, had a prominent position in the military and political set-up of the Punjab kingdom. They married Indian, Punjabi or Kashmiri women from whom they had children, and they developed a keen interest in the culture, history and archaeology of the Punjab. We know from many testimonies and detailed descriptions by European travellers that they had their residences decorated by local artists with grand frescoes but also more intimate scenes, some of them entirely "native" and others blended with French and Italian traditions.

General Court wrote his *Mémoires*, rediscovered in 1986 but still unpublished, which cover 26 years from 1818, when he left Marseilles for Syria, till 1844 when he returned home with his Kashmiri wife and their three children [No 209]. The 90 illustrations of this

[207] General Allard and his family at Lahore
Oil on canvas
"Paris, 1836"
Author unknown
Size not recorded. c. 60 x 40 cm
Private collection. Stolen in 1977

[216] Habitant of the Khyber Pass: Shinvari, Afridi, Orakzais
"Habitants d u Khéyber. Chinvari. Aféridi. Ouroukzeï"
Watercolour on European paper
By Imam Bakhsh L ahori. Peshawar, 1837-1843
171 x 249 mm
Court collection, Musée Guimet
MG 78 III 39736

1200-page manuscript in five volumes are stored in five boxes. While the first three volumes deal with Persia and Afghanistan, volumes 4 and 5 deal specifically with the Punjab, where Court spent sixteen years of his life. Volume five is entitled "*Du Maharaja Ranjit Singh*". Out of the 90 miniature paintings, 35 concern the Punjab kingdom. These volumes also contain many maps drawn by Court which are among the first scientific maps of the Punjab.

In his *Mémoires* Court declared that for painting these miniatures he engaged Imam Bakhsh Lahori, an artist who accompanied him wherever he went with his brigade. While posted in Peshawar (1834 to 1843), Court sent this artist on a tour to Kafiristan. Imam Bakhsh went up to Dir and Chitral, but was too afraid to go further up in the Himalayas. The amusing story told by Court as to how Imam Bakhsh made a drawing of the Kafir family is given in the caption of N° 215. Imam Bakhsh also went to Bannu and Tonk with General Court and his brigade, and he probably drew several paintings of Afghan folk and military men in the Khyber Pass and in Peshawar.

This association of Imam Bakhsh with the French generals of Maharaja Ranjit Singh proved fruitful in a more comprehensive artistic programme, the illustration of La Fontaine's *Fables* from 1837 onwards. In 1835, while on leave in France, General Allard met Feuillet de Conches, Head of Protocol in the Ministry of Foreign Affairs and a distinguished member of the Société Asiatique. Feuillet gave him a copy of the Didot edition of the *Fables* of La Fontaine in two volumes (1827) and asked him to find a Punjabi artist to fill up the blanks according to his inspiration. The topic of each fable was indicated in Persian by Biberstein-Casimirski, a noted orientalist who had translated the *Koran* into French. Allard returned to Lahore in March

[219] La Fontaine, "La forêt et le bûcheron"
"The Forest and the Woodman"
Gouache and gold on paper
Imam Bakhsh L ahori. Attock/Peshwar
1837-1839
Musée Jean de La Fontaine, Château-Thierry

[215] A Kafir Family
"Famille Kafférienne"
Watercolour on European paper
By Imam Bakhsh Lahori
Chitral / Peshawar 1837-1843
194 x 298 mm
Court collection, Musée Guimet
MG 78 III 41832

[213] Habitant of Bajaur
"Habitant de Badjore"
Watercolour on European paper
By Imam Bakhsh Lahori
Probably Peshawar, 1837-1843
108 x 196 mm
Court collection, Musée Guimet
MG 78 III 41824

1837, just in time for the wedding of Prince Nau Nihal Singh. He delivered his credentials as Agent de France [N° 264] to the Maharaja and was immediately engaged with the *Fauj-i-khas* to go to the relief of Hari Singh Nalwa's army trapped by the Afghans in Jamrud. He was then appointed military governor of Peshawar and its province, where at last he had some time for artistic considerations.

Imam Bakhsh Lahori started working on the illustrations of the *Fables* at Attock in November 1837, and a first batch was sent by Allard to Feuillet before May 1838, as indicated by Allard himself in a letter written to Feuillet. There is no information concerning the number of paintings completed at that time. The title page of Didot's volume 1 has the signature of Imam Bakhsh and a date : "10th of the month of Makara of the year [vikrama samvat] 1894", which is equivalent to 21 January 1838.

But Imam Bakhsh Lahori's colophon (page 608 at end of volume 2) gives three dates –

[221] La Fontaine, "Phébus et Borée"
"Phoebus and Boreas"
Gouache and gold on paper
Imam Bakhsh Lahori. Attock/Peshawar, 1837-1839
Musée Jean de La Fontaine, Château-Thierry

"25th November 1837, equivalent to the 10th day of the month of Makara of the year 1894, equivalent to 24th of Sha`ban of the Hijra year 1255". The problem of datation arises because these three dates – corresponding to 25th November 1837, 21st January 1838 and 18th November 1839 – do not concord. From these dates it seems that the work was done in about two years.

After Allard's death in Peshawar in January 1839, Ventura took over the completion of the work. According to Feuillet in an article he published in 1881, Ventura told him that more than a hundred paintings were done under his supervision by two artists, one from Patna and one from Kashmir, who had been working under his supervision during the siege of a formidable fortress in the hills. That was the siege of Kamlagarh, in Mandi, by the *Fauj-i-khas* which lasted from August to November 1840. But now we are beyond the dates given by Imam Bakhsh in the colophon of the collection. If Ventura can be trusted (see caption of N° 58 for the fabrication of his career in Napoleon's army), this is probably the second batch of the illustrations. But when the collection came up for auction in Versailles in 1968, there were only 66 "Indian paintings", which are now in the La Fontaine Museum at Château-Thierry.

Imam Bakhsh's creative genius in illustrating these *Fables* is astounding. Still we can trace influences in these paintings : from classical Mughal art, possibly from a famous *Tutinama* illustrated for Akbar in the 1560's which belonged to General Allard, to the 17th century European ships represented in one fable and the persiennes from contemporary Provence which are represented in most of the buildings shown on the miniatures.

Other Europeans came to the Punjab and were employed by the Maharaja according to their skills. Dr. Martin Honigberger was born at Kronstadt (Transylvania, Hungary) in c. 1795, and he travelled widely before reaching Lahore in 1829. Introduced to the Maharaja by General Allard, he was appointed physician at the court – he provided the Maharaja with a potion reputed to be the strongest ever made in the world - and given charge of the gunpowder and ammunition factory.

Honigberger was very close to the French officers and, like them, took interest in the history and archaeology of the country. Before he returned to Europe in 1833 he made extensive excavations at Hadda and Kabul, bringing to Vienna, Paris and London an

[230] Honigberger's Thirty Five Years ...
Plate X "Bhangee (Hemp-plant drinker)"
Probably from an original painting by
Imam Bakhsh Lahori, 1829-1849
Punjab State Archives. Acc. N° 279

[231] Honigberger's Thirty Five Years ...
Plate XI "Kar-khana Abkaree (distillatory)"
Probably from an original painting by Imam
Bakhsh Lahori, 1829-1849
Punjab State Archives. Acc. N° 279

impressive collection of coins and artifacts. Back in Lahore in 1838, he attended to Prince Nau Nihal Singh after the fatal accident of 5 November 1840 and was also present when Maharaja Sher Singh was murdered in 1843. He remained in Lahore after 1849 as director of the lunatic asylum which he had founded. According to Grey, he then returned to Hungary with the two daughters he had from his Kashmiri wife. He died there in 1865.

Honigberger was lucky enough to find a publisher for his memoirs which appeared in 1852 under the title *Thirty-Five Years in the East*. They were illustrated with plates coming, as he says, from "portraits and sketches taken by a native at Lahore". Since one of his plates is a faithful copy of a painting by Imam Bakhsh in General Court's collection [N° 78], we can safely assume that Honigberger's collection came from the workshop of Imam Bakhsh at Lahore.

Through replicas in other collections of Imam Bakhsh's drawings done for General Court, we are able to assess the extent and influence of Imam Bakhsh's workshop from c. 1827 to the 1850's. As we have just seen, they include the whole of Honigberger's collection, still untraced but known through the engravings in his book, as well as some collections of Punjab paintings in the India Office Library, London (Add. Or. 1347-1396), miniature paintings scattered in various colllections

[238] **"Foundry"**
Punjab State Archives, Chandigarh. Acc. N° 116

all over the world, and illustrated manuscripts.

Till the 1870's one can easily trace Imam Bakhsh's influence on the "bazar" miniatures showing the *who is who* of the Lahore *darbar* under Maharaja Ranjit Singh and his successors, as well as various skilled men and craftsmen in the process of doing their job. Till 1849 Maharaja Dalip Singh had many artists with him in the Lahore fort, some of them drawing birds etc., some drawing a view or two of the Summun Boorj for John Login who wrote : "Some [paintings] are very curious and interesting indeed, representing domestic life in the Punjab and various trades and professions. He [Dalip Singh] has also selected likenesses of the great chiefs and men of note". A continuation indeed of Imam Bakhsh's workshop in the Sheesh Mahal of the Lahore fort.

The great libraries of the Punjab of Maharaja Ranjit Singh have disappeared. But we know the Maharaja had his *Kitabkhana*. We know – a calculated guess can be made for others - that Hari Singh Nalwa, Lehna Singh Majithia, the Fakir brothers, Ajudhya Prasad, the French officers had Persian, Sanskrit and Punjabi manuscripts in their libraries : old ones from family tradition or purchased in the book market, and new ones commissionned at Lahore, along with collections of miniature paintings : these were the literary equivalent of the magnificent frescoes and gilded decorations which adorned their palaces and residences or which they sponsored in the religious buildings in Lahore, Amritsar and other cities in the kingdom.

[241] **"Brewer"**
Punjab State Archives, Chandigarh. Acc. N° 122

[239] "Matchlock Manufacturer"
Punjab State Archives, Chandigarh
Acc. N° 117

[232] Maharaja Ranjit Singh in Darbar
Signed by Imam Bakhsh Lahori
Gouache on paper
30.9 x 18.2 cm
Chandigarh Museum. Acc. N° 3722

[243] Great Stupa of Manikyala
"Coupole Manekyala"
Watercolour on European paper
By Imam Bakhsh Lahori. Manikyala, 1830-1843
190 x 297 mm
Court collection, Musée Guimet
MG 78 III 41830

IX

Archaeological Excavations: Manikyala-Jhelum-Peshawar

Before opening the stupa of Manikyala (near Rawalpindi) in 1830, General Ventura asked the peasants around what was lying under the tope. They all replied "the horse of Sikandar" [Alexander the Great]. The *Sikandarnama*, as we have seen, was part of the syllabus in the Punjab schools.

Ventura's findings excited the curiosity of the Punjabi people. Maharaja Ranjit Singh was the first to be informed of their discoveries by his French generals, and he in turn informed Ludhiana and Calcutta of the excavations at Manikyala. This created a sort of passionate curiosity in Lahore since everybody wanted to look at the reliquaries. Allard and Ventura obliged, and the liquid in the reliquaries dried up because of being exhibited too often.

Excavations were conducted by the French generals at Manikyala, Jhelum and later on Peshawar. Some of the discovered items and coin collections were sent to France. They were immediately studied and published in the specialised journals. Honigberger excavated at Hadda, near Jalalabad (Afghanistan), on his way back to Europe in 1834 and his collection was also widely talked about in the European press. Some "natives" in turn excavated the stupa of Pahller (Bhallar), on the actual site of Taxila. There is a painting of that stupa by Imam Bakhsh Lahori in Court's collection, but unfortunately no record has been preserved of what they discovered.

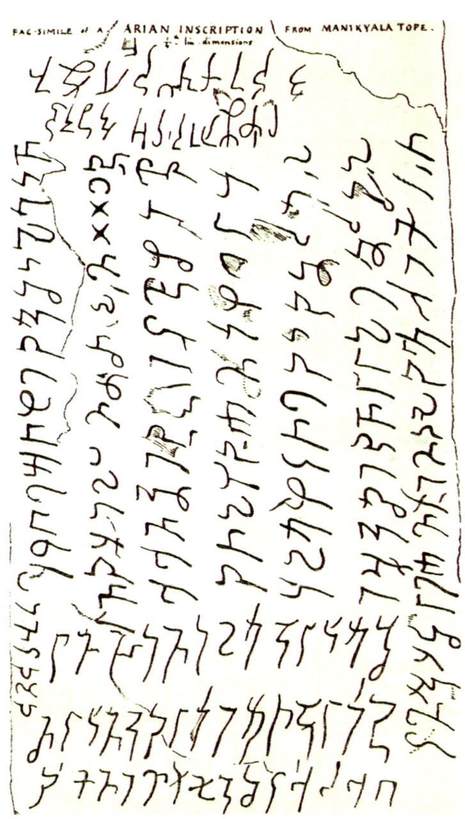

[247] Kharoshthi inscription discovered by General Court at Manikyala
From H.T. Prinsep, *Note on … Discoveries in Afghanistan*, London, 1844
"Facsimile of a Aryan inscription from Manikyala Tope taken by James Prinsep from a wax impression received from General Court"

The Allard [Ventura] collection of Graeco-Bactrian and Indo-Greek coins was till recently the largest section of such coins in the whole collection in the Bibliothèque nationale, Paris. In 1994 it was discovered that about 300 coins of the famous Cunningham collection in the British Museum were in fact the best part of General Court's numismatic collection sold after 1880. Honigberger's collection of coins has still to be traced or identified in the European museums and private collections.

Charles Masson (James Lewis by his real name), was a British deserter, who sometimes posed as an American, at others as Italian. He travelled extensively in Afghanistan and was well received by the French officers at Lahore. He got his passion for archaeology from Ventura's excavations at Manikyala and Honigberger's research at Hadda. Other

British civil or military officers like Claude Martine Wade, James Prinsep, Alexander Burnes, Dr. Gerard and young Alexander Cunningham corresponded extensively with the French generals on their archaeological discoveries. The Asiatic Society of Bengal, the Royal Asiatic Society in London, the Société Asiatique and the French Academy in Paris were the four main places where these discoveries were discussed and published in learned journals and proceedings. In British India and Europe, from London and Paris to Saint-Petersburg, these excavations were acclaimed as a landmark in the fields of classical studies as well as Indian history, and they created a lot of sympathetic curiosity for Punjab in the continental press. In 1836 the French Academy prepared a draft for an "Archaeological Survey of Punjab and Afghanistan".

We know by chance allusions of the interest of Lahoris for these excavations and of the diggings of the stupa of Bhallar by local people. We know of the interest taken by Maharaja Ranjit Singh in this research : in 1836 the Maharaja was elected an

[245] Buddhist reliquaries and coins from the great stupa of Manikyala
Discovered by General Ventura in 1830
British Museum. OA 1848.6-2, 1-4 and 5
Detail

[246] Stupa of Bhallar, near Taxila
"Coupole Pahller dans le canton d'Osman Katter"
Watercolour on European paper
By Imam Bakhsh Lahori. Taxila? 1830-1843
195 x 291 mm
Court collection, Musée Guimet. MG 78 III 39735

honorary member of the French Asiatic Society. But we are not yet able to assess the impact they had on the cultured elite of the Punjab, with one glaring exception : the *Sikandarnama* rumal of the Chandigarh Museum (Acc. N° 59.395) done in 1852 for Raja Gulab Singh, who had become Maharaja of Jammu and Kashmir in 1846. The winged "peris" of the Lahore fort, the foxes of the La Fontaine's *Fables*, the parrots of Bannu Pan Dei's shawls and the European chair of Maharaja Ranjit Singh all make an appearance on this exceptional piece of work. The *Sikandarnamas*, illustrated or not, but copied in the Punjab kingdom under Maharaja Ranjit Singh have not yet been listed. But in British India, at least two Indian political agents of the East India Company, Mohan Lal (assistant to Alexander Burnes) and Syed Keramat Ali (for a time posted in Kandahar where he collected coins), actively participated in these discoveries and became famous in Europe for their knowledge and numismatic collections.

These intense archaeological activities in the Punjab kingdom, the Peshawar area and southern Afghanistan initiated the discovery of what is internationally known today as Gandhara or Graeco-Buddhist Art. In the turmoil of the years 1839 to 1857, which witnessed the first Anglo-Afghan War (1839-1842), the Anglo-Sindh war (Annexation of Sindh in 1843), the Anglo-Sikh wars (1845-46 and 1849) and the Revolt of the Sepoys (1857), archaeology receded in the public mind. When the Archaological Survey of India was created and Alexander Cunningham visited Manikyala again, there was an unwritten decision to forget all that had been done in these fields by non-British people, whether Punjabi or French. Cunningham secretly purchased the numismatic collection of General Court after his death in 1880, and H.H. Wilson attributed the main discoveries in this field to "Charles Masson".

[252] Bronze mask of Lord Shiva discovered by General Court at Peshawar
Profile
"Tête antique découverte à Peshawer entre Caboul et Attock Près du haut Indus, par Mr le Général Court"
5th / 6th century AD. H. 46 cm. W. 25.5 cm
Weight 4730 gm
Bibliothèque nationale. Cabinet des Médailles. Paris

[245] Buddhist reliquaries and coins from the great stupa of Manikyala
Discovered by General Ventura in 1830
British Museum. OA 1848.6-2, 1-4 and 5
Detail

[254] Portrait of Victor Jacquemont (1801-1832)
Lithograph by Lemercier, from a portrait by Mrs. Léonor Mérimée
Private collection

[257] Map of Kashmir
Given by General Court to Jacquemont
1831
Lettres de Victor Jacquemont
Ref. 2532, document 347
Bibliothèque centrale
Museum d'Histoire Naturelle, Paris

X

Geological Exploration of the Himalayas

In 1828 the Museum of Natural History, Paris, decided to send a brilliant, young naturalist, Victor Jacquemont, to India to study the fauna, flora and geology of the Himalayas.

Born in 1801, Jacquemont had already conducted a geological survey of the Hudson valley in the USA. He reached Calcutta in May 1829, met William Bentinck, the governor-general, and started exploring the Himalayas under British authority, going up to the Kedar Kanta, Kotgerk, Kanum, and crossing twice into Chinese territory. He was back in Delhi in December 1830.

While at Nako, "frontier between Ladakh and Chinese Tartary", Jacquemont received an invitation from General Allard to visit the Punjab and extend his research to Kashmir. He crossed the Sutlej in March 1831 and went to Lahore where he was well received by his French compatriots. He met Maharaja Ranjit Singh several times, and was impressed by his deep curiosity. He had long, vivid conversations with him, especially on some medical points since Jacquemont was also a physician and Ranjit Singh had some health problems at that time.

Coming in the wake of Alexander Burnes's travel on the Indus, Maharaja Ranjit Singh wasn't sure of the real purpose of Jacquemont's visit, political or scientific. When he saw that Jacquemont did not evince any interest for material benefits or appointments, he gave him permission to travel freely in the kingdom. He also gave him generous gifts (Rs. 5,000 in cash and the same amount in kind) : for Jacquemont this was providential at a time when his finances were at their lowest ebb.

[258] Shalimar Gardens at Srinagar
Illustration "Shalibagh"
Victor Jacquemont's *Voyage dans l'Inde*, tome 5, *Atlas*, plate 69
Bibliothèque centrale
Museum d'Histoire Naturelle, Paris

General Allard provided Jacquemont with an escort of his own cavalry, and Ranjit Singh gave him letters for his officers in the province. The naturalist then got a map of Kashmir copied by Court from his own papers [N° 257] and he first went to Khewra where he visited the Salt Mines with Raja Gulab Singh. From May to September he explored the valley of Kashmir, amassing a huge collection of plants and minerals and acquainting himself with the most interesting cultural and historical aspects of the valley.

Back in Amritsar he met Ranjit Singh again in October 1831. Ranjit Singh wanted Jacquemont, who knew Lord and Milady Bentinck, to attend the Rupor meeting. But Jacquemont preferred to return to Delhi

[255] View of Dhankar
Illustration "Vue de Dhankar"
Victor Jacquemont's *Voyage dans l'Inde* ,
tome 5, *Atlas*, plate 46
Bibliothèque centrale
Museum d'Histoire Naturelle, Paris

through Mandi where he studied the iron and salt deposits in that state. From February to December 1832 he travelled to Bombay, where he died on 7 December. He was only 31 years old.

[260] Ornithological plate : "Heron brag"
"Héron brag"
Victor Jacquemont's *Voyage dans l'Inde*,
tome 6, *Atlas*. Plate 8
Bibliothèque centrale
Museum d'Histoire Naturelle, Paris

Jacquemont's mortal remains and packages - boxes full of stones, herbs, plants and papers - were sent to France. A year later his correspondance in two volumes was printed in Paris (Dec 1832). When Honigberger arrived in Saint-Petersburg in 1834, he was surprised to see people reading Jacquemont's *Correspondance*. It contains so much interesting information on British India and the Punjab kingdom that it was translated into English in 1834. Jacquemont's *Voyage dans l'Inde* was published in six volumes between 1835 and 1841.

[259] Botanical plate : "Allardia Tomentosa"
Victor Jacquemont's *Voyage dans l'Inde*,
tome 6, *Atlas*. Plate 95. Bibliothèque centrale
Museum d'Histoire Naturelle, Paris

[256] The head of the Tibetan Church in Kanawar
"Le Chef de l'Eglise thibétaine en Kanawer"
Victor Jacquemont's *Voyage dans l'Inde*,
tome 5, *Atlas*, plate 55
Bibliothèque centrale
Museum d'Histoire Naturelle, Paris

[261] Entomological Plate : Butterflies"
"Insectes. Papillons"
Victor Jacquemont's *Voyage dans l'Inde*, tome 6, *Atlas*. Entomologie, Plate 1
Bibliothèque centrale
Museum d'Histoire Naturelle, Paris

[198] Inside a Punjabi residence
La Fontaine, "Le vieillard et ses trois fils" "The old Man and his children"
Gouache and gold on paper. Imam Bakhsh Lahori. Attock, 1837-1839. Musée Jean de La Fontaine, Château-Thierry

XI

Materia Medica of the Punjab

Medical studies in Punjab followed the systems in use in northern India and which were taught in the various schools, Hindu, Muslim and Sikh (Leitner). Among his close friends, Maharaja Ranjit Singh had excellent physicians like the Fakir brothers. He established a *Dar-ul-Shefa* or public hospital in Lahore, which was directed by Fakir Nuruddin to dispense free consultation and medicine.

Dr. Honigberger reached Lahore in 1829. He had been trained in allopathic medicine, was appointed physician to the court and practised in Punjab where he introduced vaccination. When Jacquemont met him in Lahore in 1831, he observed that this man was "very devoted to his profession and it is the chief object of his life. One would call him a good surgeon, and he appears to me to be well versed in oriental Materia Medica". During his leave in Europe (1833-1837) Honigberger met Dr. Hahnemann, the founder of homeopathy, in Paris and he returned to Lahore as a homeopathic physician. From 1839 to 1849 Honigberger was in charge of the government hospital at Lahore, along with Fakirs Azizuddin and Nuruddin.

Honigberger published his Memoirs in two volumes in 1852, volume 1 being his *Adventures in the East*, and volume 2 a *Materia Medica* of plants and products mainly from Kashmir which were found in the bazars of Lahore and were used by the local physicians. Volume 2 is accompanied with drawings of plants. Honigberger gives interesting descriptions of diseases he cured (e.g. Raja Suchet Singh), or could not cure, at Lahore. He exchanged information and even patients with Fakir Nuruddin, and gives the information that Amritsar was the great market for medical plants where people used to come from all over Punjab to procure them.

[229] Honigberger's Thirty Five Years ...
Plate IX "Attar, or Uttar (Druggist)"
Probably from an original painting by
Imam Bakhsh Lahori, 1829-1849
Punjab State Archives. Acc. N° 279

[262] Honigberger's Thirty Five Years ...
Plate VIII "Hakim, or Hakeem
(Mohammedan or Mahommedan Doctor)"

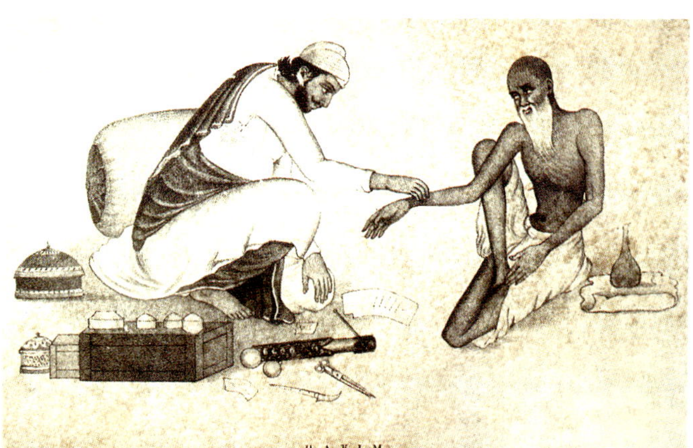

[211] Raja Suchet Singh
"Rajah Sutcheyt Singh" /
Rajah Semtcheyt Sing"
Gouache on European paper
By Imam Bakhsh Lahori.
Lahore, 1827-1843
169 x 251 mm
Court collection, Musée
Guimet. MG 78 III 41831

GLOIRE A DIEU

Du doigt il pèse les mondes comme un grain de poussière, il fait mouvoir les phalanges célestes il fait rouler les astres sur eux-mêmes pour ramener ou les fléaux ou les fêtes des saisons. Principe et fin de toute chose, c'est de lui que part l'éclair que nous appelons existence, et c'est en lui que cet éclair va s'éteindre. Dieu des armées, il aime, il soutient, il anime les braves, leur ceint l'épée et fait flotter pour eux au front de bataille l'étendard de la victoire. Il marque du sceau de sa puissance ceux qu'il appelle à commander aux nations : et, quand il le faut, met au cœur des Princes et des peuples l'esprit de conciliation, de concorde et de clémence. Un fleuve de lumière et de sagesse, d'affection et de vérité coule de ses lèvres, et sa main jète au même moule, teint des mêmes couleurs, purifie au même foyer les âmes heureuses destinées à sympathiser malgré les lieux qui les séparent.

Louis Philippe Empereur des Français

Au très Grand, très Magnifique et très Puissant Prince Le Maharadjah

Rendjit Sing, Bahadór, Padichah du Pendjab,

Conquérant du Cachemire, du Moultan, de Mangara, d'Attok, de Péhawer, &c. &c. &c.

Guerrier invincible et magnanime, Notre très-cher et parfait Ami : Salut.

[illegible]

Votre très-cher et parfait Ami,

Louis Philippe

V. Broglie

Ministre et Secrétaire d'Etat de Sa Majesté l'Empereur des Français.

[264] Letter of Louis-Philippe, King of the French, to Maharaja Ranjit Singh
appointing General Allard as Agent de France to the Punjab
Tuileries Palace, Paris,
27 October 1835.
Seal in Gold "Charte de 1830"
Last place known :
the *toshakhana* in the Lahore fort
British Museum, Mss. Eur. G 59

XII

The Punjab in 1839 The Maharaja's death: The days before. The years after

What Maharaja Ranjit Singh managed to achieve in Punjab was done in the regional context of British consolidation in India on the east, Islamic reassessment in Iran and Afghanistan on the west-north-west axis, and the growing Russian shadow in central Asia and Afghanistan.

In the last years of the 18th century and the first half of 19th century, England had no intention to let India go the way the Thirteen Colonies of North-America had done in 1783. The money from India formed a substantial part of the British exchequer, and when Europe was engulfed in the revolutionary and Napoleonic wars (1792-1815) the East India Company moved swiftly : 1792 (first siege of Srirangapatnam), 1798 (Hyderabad), 1799 (second siege of Srirangapatnam and death of Tipu Sultan), 1802 (Treaty of Bassein), 1803 (capture of Delhi). Holkar with his army was at Amritsar in 1805, while the army of Lord Lake was camping on the Beas. In 1809 the frontier between Punjab and British India was fixed on the Sutlej, and Calcutta opened a series of political post at Karnal, Ambala, Subathu and Ludhiana, the last one being more particularly in charge of monitoring the Punjab. Ranjit Singh had his *vakils* there (Anand Singh, then Kishen Chand) and in Delhi. From 1825 onwards the *Fauj-i-khas* controlled the border on the right bank, and a squadron of cavalry was permanently posted at Ludhiana for the security of the *vakil* and the diplomatic correspondence. Skinner's Horse was in charge of the left bank, the "British" side of the river.

[263] **Fakir Syed Aziz-ud-Din**
Watercolour on paper
20.7 x 10.8 cm
Chandigarh Museum. Acc. N° D-29

The question whether the Indus threw itself into the Sutlej, or the Sutlej into the Indus, was hotly debated between Lahore and Calcutta since it entailed the inclusion, or exclusion, of Sindh among the territories where Ranjit Singh could freely move according to the treaty of 1809. In 1832 the Maharaja thought he had been diplomatically beaten by Lord William Bentink and excluded from Sindh. But the prospect of Bentinck being replaced by Charles Metcalfe in 1834 gave him the hope that he could move and annex Sindh. An old acquaintance and a friend of Maharaja Ranjit Singh's, Metcalfe was known to advocate the creation of a "Sikh" buffer-state extending from the Indian Ocean (Sindh) to the Himalayas (Ladakh) as a protection for British India against the *Dar-ul-Islam* and Russia.

The prospect of having a Punjab empire extending from the Himalayas to the Indian Ocean, and from the Khyber Pass to the Sutlej river was one of the factors that convinced the Maharaja to allow General Allard to go on leave to France. Allard, who had to travel through British territories to board a ship to Europe, did not carry an official letter to hand over to the French government. But he certainly had a message to deliver, which was to help the Punjab kingdom reinforce itself both militarily and diplomatically. The French government on its side was anxious to fix the English military forces in the east at a time when the conquest of Algiers (1830) was expanding quickly towards Constantina and Tunisia (1835). The French decided to appoint Allard as Agent de France (French ambassador) at Lahore and to send military equipment and a few experts to further modernize the Punjab army. This appointment created difficulties between Calcutta and Lahore : London asked Paris to cancel the nomination, but France refused to oblige. However the replacement of Bentinck by Auckland, instead of Metcalfe, cut short any possibility of modifying British policy in Sindh.

If we turn now to the north-west frontier, we must not forget that the Iranians and then the Afghans had been the dominant power in the Punjab (between Indus and Sutlej) since 1739. When Ranjit Singh captured Multan in 1818, Kashmir in 1819, the Derajat in 1821, and when ultimately he started crossing the Indus towards Peshawar in 1823, he was indenting on Afghan principalities and disturbing Afghan interests in these areas. Dost Muhammed Khan tried to reunify whatever Afghan principalities and forces he could around the Hindukush against "the Sikhs". In the meantime in the early 1830's the Iranians were closing towards Herat, and the renewed prospect of an invasion of Punjab by a Persian army deeply perturbed Maharaja Ranjit Singh. Between 1827 and 1839, the major preoccupation of the Punjab government was the north-west province, Peshawar till the Khyber Pass, and their relations with the states beyond the Khyber Pass. This preoccupation increased when Dost Mohammed Khan asked for Russian "protection", following which a Russian emissary, Captain Vitkevitch, reached Kabul in December 1837. Vitkevith's instructions were to inform Dost Mohammed Khan that Russia did not recognise any of the Punjab acquisitions since 1813 : "Captain Vitkevitch said [to the Prime Minister of Afghanistan] that his presence at Lahore with the letters of the Emperor [of Russia] and of the Shah of Persia of which he was the bearer will induce the ruler of the Punjab to accede to the terms of the Amir [Dost Muhammed Khan] in giving Multan, Derajat, Kashmir and Peshawar to their original masters, the Afghans" (Mohan Lal). Vitkevitch asked for permission to come to Lahore, which was denied by the Maharaja. Lord Auckland was also worried about this Russian influence which pretended to dictate terms to the Government of Punjab and was threatening his own authority in India. The field was clear for the First Anglo-Afghan War.

Facing these formidable challenges, not to speak of the minor irritants of everyday life in international relations, Ranjit Singh's foreign policy, backed by a powerful military machine which he methodically built up all over his reign, was a subtle and difficult balance and check of these factors. He had

[1] Maharaja Ranjit Singh
Gouache on paper
Artist unknown. c. 1850
Lahore Museum. Pakistan
Ref. S. 229 / S.N. 1086

[265] "Treaty of Alliance and Friendship between Maharaja Ranjit Singh and Shah Shuja-ul-Mulk, with the approbation of and in concert with the British Government"
(Done at Lahore. 26th June 1838, ratified at Simla, 23rd July 1838)
National Archives of India. Acc. N° 121

[266] Cremation of Maharaja Ranjit Singh
Central Sikh Museum, Amritsar
Shiromani Gurudwara Parbandhak Committee

trusted advisers like Raja Dhyan Singh, Fakir Syed Azizuddin (his minister of foreign affairs), Raja Dina Nath (who favoured the reception of the Russian envoy at Lahore) and on some occasions General Allard. But he decided alone, acknowledging the fact that the British had outwitted him in Sindh in 1832, annexing Peshawar in 1834 and trying to open communication with France at that time, restricting Zorawar Singh in Ladakh in 1835 in order not to bring a direct conflict with the Chinese and all along keeping a secret channel open with Nepal through a few senior officers of the *gurkhas* of the *Fauj-i-khas* who went on leave to Kathmandu whenever deemed necessary.

The Maharaja's death

The days before. The years after

After consulting Fakir Azizuddin on 20th June 1839, Maharaja Ranjit Singh declared that Prince Kharak Singh was the heir-apparent, and Raja Dhyan Singh must continue as prime minister. That put an end to the speculations that Prince Nau Nihal Singh, whatever his statesmanship, could succeed his grandfather on the *gaddi* of Lahore. On 27 June 1839 Maharaja Ranjit Singh breathed his last.

On 23 July the British army captured Ghazni in Afghanistan and on 7 August Shah Shuja-ul-Mulk was restored on the throne of Kabul. From 20 to 25 July, the five thousand Punjabi musulmans under Brigadier Sheikh Basavan (*Fauj-i-khas*) and Colonel Lafont forced the Khyber Pass. The Punjabi army reached Kabul on 2 September 1839, where "the Sikh troops were inspected in full dress, and their appearance brought for the Colonel's eulogium" (Barr). After one month in Kabul, they returned safely to their headquarters at Peshawar..

The British army also returned to India, leaving a strong occupying force in Kabul. That force was exterminated during the Afghan revolt of 1841-1842. This in turn led to a series of wars with the English army of retribution in Afghanistan being followed by the conquest of Sindh (1843), the First (1845-6) and Second (1849) Sikh Wars with the annexation of the Punjab. As Maharaja Ranjit Singh had once sadly prophesied, the whole of India had turned red.

Next was 1857, and then again 1947.

[56] Maharaja Ranjit Singh on horse back
Artist unknown. 1830. 23.6 x 18 cm
Chandigarh Museum. Acc. N° 3305

CONCLUSION

Ranjit Singh started his political career in 1792 as the head of the Sukerchakia *misl* with a tiny territory extending around Gujranwala at a time when the Punjab was parcelled into so many petty powers of every creed and race that the political map of the country would have looked more like a patchwork. In January 1839 he was Maharaja of the Punjab Kingdom, an empire extending over 390,000 sqare km with a population of c. 15 million people, a prospering agriculture, a booming traditional economy and a full treasury. A powerful army (130,000 strong), spear-headed by the "French" and other regular brigades, assured the defense of the country and internal peace within the borders.

This life-long achievement was not an easy task. Just like the great European statesmen of 19th century who had to reunify a country and give it its right place in the concert of nations, Maharaja Ranjit Singh needed an exceptional foresight of what he wanted to achieve, and then he needed patience and perseverance to attain his goals, restraint when encountering success and courage in the face of adversity and setbacks. This restraint was perhaps the most humane aspect of Ranjit Singh : he took care of individuals after he had won a victory or achieved the political purpose of an annexation. He never took life for raison d'état or out of vindication, and he did his best to control and restrain his administrators sometimes too prone in doing so. The presence in his court of so many former sovereigns and heads of principalities he had annexed, from Kangra to Multan and Peshawar, shows a respect for life much greater than what had been the case in these areas in the previous centuries. The "save the child" he shouted to his bodyguards in the midst of a battle at Multan rescued the two-year-old Syed Poor from certain death : he was later adopted by General Allard and Bannu Pan Dei.

A major quality of Maharaja Ranjit Singh was the way he attracted people, discerning talent wherever it was -including in the *farenghis*- and received in return faithful service for the betterment of the state. But he received more than that : affection no doubt, and often admiration from the people who came close to him. Ranjit Singh knew the charm he affected on people and turned it into an element of his governance and policy. The care he took of his subjects - be it in the villages when he was touring the countryside, in the salt mines when he sat on a rock and had discussions with the workers, or in his court when he directed the relief operations for Kashmir - is an indication of his sollicitude for the common folk . He had a constant desire to get in touch with them beyond the screen of administration. He never spared his friends when he found them at fault with their duty towards the State, and some of his most flamboyant outbursts of anger were directed against his own administrators when he found them guilty of injustice or extorsion.

[10] Maha Singh Sukerchakia father of Maharaja Ranjit Singh
27.5 x 20.6 cm
Chandigarh Museum. Acc. N° 364

During the forty seven years of his reign, Ranjit Singh met with tense, sometimes desperate situations where he needed all his courage and perseverance to hold on till better times. The *jihad* of Syed Ahmed Barelvi from Peshawar (1827-1831) was one such case of permanent tension in his mind. The fear of an Iranian invasion of Punjab in the early 1830's was another one: Wade was at one time surprised to see the Maharaja, apparently calm and composed, appose by mistake his seal on his own thigh, instead of the document he was supposed to validate. When Wade inquired from his confidants about this hidden tension, he was told that the Maharaja was extremely worried by the Persian military build

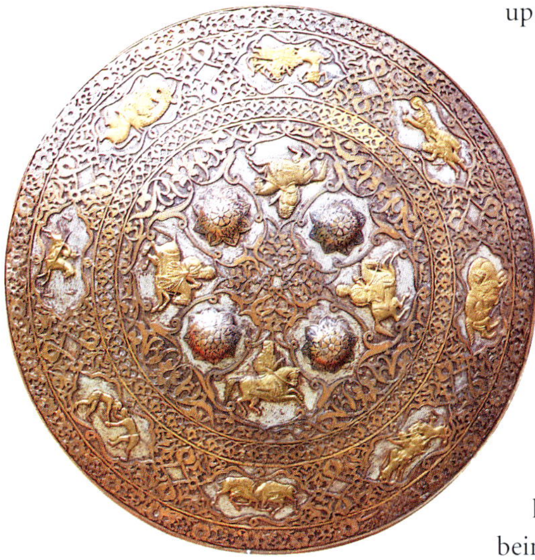

[22] Shield "of Maharaja Ranjit Singh"
Iron and brass
Diameter 49 cm
Lahore, 1891
Maharahja Ranjit Singh Museum.
Amritsar. Acc. N° nil

up and the Iranian armies moving into Khorassan. Another difficult situation, on the economic front that time, was the rarification of silver in India in the late 1820's and early 1830's, when the great banks of Calcutta collapsed and the cash revenues decreased in the Punjab kingdom. The Maharaja found himself obliged to cut salaries and impose forced payments to his closest aids and friends, which led to considerable tension in the *darbar* and veiled accusations of "avarice". Ranjit Singh stuck to his policy, and the tension subsided. We could list endless instances when the Maharaja spent sleepless nights worrying for his kingdom and working for his people.

To compensate for such tensions, he partook of the pleasures of life fully. We do not know much about Ranjit Singh's pastimes since they belonged to his private life and are rarely recorded in Persian chronicles, the *Umdat-ut-Tavariikh* for instance. The Maharaja loved riding splendid horses, organised ram fights, went on hunting expeditions which sometimes were conducted on a great scale, the regular army being put into action for beating drums and flying nets. We know that within his circle of friends the Maharaja liked to spend his evenings drinking and discussing an infinite number of interesting topics ranging from the etymology of the word "*Shalimar*" down to the subject of whether ghosts existed or not. Ranjit Singh also had his own painters whose style he liked and whose paintings he offered when he knew they would be appreciated. He loved music, and he was particularly fond of the flute when played by an Atar Khan. He listened to the Punjabi poetry of Hashim, but he also knew the *Sikandarnama* well enough to be excited by the possible discovery of the tomb of Sikandar's horse at Manikyala.

Of course he loved women. Not only the women of his official harem, filled through political marriages which consolidated alliances and extended his kingdom, although he was deeply attached to some of them, the mother of Prince Kharak Singh for instance. He married some beautiful women till the end of his years : Rani Jindan, the mother of Prince Dalip Singh. But he liked the beautiful women he could meet in Lahore, even when they came as part of the tribute of Kashmir, and his biographers have put up lists of lovely young persons and dancing girls who gave the Maharaja a happy interlude in the tense life to built up and strengthen the Punjab kingdom. Most of the foreigners who visited Lahore, the less hypocrite at least, acknowledged the beauty of the "Lahori" women the Maharaja entertained in his dancing troops, the "state dancing girls", and the young girls in tight uniforms forming his Amazon "regiment". General Court, the prude Christian, and Victor Jacquemont, the Parisian dandy, were particularly impressed by the beauty of the young women Ranjit Singh sent them for their own leisure or temptation. Some of his biographers, with their Victorian values and influenced by most of the English contemporary accounts insisting equivocally on the "debauche" of the Maharaja, have tried to overlook that aspect of his life. But Ranjit Singh was quite frank

[50] "Arrival of contingent force of Sikh irregular cavalry"
Director of Culture, Government of Punjab

[13] Maharani Jindan
Gouache on paper
Artist unknown
Lahore Museum. Pakistan
Ref. S. 234/ S.N. 1087

about it, and the almost official *Umdat-ut-Tawarikh* has recorded his declaration at Jallandar in 1831 that "in his life he had been making so much of merriment and pleasure that it could not be described in words". That was part of a life so full, animated as it was by a curiosity of mind for all the good and beautiful things of the world, that no pen can circumscribe it in the compass of words.

More than any other son born in the Land of the Five Rivers, Maharaja Ranjit Singh incarnated the best qualities of the Punjab people : a deep attachment to the soil, a practical foresight and a logical way to implement on the long term what has been decided, a resilience against adversity, a will to fight and to win. Also a love for mankind and nature which the anonymous artist of the *Janamsakhi B-40* had marvellously encompassed in the 1730's.

[14] Maharani Chand Kaur
Gouache on paper
Artist unckown. c. 1850
Lahore Museum. Pakistan
Ref. S. 232 / S.N. 1088

This extraordinary dynamism of Ranjit Singh is one of the most striking elements of his personality. Punjab moved systematically under him from a cluster of fragmented tiny principalities to a formidable kingdom or empire whose modern armies challenged the first world power of the time at Firozeshah and Chillianwala. In that way, Ranjit Singh embodied a long Punjabi aspiration of self-confidence and self-achievement. This is one of the reasons of his "everlasting" kindness towards his own people and human beings at large, and that was the reason of the deep attachment he received from men of every walk of life in the kingdom. In return, he strengthened and highlighted this Punjabi identity which, beyond race, religion and local culture, had its core between the Indus and the Sutlej river, from the Himalayan foothills to the frontiers of Sindh. This might be called today Punjabi ethos, or culture. In doing so, the Lord of the Five Rivers has left a legacy which is very much alive in the minds and hearts of the present generations.

[23] Lithoprint of jewel studded horse of Maharaja Ranjit Singh
From an original drawing by Emily Eden
Lahore, 1838. 20.5 x 30 cm
Maharahja Ranjit Singh Museum. Amritsar
Acc. N° 46 A

[Map 5]

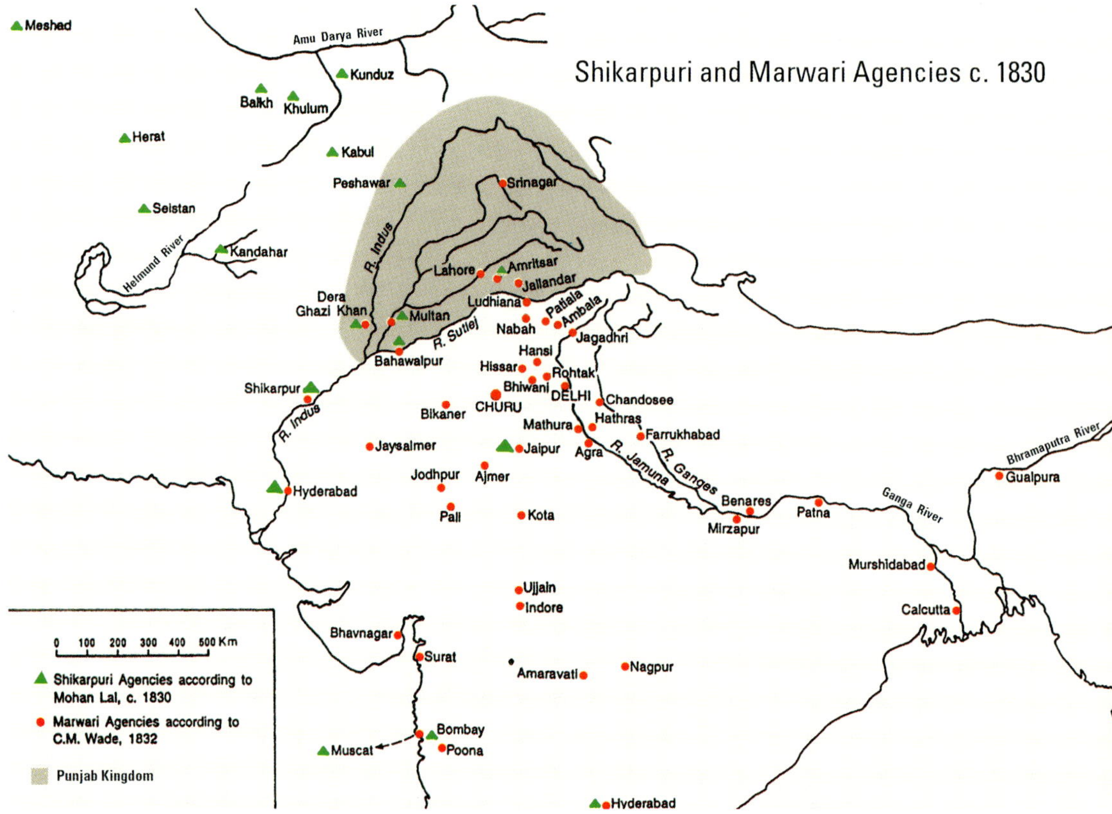
Shikarpuri and Marwari Agencies c. 1830
Meshad
Amu Darya River
Kunduz
Balkh
Khulum
Herat
Kabul
Peshawar
Srinagar
Seistan
Helmund River
Kandahar
R. Indus
Lahore
Amritsar
Jallandar
Ludhiana
Dera Ghazi Khan
Multan
Patiala
Ambala
Nabah
R. Sutlej
Jagadhri
Bahawalpur
Hansi
Hissar
Rohtak
Bhiwani
DELHI
Shikarpur
Chandosee
Bikaner
CHURU
Hathras
Mathura
Farrukhabad
Jaysalmer
Jaipur
Agra
R. Jamuna
R. Ganges
Bhramaputra River
Gualpura
Jodhpur
Ajmer
Hyderabad
Benares
Patna
Ganga River
Mirzapur
Pali
Kota
Murshidabad
Ujjain
Indore
Calcutta
Bhavnagar
Surat
Amaravati
Nagpur
Bombay
Muscat
Poona
Hyderabad
0 100 200 300 400 500 Km
Shikarpuri Agencies according to Mohan Lal, c. 1830
Marwari Agencies according to C.M. Wade, 1832
Punjab Kingdom

[Map 6]

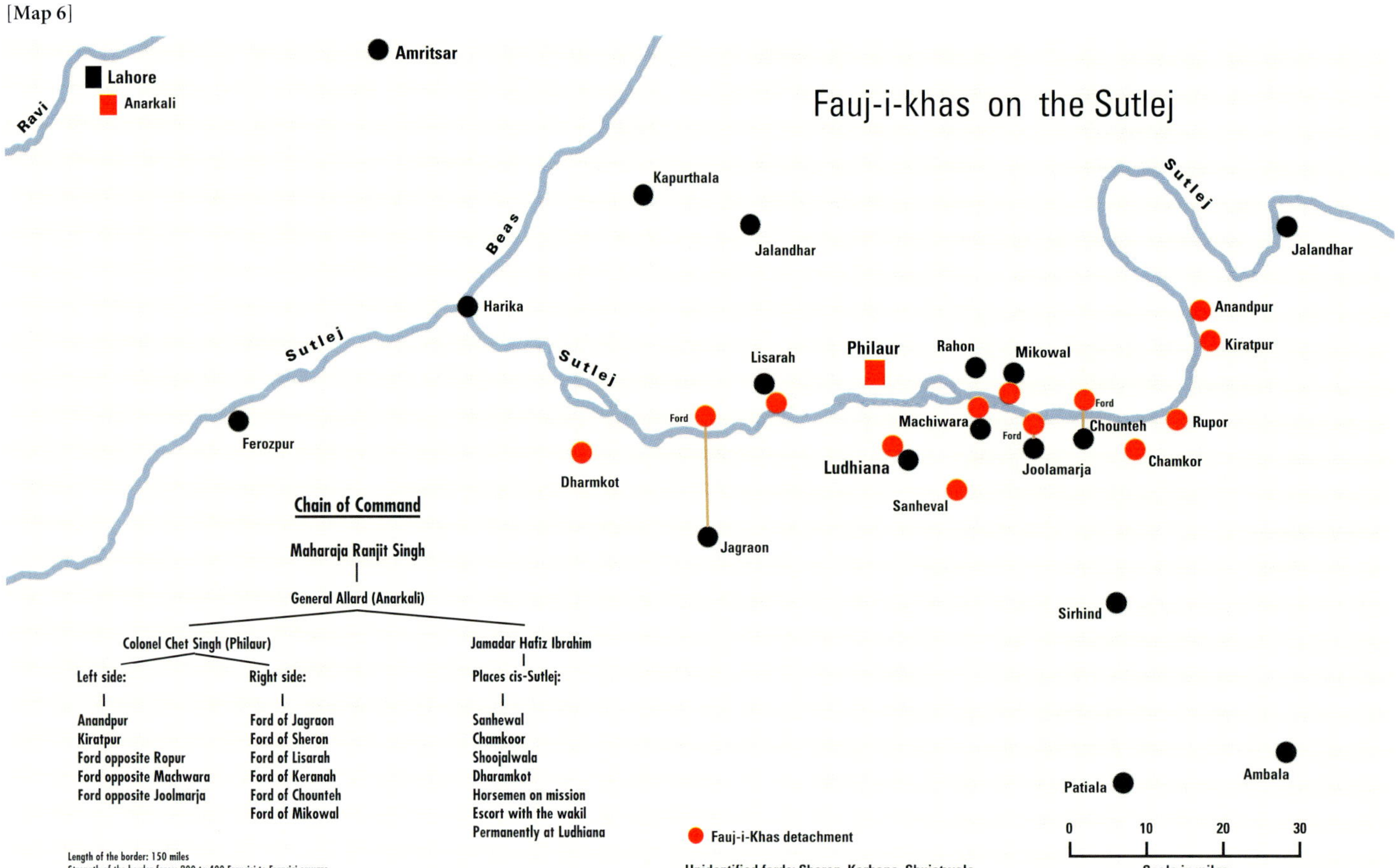
Fauj-i-khas on the Sutlej
Amritsar
Lahore
Anarkali
Ravi
Kapurthala
Jalandhar
Sutlej
Jalandhar
Beas
Harika
Anandpur
Kiratpur
Sutlej
Sutlej
Lisarah
Philaur
Rahon
Mikowal
Ford
Ford
Ferozpur
Machiwara
Chounteh
Rupor
Ford
Dharmkot
Ludhiana
Joolamarja
Chamkor
Sanheval
Chain of Command
Maharaja Ranjit Singh
General Allard (Anarkali)
Jagraon
Colonel Chet Singh (Philaur)
Jamadar Hafiz Ibrahim
Sirhind
Left side:
Anandpur
Kiratpur
Ford opposite Ropur
Ford opposite Machwara
Ford opposite Joolmarja
Right side:
Ford of Jagraon
Ford of Sheron
Ford of Lisarah
Ford of Keranah
Ford of Chounteh
Ford of Mikowal
Places cis-Sutlej:
Sanhewal
Chamkoor
Shoojalwala
Dharamkot
Horsemen on mission
Escort with the wakil
Permanently at Ludhiana
Patiala
Ambala
0 10 20 30
Scale in miles
Fauj-i-Khas detachment
Unidentified fords: Sheron, Kerhana, Shujatwala
Length of the border: 150 miles
Strength of the border force: 200 to 400 Francisi to Francisi sowars

[Map 4]

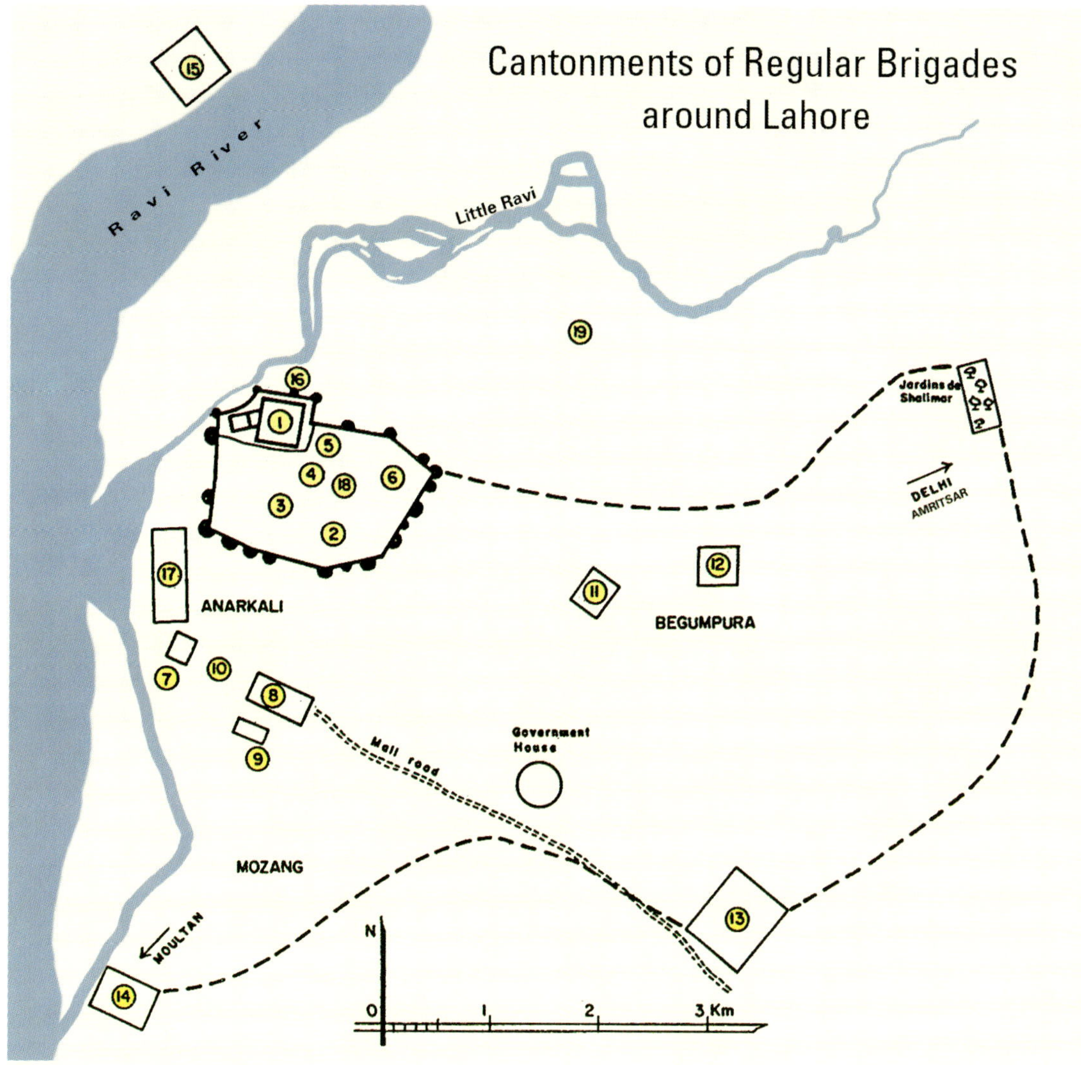

1. Lahore Fort
2. Walled City
3. Fakir Khana, residence of Fakir family
4. Raja Dhyan Singh's residence
5. Raja Tej Singh's residence
6. Raja Dina Nath's residence
7. Anarkali. Headquarter of Fauj-i-khas and residence of Generals Allard and Ventura
8. Cantonments of the Fauj-i-khas
9. General Allard's *baradari*
10. Training ground of Fauj-i-khas
11. Naulakha. Headquarter of General Court's brigade and residence of the General
12. Budhu-ka-awa. Headquarter of General Avitabile's brigade and residence of the General
13. Mian Mir. Cantonments of the Campu-i-mualla
14. Nawankot. Cantonments of troops from the Campu
15. Shahdara. Headquarter of General Oms' brigade and residence of the General
16. Royal Training ground
17. The 'Soldier's Garden', laid out by Allard and Ventura along the riverside
18. Sohnari Masjid
19. Three villages given in *jaghir* by Maharaja Ranjit Singh to General Court

-----Approximately the limits of ruins of Lahore: tombs, mosques, gardens, baradaris

[126] The Sonahri Masjid, Lahore
Gulgashat-i-Punjab
Lahore, 1860
Maharaja Ranjit Singh Museum. Amritsar
Acc. N° 38

[189] The Tomb of Anarkali. Lahore
Gulgashat-i-Punjab
Maharaja Ranjit Singh Museum. Amritsar
Acc. N° 38

[181] The Harmandir, or Golden Temple, Amritsar
Gulgashat-i-Punjab
Maharaja Ranjit Singh Museum. Amritsar
Acc. N° 38

[187] The Shalimar Gardens, Lahore
Gulgashat-i-Punjab
Maharaja Ranjit Singh Museum. Amritsar
Acc. N° 38

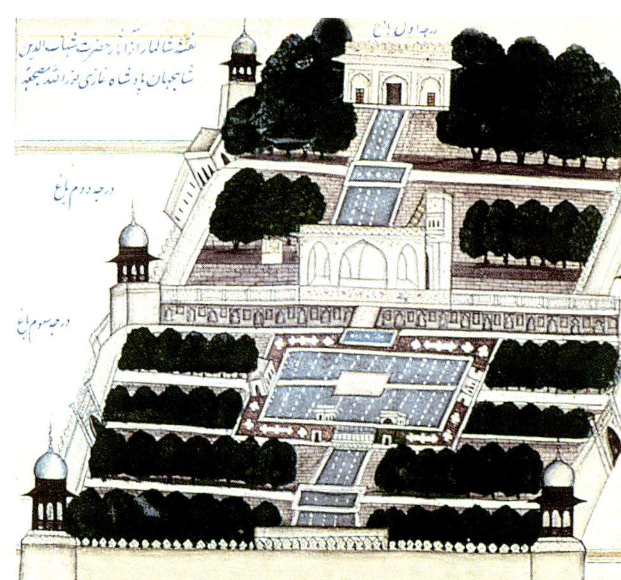

Catalogue

List of Maps

[1] Maharaja Ranjit Singh
Gouache on paper
Artist unknown. c. 1850
Lahore Museum. Pakistan
Ref. S. 229 / S.N. 1086

[2] Sardar Fateh Singh Ahluwalia
Courtesy : Brigadier Sukhjit Singh, MVC

Fateh Singh Ahluwalia (r. 1801-1837) succeeded his father Bagh Singh on the *gaddi* of Kapurthala and immediately formed an alliance with Ranjit Singh, sealed by an exchange of turbans. During their first dealings with the English, both of them were called "Sardar" and were treated on an equal footing. Fateh Singh participated with his troops in the military campaigns of the Lahore army: Jhang and Kasur (1807), Kangra (1809), Attock (1813), Multan (1818), Kashmir (1819), Mankera (1821). But apparently apprehensive of the policy of consolidation of the Punjab under Ranjit Singh's rule, Fateh Singh fled to the British territories in 1825. Aggrieved by the departure of his old friend, Maharaja Ranjit Singh did his best to reassure him and Fateh Singh returned to Kapurthala in 1827. Ranjit Singh faithfully respected all his possessions and sovereign rights, which in 1837 passed to his son Nihal Singh.

[3] Letter issued by Maharaja Ranjit Singh to Raja Fateh Singh of Kapurthala.
Dated 1871 B.K. (1814 AD)
20 x 10 cm
Maharaja Ranjit Singh Museum. Amritsar
Acc. N° 2
The letter in Persian has the seal of Maharaja Ranjit Singh in Gurmukhi script "*Akal Sahae*". It also bears the word "Sahi" in Gurmukhi script.

[4] Treaty between Maharaja Ranjit Singh and Raja Fateh Singh of Kapurthala
Dated 9th March 1825. 44.5 x 13 cm
Maharaja Ranjit Singh Museum. Amritsar
Acc. N° 9

The treaty in Persian bears the palm impression of Maharaja Ranjit Singh in saffron and also his seal in Gurmukhi script.

[5] *Iqbal Nama-i-Maharaja Ranjit Singh*
by Raja Ram Kaul Tota, Pandit. Persian
Dated 1849 AD
PSA. Acc. N° M 649
Exhibited in Maharaja Ranjit Singh Museum Amritsar

This Persian manuscript gives an account of the forty years of Maharaja Ranjit Singh's reign.

[6] Persian edition of Lala Sohan Lal Suri's *Umdat-ut-Tawarikh*
5 volumes, Arya Press, Lahore, 1885-1889 AD
Punjab State Archives, Patiala

[3]

"By far the most authoritative, comprehensive and coherent chronicle among all the extent original indigenous sources of the history of the Punjab. It purports to cover the period from the foundation of the Sikh religion under Guru Nanak Dev to the annexation of the Punjab by the British (1469 to 1849)". (V.S. Suri). Lala Ganpat Rai, father of Sohan Lal, was a *vakil* and *akhbar nawis* of Sardar Charat Singh, Sardar Mahan Singh and then Maharaja Ranjit Singh. After his death in 1812, Sohan Lal took over his father's charge and completed the manuscript of more than 7000 pages in Persian *shikesta* in 1849. The manuscript copy of the book was exhibited at the International Congress of Orientalists at Florence in 1879.

[7] *Tawarikh-i-Panjab*
by Bute Shah. Persian. Copies in Punjab State Archives (Acc. N° M 347, Patiala), Bhai Vir Singh's Library (Delhi), *Khalsa* College (Amritsar), Ganda Singh's Library (Patiala)

"Bute Shah's *Tawarikh-i-Panjab*, completed in Persian in 1848 AD, is a comprehensive history of the Punjab from the earliest time to the break-up of the Sikh empire" (Ganda Singh)

[8] Maharaja Ranjit Singh at Ropar in 1831
Oil on canvas
31 x 36 cm. No date. No signature
Private collection

This portrait of the Maharaja is attributed to Marie de Tournemine, half-sister of the famous Orientalist painter Vacher de Tournemine, who had married Jean-François Allard, alias "Poulou", the eldest son of General Allard and Bannou Pan Dei. However, the origin of this portrait goes back to the famous Ranjit Singh/Bentinck meeting at Ropar in 1831. Jiwan Ram, an artist in Lord William Bentinck's entourage, made a drawing of Maharaja Ranjit Singh, which was engraved as the frontispiece of H.T. Prinsep, *Origin of the Sikh Power in the Punjab and Political Life of Maharaja Runjeet Singh*, Calcutta, 1834. A French translation by Xavier Raymond was published in France in 1836, with the same frontispiece and a portrait of General Allard : Marie de Tournemine's portrait is a copy from the engraving on the French edition of the book.

[9] Family tree of Maharaja Ranjit Singh
Iqbalnama-i-Maharaja Ranjit Singh
Maharaja Ranjit Singh Museum. Amritsar
Acc. N° nil

The family relations of Maharaja Ranjit Singh played a crucial role in his early political career. His grand-father and father had already started building up a reasonably strong principality around Gujranwala. From his mother's side, he was particularly close to his 'mama', Bhag Singh of Jindh, who more than any other chief knew what was going on in Hindustan and gave him friendly advice on the Marathas, the French and the English. From his first mother-in-law, Sada Kaur, the grand-mother of Prince Sher Singh, he received the powerful backing of the Kanhaya misl, who helped him consolidate his position in the Sikh community, increase his territories and was a great help in his capture of Lahore and Amritsar.

[10] Maha Singh Sukerchakia, father of Maharaja Ranjit Singh
27.5 x 20.6 cm
Chandigarh Museum. Acc. N° 364

Maha Singh, the head of the Sukerchakia misl, built a fort at Gujranwala and started extending the

[101]

territory of the Sukerchakia chiefs, from Sahiwal and Isakhel to Sialkot. He raided Jammu, and defeated the forces of the Kanhaya misl. Following that he arranged the marriage of his son, the future Maharaja Ranjit Singh, to Mehtab Kaur, grand-daughter of the Kanhaya chief. Mehtab Kaur's mother was the remarkable Sada Kaur, who inherited the Kanhaya estates and proved a useful, though sometimes a dangerous and overpowering ally of her son-in-law.
In Gujranwala Ranjit Singh built a very handsome structure with a golden pinnacle and inner rooms adorned with paintings as a *samadh* for his father, and he venered his memory all his life. According to the *Handbook of the Punjab* published in 1883, in the building there were "knobs which mark the place where the ashes are deposited" (sic. p. 226), some of them identified by Persian inscriptions: Maha Singh Padsha, Maharaj Sher Singh, Kanwar Nau Nihal Singh.

[11] Sword of Bagh Singh of Jind (1768-1819), maternal uncle of Maharaja Ranjit Singh.
Size 92.5 cm
Sangrur Museum. Acc. N° nil

Ranjit Singh's mother, Raj Kaur or Mai Malwain as she was called in her family, was the daughter of Raja Gajpat Singh of Jind. Bhag Singh, her brother and the 'mama' of Ranjit Singh, reigned from 1786 till 1819. Well informed of the politics of the Delhi *darbar* and of the powerful influence of the "French" Brigades of Hindustan under de Boigne and Perron (1784-1803), he personally led the delegation of Sikh sardars to Perron to ask for help against George Thomas at Hansi. He then accompanied a delegation of Perron and Bourquien's emissaries to Lahore to meet Ranjit Singh. After the Maratha disasters of 1803, Bhag Singh turned to Lord Lake and the English as the paramount power in Hindustan. He again gave judicious advice to his nephew concerning his conduct with the East India Company.

[12] Young Ranjit Singh
from the *Iqbalnama-i-Maharaja Ranjit Singh*
Maharaja Ranjit Singh Museum. Amritsar
Acc. N° nil
This is an imaginary painting of Maharaja Ranjit Singh reconstructed by the artist. Ranjit Singh is sitting on his famous golden throne made in the early 1820's by Hafeez Muhammad Multani. The general set up, building in the back, *qanat* in the forefront with a horse ready for the Maharaja, is a reminder of two similar paintings by Imam Bakhsh Lahori : the frontispiece of the *Military Manual* and the frontispiece of the *Fables* of La Fontaine. Even more, the three closed doors of the building are the typical persiennes from Provence which General Court had built in his house at Lahore and which we see represented several times in the miniature paintings of the *Fables* .

[13] Maharani Jindan
Gouache on paper
Artist unknown
Lahore Museum. Pakistan
Ref. S. 234/ S.N. 1087

Born in 1817, she was "one of the most beautiful creatures of the world" (A.S. Gill). Maharaja Ranjit Singh, who knew her from her childhood, married her in 1835, and she gave him Prince Dalip Singh in 1838. After the death of Sher Singh in 1843, she was appointed regent for little Maharaja Dalip Singh. She had a great responsibility in the events of 1844-1845 and the way the first Anglo-Sikh war evolved. She was interned by the English at Sheikupura in 1846, then exiled to Benares from where she escaped to Nepal. In 1861 she was finally allowed to settle in England with her son, where she died in 1863.

[14] Maharani Chand Kaur
Gouache on paper
Artist uncknown. c. 1850
Lahore Museum. Pakistan
Ref. S. 232 / S.N. 1088

Chand Kaur, daughter of Jaimal Singh Kanhaya, married Prince Kharak Singh in 1811. She was the mother of Prince Nau Nihal Singh.

[15] Maharaja Kharak Singh
Gouache on European paper
By Imam Bakhsh Lahori. Lahore, 1841-1843
Court collection, Musée Guimet

Eldest son of Maharaja Ranjit Singh, Kharak Singh was born from his second and beloved wife Rani Raj Kaur in 1801. There is not a single favourable description of Prince Kharak Singh, despite which he was declared heir by Maharaja Ranjit Singh in 1816. In 1811 he married Rani Chand Kaur, and in 1821 he fathered Prince Nau Nihal Singh, a brillant personality and most respected member of the royal family. In June 1839 Kharak Singh succeeded his father on the *gaddi* of Lahore, with Raja Dhyan Singh as Prime Minister, who was soon replaced by Chet Singh, a friend of the Maharaja. Chet Singh was murdered in October 1839, and Nau Nihal Singh practically assumed the direction of the government. The Maharaja died from a fever in November 1840, and Prince Nau Nihal Singh was to succeed him as Maharaja of the Punjab.

[16] Prince Nau Nihal Singh
"Le Prince Noh Néhal Singh. Kover Novn Nehal Sing"
Watercolour on European paper
By Imam Bakhsh Lahori. Lahore, 1837-1843
172 x 245 mm
Court collection. Musée Guimet. MG 78 III 41826

Prince Nau Nihal Singh was much loved by his grand-father Maharaja Ranjit Singh, and most of the time he is represented sitting next to the Maharaja when most of the courtiers are standing. Trained in military affairs by Hari Singh Nalwa, who also taught him Persian, and with a sound scientific education from his teacher Akhwand Ali Ahmad, he seemed the most promising successor to the ailing Maharaja right from the mid 1830's. His marriage in Lahore in March 1837 with a daughter

[21]

of General Sham Singh Attariwala was a splendid affair. However, on his death-bed Maharaja Ranjit Singh reiterated that Prince Kharak Singh be his successor. After the murder of Chet Singh, Nau Nihal Singh became the *de facto* ruler of the Punjab. His firm conduct at Peshawar against British intrigues and the way he conducted himself till November 1840 spoke highly of his ability to succeed his grand-father. When Maharaja Kharak Singh died on 5 November 1840, the stage seemed clear for Nau Nihal Singh to officially assume the direction of the state. But the young prince was crushed by the falling of the Roshnai Darwaza while returning from the cremation ground of his father and he died on 6 November, aged 22 years.

[17] **Prince Sher Singh**
"Maharaja Cheyr Singh" / "Maharaja Shair Sing"
Watercolour on European paper
By Imam Bakhsh Lahori. Lahore, 1841-1843
181 x 257 mm
Court collection, Musée Guimet. MG 78 III 39749

Maharaja Sher Singh (reign 1841-1843) was the reputed son of the Maharaja from Rani Mehtab Kaur, his first wife. Sher Singh was a close friend of generals Allard and Ventura, and in January 1841 he obtained the *gaddi* through what British political agents called a coup d'état of General Ventura. Extremely courageous, he ignored Court and Ventura's information concerning a machiavelic plot against him, and he was assassinated along with his son Partab Singh (10 years old) and Prime Minister Dhyan Singh on 15 September 1843. In his *Memoirs*, Court says that the French generals took care of the cremation of Sher Singh and young Partab Singh. General Ventura then resigned from the *darbar*, and he left Lahore just before generals Avitabile and Court.

[18] **Maharaja Dalip Singh**
"Maharajah Dhélip Singh" / "Maharajah Duleep Sing Bhadoor"
Watercolour on European paper
By Imam Bakhsh Lahori. Lahore, 1843
187 x 258 mm
Court collection, Musée Guimet. MG 78 III 39750

Prince Dalip Singh, the youngest son of Maharaja Ranjit Singh from his beautiful, young wife Rani Jindan, was born on 4th September 1838. He was proclaimed maharaja in 1843, under the regency of his mother. Deposed by Dalhousie in 1849, he was exiled to Futtehgar, then went to England and lived a comfortable life, "protected" by Queen Victoria, until he resolved to return to Punjab. Arrested by the British authorities in Aden in 1886, he managed to escape to France, asking for French protection and setting up a kind of government in exile at Pondicherry. He then went to Russia and offered the Tsar to lead a revolt against the English in India. Meeting with no success and having no more money, he begged Queen Victoria for forgiveness and was 'pardoned'. He died in Paris in 1893.
His youngest daughter from his first wife was Princess Bamba, who inherited the collection of paintings and artefacts, which are housed today in the Lahore fort.

[19] **Golden Throne of Maharaja Ranjit Singh (Replica)**
Gold leaves on wood, with repoussé work
Height c. 93 cm
Victoria & Albert Museum, London
Acc. N° 2518 IS

This throne was made in Lahore after 1818, probably in the early 1820's, by Hafeez Muhammad Multani. The base is the same as can be seen in a painting of the *Iqbalnama-i-Ranjit Singh* (N° 12), and the complete throne is represented for example in N° 33 and 232. Taken by the British in 1849 from the *toshakhana* in Lahore, it was sent to London in 1853. It is now on display in the Victoria and Albert Museum, London.

[20] **Inscribed sword of Maharaja Ranjit Singh**
Used during the conquest of Kasur in 1807
Central Sikh Museum, Amritsar

Kasur, founded by Kusa, son of Rama, was the mythological rival city of Lahore, founded by Loh or Lava, son of Rama and brother of Kusa. Historically, it belonged to a colony of Pathans established there under Babur or Akbar. When the Sikhs rose to power, they were fiercely opposed by the Pathans of Kasur. Maharaja Ranjit Singh captured the place after a month of resistance by Qutb ud-Din, its chieftain, who then retired to his estate at Mamdot. Ranjit Singh then annexed Kasur to Lahore.

[21] **Sword offered by Maharaja Ranjit Singh**
Length: 104.5 cm
Maharaja Ranjit Singh Museum. Amritsar.
Acc. N° 232

Maharaja Ranjit Singh presented this ceremonial sword (c. 1830-1839) to Captain Robert Brown. It has a horse-shaped jade handle with rubies set in gold for eyes. In the centre of the quillon is a portrait of the Maharaja which is also adorned with rubies. The steel blade is decorated with hunting scenes, while the scabbard is richly embellished with rubies and emeralds in a gold setting.

[22] **Shield "of Maharaja Ranjit Singh"**
Iron and brass
Diameter 49 cm
Lahore, 1891
Maharaja Ranjit Singh Museum. Amritsar.
Acc. N° nil

A splendid piece of workmanship, signed by Asad-Ullahi and dated from 1891 AD, i.e. after the fall of the Sikh kingdom. The four figures on horseback represent the Maharaja, sons Kharak Singh and Sher Singh, and grandson Nau Nihal Singh. On the outer band are scenes of wrestlers, tent pegging, hunting scenes and goddess Durga killing demons.

[184]

[23] **Lithoprint of jewel studded horse of Maharaja Ranjit Singh**
From an original drawing by Emily Eden
Lahore, 1838
20.5 x 30 cm
Maharaja Ranjit Singh Museum. Amritsar
Acc. N° 46 A

"The first show of the day [23rd December 1838, Lahore] was Runjeet's private stud. I suppose fifty horses were led past us. The first had on it emerald trappings, necklaces arranged on its neck and between its ears, and in front of the saddle two enormous emeralds, nearly two inches square, carved all over and set in gold frames, like looking-glasses. The crupper was all emeralds, and there were stud-ropes of gold put on something like a martingale. Hira Singh said the whole was valued at 37 lakhs (3,700,000). But these valuations are fancyful as nobody knows the worth of these enormous stones. They are never bought or sold. The next horse was simply attired in diamonds and turquoises, another in pearls, and there was one with trappings of coral and pearls that were very pretty. Their saddle-cloths have stones woven into them. It reduces European magnificence to a very low pitch". (E. Eden, *Up the Country* , p. 227).

[24] **The Court of Lahore**
Oil on canvas
by August Schoefft. Lahore 1841-Vienna 1855
120" x 192"
Princess Bamba Collection
Sikh gallery, Lahore Fort
Director of Archaeology, Govt of Pakistan

August Schoefft, an Austro-Hungarian artist born in 1809, came to India and was invited to Punjab in

1841-1842 by his compatriot Dr. Honigberger. He was welcomed by Maharaja Sher Singh, who sat for him and commissioned several paintings. He also made paintings "for several of the principal persons of the court" (Honigberger) and for private sponsors, like the lovely Fezli Azam Joo, the Kashmiri wife of the French General Court, who sat for him in 1841 in her residence at Naulakha (cf. N° 209).
Schoefft collected all the drawings and paintings he could get of absent or deceased people (Maharaja Ranjit Singh, Kharak Singh, Nau Nihal Singh, Udham Singh, General Allard, Fakir Haridas) which he kept in his portfolio. Back in Europe, he painted *The Court of Lahore* which Honigberger thought had been purchased by King Louis-Philippe of France. That sovereign had sponsored historical paintings of exceptional dimensions for the Versailles palace. If Schoefft had not received a French commission, he was inspired by that impressive program. But Louis-Philippe lost his throne in 1848, and Schoefft completed his painting by 1852. Exhibited in Vienna in 1855, the painting was ultimately purchased by Maharaja Dalip Singh and remained in his family till Princess Bamba's death in Lahore in 1957. She bequeathed her collection to her secretary, who sold it to the Government of Pakistan in 1959.
The indispensable companion to this painting is F.S. Aijazuddin's book, *Sikh Portraits by European Artists*, Sotheby Parke Bernet, London-New York, OUP Karachi, 1979.

[25] Tavernier: The "Great Mughal" in the Delhi Red Fort, c. 1660
From Tavernier's *Travels in India*, chapter XII "Figures of large diamonds"
First French edition Paris, 1676, 2 vol
Engraving. Private collection

In 1665 Aurangzeb allowed the French jeweller Tavernier to examine (and draw if he so wished) the fifty most beautiful diamonds of the Mughal Empire kept in a small room in the Red Fort of Delhi. They were presented to him on two large golden trays. The first and the biggest diamond he was shown, called the "Great Mughal", weighed 280 carats, and Valentine Ball identified it (1889) as being the Koh-i-noor. This remains a hypothesis, but probably the best we have till now.

[26] "The Jewels of Maharaja Ranjit Singh"
From an original drawing of Emily Eden
Lahore, 1838
20.5 x 30 cm
Maharaja Ranjit Singh Museum. Amritsar
Acc. N° 46

[26]

Maharaja Ranjit Singh received the Koh-i-noor from Shah Shuja-ul-Mulk, the dethroned sovereign of Afghanistan, on 1 June 1813, as a reward for helping to free the Afghan king imprisoned by his own revolted subjects in Kashmir.
Maharaja Ranjit Singh kept it mounted on different settings: as a bracelet, on his turban and even on his horse's bridle. Ultimately, he set it on an armlet between two other diamonds which he purchased for rupees one lakh each, and put them around his arm.
The diamond was shown to high ranking visitors, who described it in their *Memoirs* and correspondence. The Koh-i-noor was shown to Lord Auckland, Governor-General, and his sister Emily Eden on 31 December 1838.

[27] Terms granted to, and accepted by Maharaja Dulleep Singh, 1849
"Granted and accepted at Lahore, on 29th March 1849, and ratified by the Right Honourable the Governor-General on the 5th April 1849"
National Archives of India, New Delhi. Acc. N° 90

This is the Persian text of the terms imposed by the East India Company to the Punjab Government after the decisive battle of Gujrat, 21 February 1849.
Dalhousie never made any mystery that the conquest of Punjab was for the material and financial benefit of England. Paragraph 3 of the document stipulated, in its English official translation, that "The gem called the Koh-i-noor, which was taken from Shah Shuja-ul-Mulk by Maharaja Runjeet Singh, shall be surrendered by the Maharaja of Lahore to the Queen of England".
Writing to Hobhouse some days later from Ludhiana, he stated with unconcealed satisfaction: "The Koh-i-noor has become in the lapse of ages a sort of historical emblem of conquest in India. It has now found its proper resting place".

[28] Minute by Dalhousie concerning the Koh-i-Noor
13 May 1850. [14 June 1850]
National archives of India, New Delhi. Acc. No. 90

Instructions were received from Queen Victoria to dispatch the Koh-i-noor to London. Dalhousie forwarded them to Henry Lawrence at Lahore, who in the board meeting called for this topic reminded his brother John that the diamond was with him. John had forgotten it in his waistcoat some time ago, and quietly asked his old bearer if he had found a small box in his pocket : "Yes, Sahib. I put it in one of your boxes".When the little box was brought and opened, the bearer added : "There is nothing here, Sahib, but a bit of glass".
The first page of Dalhousie's minute reproduced here describes the departure of the Koh-i-noor from the Lahore fort (para. 4). The second page reproduced mentions the golden chair of Maharaja Ranjit Singh and the Muslim relics kept in the

[30]

toshakhana of the fort.
The Koh-i-noor was secretly brought to Bombay by Dalhousie himself, and the diamond sailed for London on 6th April 1850 on HMS *Medea*, a steamboat. It was delivered to the Queen at Buckingham Palace on 3 July 1850, and presented during the Great Exhibition in the Crystal Palace at Hyde Park in 1851.

[29] The Koh-i-Noor on the English crown (Replica)
Maharaja Ranjit Singh Museum. Amritsar
Acc. N° nil

On 17 July 1852 the cutting of the Koh-i-noor (186 carats) started in London. The Duke of Wellington initiatied the process himself at Garrards, Panton Street, off the Haymarket. It lasted thirty-eight days, cost £ 8,000 and reduced the stone to 108.95 metric carats, a loss of 43 per cent from its original weight.
The "new" Koh-i-noor, which was examined by Maharaja Dalip Singh at Buckingham Palace in 1854, was mounted on a different setting : tiara for Queen Victoria in 1855 along with 2,000 diamonds. Five years later, it was reset for Queen Victoria

again in a regal circlet. In 1911 it was mounted on Queen Mary's new crown which she wore for the coronation. The present setting was done in 1937 for Her Majesty, Queen Elisabeth, the Queen Mother. It is fixed in the Maltese cross at the front (base) of the crown.

[30] Lithoprint of Prince Partab Singh
From an original drawing of Emily Eden
Lahore, 1838. c. 36 x 15 cm
Maharaja Ranjit Singh Museum. Amritsar
Acc. N° 42

'We had little Partab to sketch this morning, and he was very pleasant. I asked him to fix his eyes on Captain M., who was acting as interpretor. After a while he began to fidget, and his stern old Sikh tutor reproved him for it. Partab declared he could not help it... We gave him a diamond ring, which seemed to delight him". (E. Eden, *Up the Country* , p. 217)

[31] Lithoprint of Raja Hira Singh
From an original drawing of Emily Eden
Lahore, 1838. c 38 x 24.5 cm
Maharaja Ranjit Singh Museum. Amritsar
Acc. N° 44

"Hira Singh, Runjeet's favourite, came to my tent to sit for his picture. [But as] he arrived late, it was too dark to draw him well. Runjeet sent word that he considered him 'his best-beloved son'. Dhyan Singh, the prime minister [...] of the Punjab, was coming at the same time to see G[eorge Auckland] in a private manner. He is Hira Singh's father, but Runjeet sent 'the best-beloved son' with quantities of elephants and two regiments to take care of him, while Dhyan Singh came on horseback with only four soldiers riding behind him. He is a very striking-looking man, and his manners are much more pleasing than his son's". (E. Eden, *Up the Country* , p. 226)

[32] Lithoprint of Prince Sher Singh
From an original drawing of Emily Eden
Lahore, 1838. c 38 x 24.5 cm
Maharaja Ranjit Singh Museum. Amritsar
Acc. N° 43

"Sher Singh came to my tent [near Shalimar Gardens, Lahore] for his picture. Such a gorgeous figure ! All over diamonds and emeralds. He made a very good picture. He was extremely curious about the arrangement of our tent and poked about, looking into every book and box". (E. Eden, *Up the Country*, p. 223)

[33] The Darbar of Maharaja Ranjit Singh
Gouache on paper, stuck on wood panel
Artist unknown. c. 1850
91.5 x 32 cm
Maharaja Ranjit Singh Museum. Amritsar
Acc. N° 110

This unique painting shows the *darbar* of Lahore with the Maharaja sitting on his golden throne. Behind him, the princes and attendants. In front of him, the great administrators and military officers of the state, the dead (Phula Singh Akali, Ganga Ram, probably Hari Singh Nalwa) as well as the living. Three French generals are also represented : Allard, Ventura and Avitabile.
Besides showing princes Peshora Singh and Kashmira Singh, a rarity, this painting shows the multi-ethnic, multi-confessional composition of the Lahore *darbar* under Ranjit Singh: the number of Hindus among the ministers and dignitaries, the various sections of the Muslims (Panjabis, Multanis, Peshawari-Kabuli), and the *farenghis*. Some of the persons represented here are rarely represented in the *darbar*, like Ajudhya Prasad. Last but not least, note the strange beard and mustachios of Avitabiļe - "rouflaquettes", or sidewhiskers - imitated by Dhunkal Singh, an officer trained in the British army.

[31]

[34] Sozni of Maharaja Ranjit Singh
Gold embroidery on silk
Faqir Jalaluddin Collection
Lahore Museum, Lahore
Ref. Sr. N° 646 list 27

According to the Fakir family tradition, this ceremonial dress belonged to Maharaja Ranjit Singh. It is similar to the *khilat* given by Ranjit Singh to General Allard [N° 95]

[35] Golden Gates of the Harmandir Sahib (Golden Temple)
Offered by Maharaja Ranjit Singh. c. 1830
Length 6' 3" Breadth 4' 6"
Entered in the *Toshakhana* register dated 3.10.97 at page 2, Sr. N° 17 under the title "Jalao Sri Harmandir Sahib"
Courtesy: Shiromani Gurudwara Parbandhak Committee

Four golden gates (eight panels) are kept in the *Toshakhana* and are fixed in place of the four silver gates at the time of *Jalao* (Splendor, i.e. special festivities). Two of these gates were offered by Maharaja Ranjit Singh, and two by the Temple management. They are embossed with floral decorations and panels depicting the lives of the Gurus.

[36] Sword of Maharaja Ranjit Singh
Full length 32"
Golden hilt studded with rubies and emeralds
Velvet scabbard with gold work
Entered in the *Toshakhana* register dated 3.10.97 at page 2, Sr. N° 24 under the title "Jalao Sri Harmandir Sahib"
Courtesy : Shiromani Gurudwara Parbandhak Committee

This sword is exhibited on ceremonial occasions only.

[37] Gold Chhatar studded with emeralds with neelam (blue saphire) peacock on the top.
Diameter with the string of pearls 2' 6"
Length with peacock 1' 7"
Entered in the *Toshakhana* register dated 3.10.97 at page 1, Sr. N° 1 and 2 under the title "Jalao Sri Harmandir Sahib"
Courtesy : Shiromani Gurudwara Parbandhak Committee

This canopy (*chhatar*) with the bejewelled peacock is a rare piece of Punjabi craftsmanship. It is in pure gold (about 20 lbs) studded with more than two hundred diamonds of the highest quality (*almas hire*), emeralds, rubies and pearls. The peacock, also in gold, has studded diamonds for eyes, and holds a tiny pearl necklace in its beak. The *jhalar* (fringe) of the canopy is decorated with 180 pearls of a rather large size offered by Maharaja Sher Singh.

[37 A] Jarau sehra of Kanwar Nau Nihal Singh
Length 1' 3" Breadth 2'
Studded with uncut diamonds and pearls
Entered in the *Toshakhana* register dated 3.10.97 at page 2, Sr. N° 9 under the title "Jalao Sri Harmandir Sahib"
Courtesy : Shiromani Gurudwara Parbandhak Committee

This *jarau sehra* (bejewelled headband) was ordered by Maharaja Ranjit Singh for the wedding of his grandson Nau Nihal Singh in 1837. It is said that when the Maharaja saw the splendour of the *sehra* at the time of the *sehrabandi* ceremony, he decided to offer it to the Harmandir.
The *sehra* has diamonds, emeralds and 2953 pearls that form the strings.

[38] Jewellery
Miniature painting from the *Ain-i-Akbari*
Copied at Lahore under Maharaja Ranjit Singh
Illustrated. Artist unknown
Patiala State Archives. Acc. N° M. 658

The Koh-i-noor is not the only jewel which travelled beyond the black waters from Lahore to London after 1849. Most of the English gentlemen and ladies who met Maharaja Ranjit Singh had been shown the crown jewels since he was justly proud of his collection. Just before he died, he wanted to give most of them to religious institutions, the Koh-i-noor being destined for the temple of Jaganath. It was Misr Beli Ram, the keeper of the *toshakhana*, who saved it. But after 1849, a section of the most beautiful items kept in the *toshakhana* were selected and sent to London, where some of them were presented at the Great Exhibition of 1851. After the exhibition they were offered to Queen Victoria.
Here is a painting done in Lahore in c. 1835 showing an exhibition of jewels.

[39] Jewellery
Lahore. 1825-1841
Private collections

These are some of the gold ornaments brought from Lahore by the French officers: gold bracelets, broches, rings etc.

[40] The Fort of Lahore
The Sheesh Mahal
Built by Shah Jahan in 1631-32
Renovated by Maharaja Ranjit Singh
Courtesy: Director of Archeology, Govt. of Pakistan

Maharaja Ranjit Singh restored the Lahore fort, which was in a pitiable condition in 1799. The Sheesh Mahal was renovated, with glass work and gold decorations. In the niches were painted scenes of Hindu mythology and hunting expeditions with soldiers of the *Fauj-i-khas* escorting the hunting parties. The water pipes were also restored. In March 1842 Prince Soltykoff described a splendid reception given by Maharaja Sher Singh in the Sheesh Mahal, with the "basin full of water-fowls, and fine jets of water [which] filled the air like diamond dust", shawls and gold brocades everywhere, thousand of illuminated globes of different colours which "gave a faint, soft light like that of dawn". And ultimately, as Sher Singh, Clerk and Soltykoff advanced, "we were more and more

[43]

overwhelmed by the splendour of a new hall, the walls and ceiling of which were decorated with green, white and red crystals framed in gold and looking like a pavement of precious stones upon an enormous ladder".

[41] The pavilion adjacent to the Sheesh Mahal
Lithograph by J.D. Hardinge from a sketch by C.S. Hardinge, Lahore, March 1846
Maharaja Ranjit Singh Museum. Amritsar

Built by Maharaja Ranjit Singh to hold his court, this pavilion was chosen by A. Schoefft for the setting of his grandiose "Court of Lahore" (N° 24). Paintings of Hindu mythology on the walls and a beautiful wooden ceiling similar to the ones in the Maharaja's summer palace at Amritsar still decorated it fifteen years ago. The capped tower in the back was built by Nau Nihal Singh, as observed by Fakir Syed Aijazuddin.

[42] Stand of traditional weapons
Maharaja Ranjit Singh Museum. Amritsar
Acc. N° 90-11

Coat of arms. Bows, swords, maces, lances etc. These arms were still used at the time of Maharaja Ranjit Singh by the irregular units of the army.

[43] Stand of traditional weapons
Maharaja Ranjit Singh Museum. Amritsar

The coat of arms in four pieces, used by Mughal as well as Rajput cavalry, were also the prefered armour of the *gorcharas*, the irregular cavalry of the Punjab army. The *gorcharas* were widely admired and described by English travellers in the Punjab, and especially by Emily Eden at a time when Walter Scott was read by British officers all over India, including the ones posted in Ludhiana.

[44] Stand of traditional weapons
Maharaja Ranjit Singh Museum. Amritsar

In 1836 General Allard brought modern armours

for his cuirassier regiments from France. Writing in 1839, Osborne admired "Raja Dhyan Singh dressed in a magnificent helmet and cuirass of polished steel embossed with gold, a present from King Louis-Philippe of France". However in 1841, Soltykoff described a "cuirass with helmet and gauntlets which, I understand, General Allard had brought from France, a miserable theatrical property clean enough, but in very bad taste, beyond all question. However the English, probably in sympathy for anything that reminded them of Europe, admired it much and were for trying on the gauntlets. I think this pleased the Sikhs who regarded it as a curiosity". Allard did bring a replica of a knight's cuirass since pseudo-medieval artifacts were manufactured in France in the wake of romanticism. It is this cuirass which is also worn by Raja Lal Singh in the famous engravings showing him parading on his horse.

[45] Phula Singh Akali
"Poullah Singh Naheng. Général des Akalis, fanatiques sikhs"
Gouache on European paper
by Imam Bakhsh Lahori, Lahore, 1827-1843
163 x 242 mm
Court collection. Musée Guimet. MG 78 III 39748

Phula Singh, head of the Akali or Nihang sect, joined Ranjit Singh's army after the capture of Amritsar in 1802. The total strength of the Akalis was 3,000 to 5,000 men distributed in the irregular units of the army, both infantry and cavalry. They formed the storming parties of the Punjabi troops, often opposed to the *ghazis* of the Islamic states. Although their poor performance in Amritsar in 1809 against the disciplined escort of Metcalfe was instrumental in deciding Ranjit Singh to develop his regular units, they performed well in the battlefield, be it at Chuch in 1813, Multan in 1818 and Noshera in 1823, where Phula Singh was killed while storming the Afghan positions. He was so famous that he is represented in the painting "Darbar of Maharaja Ranjit Singh", although he had been dead for a long time when the painting was done.

[46] "Nahang, or Akalee (Immortal", fanatic Sikh)"
From Honigberger, *Thirty-Five Years in the East ...*, plate V, p. 121
Probably from an original painting
by Imam Bakhsh Lahori
Punjab State Archives. Acc. N° 279

Honigberger was on one particular occasion ordered by Maharaja Ranjit Singh to take care of an Akali who had been punished. The Hungarian physician shared with all the Europeans the fascination *cum* repulsion toward this easily identifiable "sect" of the Sikhs. This painting has all the characteristics of Imam Bakhsh's workshop, including the long neck and the general attitude of the horse. It also has the precise details of the trappings of the mount and of the dress and military equipment of the man. This one is in boots, as the regular cavalry.

[47] "Three Akalis"
From an original drawing of Emily Eden
Lahore, 1838. c. 38 x 25 cm
Private collection

"[The Akalis] move about constantly, armed to the teeth, and it is not an uncommon thing to see them riding about with a drawn sword in each hand, two more in their belt, a matchlock at their back, and three or four pair of quoits fastened round their turban. Ranjit Singh has raised some irregular regiments composed entirely of Akalis, which he always employs on any dangerous or desperate service. And as they fight like devils, he continues to make them useful". Osborne, *Court and Camp ...*, pp. 144-5.

[48] Gorcharas
Oil on canvas
Detail from A. Schoefft's The Court of Lahore
Lahore 1841-Vienna 1855
Princess Bamba Collection
Sikh gallery, Lahore Fort
Director of Archaeology, Govt of Pakistan

The *gorcharas* formed the elite unit of the irregular cavalry of the kingdom. The men came from the greatest families of the land, upholding the landed nobility's tradition of chivalry.

"I requested leave to see [the *gorcharas*] and never beheld finer, nor a more remarkable striking body of men. Each one was dressed differently, and yet so much in the same fashion that they all looked in perfect keeping. The strange troop before me was most peculiary Indian. The uniform consisted of a velvet coat or gaberdine over which most of them wore a shirt of mail. A belt round the waist, richly embroidered in gold, supported the powder-horn, covered with cloth of gold as well as the Persian *katar* and the pistol which many of them carried in addition to those weapons. Some wore a steel helmet, inlaid with gold and surmounted with *kalga* or black heron's plume. Others wore a cap of steel, worked like the cuirass in rings. The left arm is often covered from and to the elbow with a steel cuff inlaid with gold. The round Sikh shield hangs on the back, fastened with straps across the chest, a quiver at the right side and a bow slung at the back being carried as part of the equipment. A bag made in the belt holds the balls, and a tall bayonet, frequently ornamented with gold, held in the right hand when the man is on foot, and carried over the shoulder when in the saddle, completes the dress" (Baron von Hügel, *Travels in Kashmir and the Punjab* , 1836, English ed. London 1845. Reed. Lahore, n.d., p. 330-1)

[49] Irregular infantry
19 x 24 cm
Middle 19th century
National Museum. New Delhi. Sr.n 79.332

Two soldiers with matchlock guns. They also have swords and shields with them. Irregular infantry in early 19th century Punjab was divided into the *sipah-i- piyadah, the sipah-i-qilajat* (fort garrison) and the *sair jammat* (guards). It rose from 5,000 in 1808 to 9000 in 1821. With no uniform and no standard equipment, it continued to grow to 25,000 in 1839.

[50] "Arrival of contingent force of Sikh irregular cavalry"
Director of Culture, Government of Punjab

This engraving, also called "Maharaja Ranjit Singh in Camp", shows the Maharaja escorted by his *gorcharas* reaching his camp on the banks of a river. It is easy to recognise one of his French officers, with his white beard and his hussar uniform, as General Allard, commanding the *Fauj-i-khas* and the regular cavalry of the Punjab army.

[51] General Hari Singh Nalwa
Detail from "The Darbar of Maharaja Ranjit Singh"
Gouache on paper, stuck on wood panel

[52]

Artist unknown. c. 1850
Maharaja Ranjit Singh Museum. Amritsar
Acc. N° 110

A rare and interesting drawing of General Hari Singh Nalwa wearing his armour in full darbar. Born in 1791 in Gujranwala, this legendary general of the Khalsa Army received his first commission as commander of 800 horse and foot in 1814. He distinguished himself at Kasur, Sialkot and in the successive expeditions against Multan and Kashmir. He was then in charge of Hazara, where he built the town of Haripur and the fort of Harkishangarh. He had a leading role in checking the *jihad* of Syed Ahmed Barelvi (1827-1831), and in 1834 he, along with General Court, annexed Peshawar to the Punjab kingdom. In 1836 he built the fort of Jamrud, at the entrance of the Khyber Pass. In 1837 Maharaja Ranjit Singh called the French generals and their brigades from Peshawar to Lahore for Prince Nau Nihal Singh's wedding. Hari Singh, also invited, declined to go as he feared an all out attack of the Afghans on Peshawar after the departure of the crack troops to Lahore. When the Afghans did attack, the Nalwa's bravery alone saved Peshawar and Jamrud until the return of the *Fauj-i-khas*, but he was fatally wounded. His samadh at Jamrud had a tablet with the date "30 April 1837". He was 46 years old. Besides his outstanding military ability, he was a fine connoisseur of Persian and a distinguished collector of miniature paintings.

[52] General de Boigne
Oil on canvas
Private collection

Benoît de Boigne (1751-1830), born in Chambéry, was trained in the Irish brigade of the French army (1768-73). After serving in the Russian navy and (maybe) joining the Russian secret service (1774-77), he came to India and joined the Madras army in 1778. In 1784 Sindhia asked him to organise his regular troops, and for fifteen years de Boigne raised and trained the three Brigades of Hindustan, from his headquarter at Aligarh (Doab). He was instrumental in establishing the Maratha supremacy in northern India. After the death of Madhoji Sindhia in 1794, the timely arrival of the First Brigade in Pune assured the smooth succession of Daulat Rao Sindhia. When de Boigne left Hindustan in December 1795, his legacy consisted of three brigades (30,000 strong) and a remarkable civil and military administrative system which gave Hindustan some peace and prosperity after fifty years of turmoil, internecine wars and invasion from Iran and Afghanistan. On his return to Europe he lived in London, Paris and Chambéry (Château de Buisson-Rond) where he died in 1830.

[53] General Perron
Engraving from an oil painting by
Robert Lefèvre, 1822
Private collection

Pierre Cuillier, alias Perron (1755-1834) came to India in 1780. After several years in the service of Indian rulers, mainly the rajas of Gohad and Bharatpur, he joined de Boigne in 1790. He

[55]

succeeded him as commander-in-chief in Hindustan in 1796 and created two more brigades, raising the total strength of Sindhia's regular army in north India to 45,000. In 1799, at the request of the cis-Sutlej states, he sent the Third Brigade under Bourquien to crush George Thomas, who dreamed of carrying the English flag to the Indus. but was defeated and surrendered at Hansi (Haryana) on 29th December 1801. However, Perron's position during the second Maratha war in 1803 is far from clear. He retired to France with his Indian family and lived in his Château du Fresne till his death in 1834.

[54] General Lake
Engraving by R. Cooper
published in London in 1807,
after a painting by George Place, Lucknow, c. 1804
52.1 x 37.5 cm
Victoria Memorial, Calcutta
Acc. N° C 347

Gerard Lake (1744-1808) entered the Foot Guard in 1758. He fought in north America during the war of Independence and served under Cornwallis in North Carolina in 1781. He fought against the French in Europe (1793-4), commanded in Ulster (1796) and Ireland (1798). Commander-in-chief in India (1801-1805), he firmly believed, like the Marquis of Wellesley, Governor-General, and Arthur Wellesley, future Duke of Wellington, that India should not be lost to England as had happened twenty years ago to the Thirteen Colonies of North America. He defeated Perron at Aligarh and captured Delhi (13 September 1803), took Agra and won the battle of Laswari against the old troops of de Boigne. After defeating Holkar in 1804, he pursued him upto the Beas in 1805. Ranjit Singh visited his camp in disguise. Lake returned to England in 1807 and died there in 1808.

[55] Major General Sir David Ochterlony, Bart., G.C.B. (1758-1825)
By Jewan Ram
Oil on canvas
Victoria Memorial, Calcutta
Acc. N° C 190

David Ochterlony (1758-1825) belonged to a loyalist family of Boston who migrated to Canada. He joined the army in 1777, was captured by the French at Cuddalore in 1783 and released in 1784. He commanded a regiment under Lord Lake in 1803, became the first British Resident in Delhi the same year. In 1808 he was ordered to organise a secret flying column and march to the Sutlej in order to back Metcalfe during his unnerving negotiations with Maharaja Ranjit Singh. Ganga Ram, the former *diwan* of Bourquien, was appointed his political adviser. Ochterlony signed the Treaty of 1809 with Lahore and issued several proclamations regulating the relations between the different Sikh states and the East India Company. In 1812 Maharaja Ranjit Singh invited him to the wedding of Prince Kharak Singh, and he came to Amritsar and Lahore. In 1814-1816 he commanded a British army in Nepal, and he then held several high ranking civil and military commands till he died in 1825. He had successfully commanded so many flying columns that after his death the people of Calcutta erected the Ochterlony Column in his honour on the Maidan.

[56] Maharaja Ranjit Singh on horse back
Artist unknown, 1830
23.6 x 18 cm
Chandigarh Museum. Acc. N° 3305

Riding a richly caparisoned horse, Maharaja Ranjit Singh is wearing a steel helmet and holding a bow and arrows. As usual, an attendant holds an umbrella over his head. Some soldiers in the escort are in the characteristic braided hussar uniform with a black heron plume on the turban.

[57] General Allard
Oil on canvas
Copy of an original painting signed "Court. 1837"
By Joseph-Désiré Court, Paris 1837
127 x 97 cm
Private collection

Jean-François Allard (1785-1839) joined the 23rd Dragoon in 1803. He served at Napoli in 1806, in Spain in 1808-1814, and was then transfered to the Imperial Guard, and later to the 2nd Hussar. During the Cent-Jours he was promoted Captain in the 7th Hussar. After Waterloo he remained on the army payrolls but got no posting, which is probably why he asked for four months leave in 1818 to go to Italy.
From Italy he went to Teheran, served Prince Abbas Mirza as a colonel. In 1822 he (and Ventura) joined Maharaja Ranjit Singh's service and created the *Fauj-i-khas*. As the senior French officer of the Punjab army, he served both as a field commander and as a diplomatic adviser to the Maharaja.
In 1834 he went on leave to France with his Hindu wife and their five children whom he settled in Saint-Tropez. Back in Lahore in 1837 with the title of Agent de France, i.e. French ambassador to the court of Lahore, he relieved Jamrud (and Hari

Singh Nalwa) from the Afghan attack. Appointed military governor of Peshawar province with the mission to modernise all the forts and settle the frontier with the Khyberi tribes, he died in Peshawar on 23 January 1839. He was buried in his garden at Anarkali, Lahore, where his tomb still stands.

[58] General Ventura
Oil on canvas
Artist unknown. 1838 ?
Size not recorded
Private collection

Reuben ben Torah (1794-1858), whose name was Italianized as Ventura, was too young to have served in Napoleon's army. His European military career was a brief enrolment in 1814 in a regiment called "Dragoni della Regina". For posterity that became a glorious career in the Great Army, a daring cavalry charge at the battle of Wagram, the long and horrible campaign of Russia and ultimately the last stand at Waterloo! In 1836 even H.T. Prinsep wrote that Ventura had been a colonel in Napoleon's army. Well educated and speaking several languages fluently, Ventura met Allard in Iran, and they came to Lahore together in 1822. Ventura took charge of the infantry of the *Fauj-i-khas* and in 1831 Ranjit Singh appointed him governor of Dera Ghazi Khan, with authority extending from Multan to Attock. In 1835 the Maharaja publicly acknowledged the remarkable work he had done as instructor of the Punjab army staff. According to Hügel he was made *qazi* of Lahore in 1836. He went on leave to Europe in 1837, and when he returned two years later, Allard was dead and Ranjit Singh dying. Ventura took full charge of the *Fauj-i-khas* and he conquered Mandi. He kept aloof from the internecine feuds of the Punjab till 1841, but he was instrumental in putting Prince Sher Singh on the *gaddi* of Lahore. He resigned after the assassination of Sher Singh and Dhyan Singh in September 1843 and returned to France. He died in his estate at Lardenne, near Toulouse, in 1858.

[59] General Court
Detail from Schoefft's 'The Court of Lahore'
August Schoefft, Vienna, 1850-1855
From drawings made in Lahore in 1841-42
Princess Bamba Collection,
Sikh Gallery, Lahore Fort
Director of Archaeology, Govt of Pakistan

Claude-Auguste Court (1793-1880) was educated at the Ecole Militaire Spéciale de Saint-Cyr. He then joined the infantry, fought in Saxony and France. His military file in 1815 stated that he was strong, educated, well-off and [politically] dangerous: to be kept under watch. An excellent mathematician, fascinated by history and geography, Court left France for the Middle-East in 1818, served in Persia till 1826 when he decided with Avitabile to join Allard and Ventura at Lahore.
Soon Ranjit Singh asked Court to renovate the artillery of the army, which he did with brilliance. He developed and modernised the casting of guns and mortars at Idgah, with shells and bombs and a new fuse which Barr admired in 1839. His brigade was said to have the best gunners of the kingdom. In 1834, since Allard had gone to France and Ventura was paralysed by a stroke, he commanded the French brigades which captured Peshawar along with the troops of Hari Singh Nalwa. In 1837 Ranjit Singh appointed him commander-in-second at Peshawar, and Court remained there till he resigned from the army and departed for France in 1843. He lived in Marseille with his Kashmiri wife and their four children, writing his *Mémoires* and looking after his collections of coins, miniature paintings and manuscripts. He died in 1880, aged 86 years.

[60] General Avitabile
Detail from "The Darbar of Maharaja Ranjit Singh" (N° 33)
Gouache on paper, stuck on wood panel
Artist unknown. c. 1850
Maharaja Ranjit Singh Museum. Amritsar
Acc. N° 110

Paolo [di] Avitabile (1791-1850) was trained as an artilleryman at Napoli. He joined the service of Persia in 1818, where he met Allard, Court and Ventura. In 1827 he arrived in Lahore, raised a brigade, but was quickly acknowledged by Ranjit Singh as a first class civil administrator. Governor of Wazirabad, he embarked upon a great programme of public work, rebuilding the main street and the great bazar, restauring the fort and the ramparts. He took deep interest in trade and agriculture, went into judicial reforms and restored peace and tranquility in the countryside in such a way that people again started building residences and gardens outside the ramparts.
On 21 June 1833 Maharaja Ranjit Singh paid an official visit to Wazirabad, inspected the city and took a particular interest in a "map" which could well be a 3-D model of Wazirabad.
In May 1837 Ranjit Singh appointed Avitabile civil administrator of Peshawar. Here again Avitabile modernised and beautified the city with large streets and a rampart. His dealings with the Khyberi tribes worked well till the first Anglo-Afghan war destabilized the whole region. Avitabile left the Punjab in 1843 for his palace in Castelamare, near Napoli, and then in his Château in Agerola where he died a mysterious death in 1850.

[61] Dr. Martin Honigberger, Colonels Mouton, de La Roche, Lafont
Oil on canvas
Detail from A. Schoefft's *The Court of Lahore*
Lahore 1841-Vienna 1855
Princess Bamba Collection
Sikh gallery, Lahore Fort
Director of Archaeology, Govt of Pakistan

The modernizing drive of the *Campu-i-mualla* on the pattern of the *Fauj-i-khas* started in 1833. General Allard went on leave to France in 1834 with a message from Maharaja Ranjit Singh to King Louis-Philippe. Did the Maharaja ask for French officers to reinforce his staff and train his new regular brigades? General Allard denied it but British intelligence networks in France were convinced of it, and both London and Calcutta put their diplomatic missions between Europe and India on red alert to arrest any young suspicious Frenchman travelling to the east.
Nevertheless, several French officers managed to reach Lahore between 1837 and 1839. Among them, Colonel Mouton, a cavalry officer who commanded the cuirassier regiments at Peshawar in 1839, and Colonel Lafont, "the expert in law and training" who took an active part in the storming of the Khyber Pass by the 5,000 Punjabi Muslims under

[64]

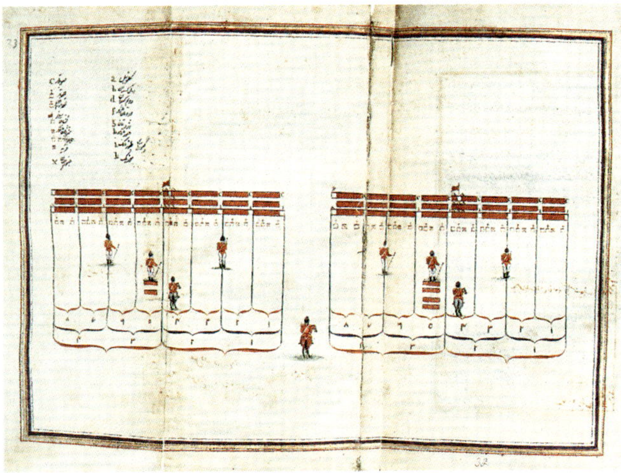

[69]

the orders of Brigadier Sheikh Basawan (*Fauj-i-khas*) in July 1839.

[62] General Ilahi Bakhsh, commanding the topkhana
Detail from "The Darbar of Maharaja Ranjit Singh"
Gouache on paper, stuck on wood panel
Artist unknown. c. 1850
Maharaja Ranjit Singh Museum. Amritsar
Acc. N° 110

Artillery was and remained a technological monopoly of the Muslims powers in India. Babur won at Panipat with the help of his guns, and Raja Mansingh of Jaipur learnt about gun-casting when he was the Mughal governor of Kabul.
The Sikh *misls* did not show much interest in artillery, and Ranjit Singh had to rely on Muslims specialists to start and develop his artillery train. His first gun-casters came from Aligarh, and his first *darogha* of artillery was Gause Khan.
Ilahi Bakhsh commanded a *dera* of artillery attached to the Maharaja before the arrival of Allard and Ventura. Ranjit Singh immediately put him and his 40 guns under the orders of Allard. The training of the *topkhana* took place regularly at Anarkali, often in the presence of the Maharaja. Ilahi Bakhsh commanded the *topkhana*, with a few exceptions, till 1849, and his gunners were mostly responsible for the Punjabi advantage at the battle of Chillianwala.

[63] Diwan Ajudhya Prasad, Bakshi of the Fauj-i-khas
Detail from "The Darbar of Maharaja Ranjit Singh"
Gouache on paper, stuck on wood panel
Artist unknown. c. 1850
Maharaja Ranjit Singh Museum. Amritsar
Acc. N° 110

Ajudhya Prasad (c. 1799-1870), nephew and adopted son of Diwan Ganga Ram, came to Lahore in 1814 and entered the service of Maharaja Ranjit Singh in 1819 as *bakhshi* of the regular units of the army. In 1822 he joined the *Fauj-i-khas* in the same capacity. When the Maharaja looked for a commander for his other regular forces, the *Campu-i-mualla*, he first offered the post to Ajudhya Prasad, who declined it on the ground that he prefered to stay with the *Fauj-i-khas*. The post was then given to Raja Tej Singh.
Very well educated, Ajudhya was a good military officer and an astute diplomat. In 1831 he was sent to escort Alexander Burnes coming up the Indus. He usually commanded the *Fauj-i-khas* infantry whenever Ventura was on leave. In 1841 he participated in the capture of the fort of Kamlagarh, in Mandi. He commanded the *Fauj-i-khas* during the first Anglo-Sikh war, including at Ferozeshah.
After the annexation of the country, Ajudhya Prasad was given charge of Maharaja Dalip Singh along with Dr. Login, and he stayed with him at Fatehgarh till September 1851. He then held several eminent positions at Lahore where he died in 1870.
A cultured gentleman, Ajudhya had a fine library with illuminated manuscripts. Considering his attachment to the French, it is no surprise that he asked their artist protégé, Imam Bakhsh Lahori, to illustrate some of them, like the *Qissa-i-Chahar-Darvesh* now kept in the Punjab University of Chandigarh.

[64] Colonel Harlan (American)
From *Central Asia. Personal Narrative ...*
Frontispiece
Private collection

Josiah Harlan (1799-1871), born in Pennsylvania, USA, joined the English army in India in 1824 as an assistant-surgeon. He resigned in 1827, but was not accepted in Maharaja Ranjit Singh's service and went to Kabul. In 1829 Maharaja Ranjit Singh offered him the brigade of Oms, which he refused. He then appointed him governor of Nurpur and Jasrota (1829-1832) and Gujrat (1832-1835). Attached to the etat-major of the Maharaja during the operations at Peshawar in 1835, he was deputed along with Fakir Aziz-ud-Din to Dost Mohammed Khan's camp for negociations, and was taken hostage. In 1836, for an unknown reason, Ranjit Singh ordered his expulsion from Punjab. Back in Kabul, Harlan travelled up to Bamyan and trained the first regular infantry units of the Afghan army. In 1837 he claimed victory at the battle of Jamrud, and he fought against the British during the first Anglo-Afghan War. Expelled from India and back in the US, he was of some influence in bringing about the import of camels for the US army, and during the Secession War he raised a regiment, the Harlan's Light Cavalry. He published several *Memoirs* and had a lot of manuscript notes in his residence. He died at San Francisco in 1871.

[65] Maharaja Ranjit Singh with generals Allard and Ventura
Military Manual of Maharaja Ranjit Singh
Illustrations : probably the workshop of Imam Bakhsh Lahori
Lahore, 1822-1830
Maharaja Ranjit Singh Museum. Amritsar
Acc. N° 1035

While raising the first units of the *Fauj-i-khas* (1822), Generals Allard and Ventura translated into Persian two French *Military Manuals* : one of infantry, which has survived, and one of cavalry (not yet traced). General Court, in c. 1830, translated the manual of artillery by Duturbie (not yet traced either).

The frontispiece of the military maual shows Maharaja Ranjit Singh sitting on a carpet with Hira Singh standing by his side, while Raja Dhyan Singh (dressed in the same colour as his son Hira Singh) is on the other side. Generals Ventura and Allard are in plain uniforms with their typical tasselled caps. Standing on the right is an officer of the *Fauj-i-khas*, with saffron uniform and épaulettes, while standing guard at the entrance is a Sikh soldier of *Fauj-i-khas*.

[66] Military Manual of Maharaja Ranjit Singh
Illustrations : probably the workshop of Imam Bakhsh Lahori
Lahore, 1822-1830
Maharaja Ranjit Singh Museum. Amritsar
Acc. N° 1035

On 20 May 1822 Maharaja Ranjit Singh put the regiment of Sheikh Basawan under the orders of Allard and Ventura. On 21 May the French officers

[81]

started training the regiment. After the briefing, the Maharaja ordered Sheikh Basawan to go every evening to the residence of Allard and Ventura in order to learn the words of command in French and understand their meaning.
In order to facilitate the process, the French Generals had a translation done from French into Persian of the Infantry Manual they had with them. The words of command are in French (red ink), while the explanations are given in Persian (black ink) and the illustrations are there to facilitate the reading.
The Manual has three sections : Drill, Weapon training, Evolutions
The marching and passing of the three arms separately as well as the combined movements were carried out at the beat of the drum or at the sound of the trumpet.
This manuscript has been studied by Fauja Singh Bajwa in his *Military System of the Sikhs*, with the deciphering of the French orders from their Persian script and an English translation and explanation.

[67] Military drill
Military Manual of Maharaja Ranjit Singh
Illustrations : probably the workshop of Imam Bakhsh Lahori
Lahore, 1822-1830
Maharaja Ranjit Singh Museum. Amritsar
Acc. N° 1035

[68] Military drill
Military Manual of Maharaja Ranjit Singh
Illustrations : probably the workshop of Imam Bakhsh Lahori
Lahore, 1822-1830
Maharaja Ranjit Singh Museum. Amritsar
Acc. N° 1035

[69] A regiment of the Fauj-i-khas at the falling-in position
Military Manual of Maharaja Ranjit Singh
Illustrations : probably the workshop of Imam Bakhsh Lahori
Lahore, 1822-1830
Maharaja Ranjit Singh Museum. Acc. No 1035

The regiment is on three lines. The ranks of the officers are given in Persian, listed under the Roman alphabet a,b,c etc.

[70] Studies on Maharaja Ranjit Singh
by Hakim Paras Ram
Urdu, date not available
Punjab State Archives. Patiala/ Acc. N° M 921

This manuscript contains many references to Maharaja Ranjit Singh's guns

[71] Hisab-i-Afwaj-i-Maharaja Ranjit Singh
Persian and Gurmukhi, date not available
Khuda Bakhsh Oriental Library, Patna, Acc. N° 622

A beautiful manuscript that details the military accounts of Maharaja Ranjit Singh. Divided under the headings of Infantry, Cavalry and Artillery, the account of each regiment or *risalah* is shown under the name of its commanding officer. The Persian entries are transcribed into *Gurmukhi* in red ink.

[72] A "French" brigade on the battle front
From the lithoprint 'The Battle of Moodkee', 18th December 1845
Engraved by J. Harris from a painting by H. Martens. Published in 1849
Maharaja Ranjit Singh Museum. Amritsar
Acc. N° 10

The regiment is on the battle-line, reinforced by the artillery. A colonel on horseback is directing the battle in the centre of the line, issuing orders to repulse the charge of the enemy.

[73] Allard's Lancer
Water colour on paper
Artist unknown
24 x 18 cm
National Museum, New Delhi. Acc. n . 79.326

Following a strongly entrenched Indian tradition, Maharaja Ranjit Singh did not believe much in regular cavalry. Nevertheless General Allard managed to raise one regiments of Lancers (*Lansia*) and two of Dragoons (*Daragun*) in 1822-23 (light cavalry). They were known all over Punjab and even in British India as "Sawaran-i-Frances". They won the prize of piquet game against Skinner's cavalry (the Yellow Boys) in Ropar in 1831.

[74] Allard's Cuirassier
"Chairana Sowar (a Cuirassier)"
Lahore, 1837-1843
From Honigberger's *Thirty Five Years in the East ...*, plate V, p. 121
Probably from an original painting by Imam Bakhsh Lahori
Punjab State Archives. Patiala. Acc. N° 279

Maharaja Ranjit Singh refused to raise regiments of heavy cavalry, but General Allard managed to convince him because when he returned from France in 1836, he brought the complete equipment for a full fledged regiment of cuirassiers. In 1839 Lieutenant Barr described them at Peshawar in the following terms : "On their right (of the parade) were two regiments of Allard's cuirassiers, the most noble-looking troops on parade. The men and horses were all picked, and among the former are to be seen many stalwart fellows who appear to advantage under their cuirasses and steel casques. Particular attention seemed to have been paid in setting the men well up, and their accoutrements are kept in the highest order. Many of the officers wear brass cuirasses, and their commandant [Colonel Mouton] is perhaps the finest man of the whole body, and looked extremely well in front of his superb regiment.[...] Lord says it used to be poor Allard's [died in January] pride and amusement to review these men, and their present soldier-like and martial appearance is no doubt owing to that officer's constant care and superintendance".

[75] Cuirass of Allard's cavalry
Lahore Museum, Lahore. Pakistan

[86]

With the money the French Government paid for the coin collection of generals Allard and Ventura in 1835 - French newspapers spoke of FF. 400.000 - Allard purchased 500 cuirasses, 2000 arms (swords and pistols), and two million detonating caps which he brough to Lahore in 1837.
This is one of the few remaining cuirass of "carabiniers" brought from France by General Allard. Each one has the serial number and place of the manufacturer engraved inside.

[76] Carbines of Allard's cavalry
Sikh Gallery, Lahore Fort. Lahore
Director of Archaeology. Govt of Pakistan

The Dragoons of Allard's cavalry were equiped with swords and carbines. These elite units were trained to fight both as cavalry and infantry, and they were particularly efficient in the hills against enemies trained in the strike and run tactics of the guerilla. These carbines were manufactured at Lahore, as Maharaja Ranjit Singh declared to Dr. Murray in 1827.

[77] Pair of carbines, flint lock guns
Made by Thomson in 1799
Length 97.6 x 88 cm. 1822-1830
Maharaja Ranjit Singh Museum. Amritsar
Acc. N° 11/4 & 11/8

Ancestors of the carbines of the Punjab light regular cavalry.

[78] Fauj-i-khas : Sikh infantry, Gurkha [Purbiah]
"Soldat Sikh. Soldat Pourpié"
Watercolour on European paper
By Imam Bakhsh Lahori. Lahore, 1827-1843
198 x 270 mm
Court collection, Musée Guimet. MG 78 III 39746

Two drawings on one leaf by Imam Bakhsh Lahori

of the elite infantry of the Punjab army. The "Pourpié", or "Purbiah", is in fact a *gurkha*, as explicitly mentioned on the similar engraving published by Honigberger in his *Thirty-Five Years in the East* , plate 6, p. 96-97 (see no 227). Right from the beginning the *Fauj-i-khas* had a regiment of *gurkhas* who wore a plume in French tricolours on their shakos. The Sikh soldier, of the *Fauj-i-khas* also, had a very recognizable appearance which can be seen on mural paintings all over the Punjab - including the recently discovered Sikh frescoes in the Sheesh Mahal of the Fort of Lahore - and even the Rambagh palace of Jammu. The number of their regiment is inscribed on the plate at the cross-section of the chest belts.

[79] Fauj-i-khas : A Muslim Gunner
"Canonnier Mahométan"
By Imam Bakhsh Lahori. Lahore, 1827-1843
186 x 278 mm
Court collection, Musée Guimet. MG 78 III 39745

A Muslim artilleryman of the *topkhana*, the heavy artillery of the *Fauj-i-khas* commanded by General Ilahi Bakhsh. As often as he could, Maharaja Ranjit Singh reviewed their training at Anarkali, Lahore. From 1827 onwards, General Court reorganised the Punjab artillery, who were trained to march quickly and follow the infantry wherever they went. This artillery, mostly manned by Muslim gunners, played havoc on the British army at the battles of Ferozeshah (First Anglo-Sikh War) and Chillianwalla (Second Anglo-Sikh War). Their blue uniform is recognizable on all the illustrations of these wars, and when overwhelmed by the enemy, they defended their guns to the last man.

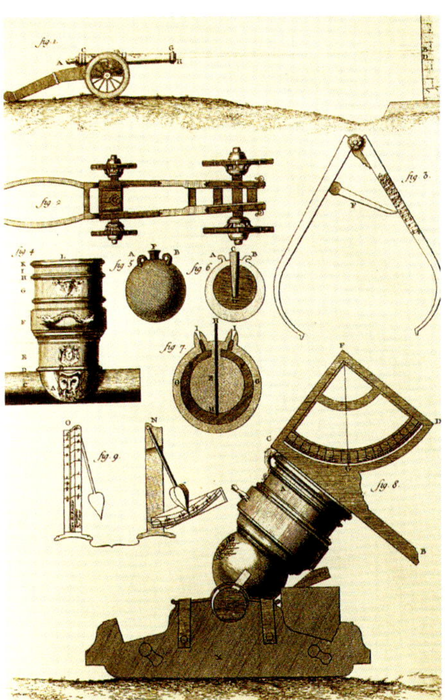

[84]

[80] Arms and artillery. Punjab army
Miniature painting from *Ain-i-Akbari*
Artist unknown. Lahore, 1838
Asiatic Society, Calcutta. Acc. N° P 128

This interesting miniature of the *Ain-i-Akbari* shows, better than any of these manuscripts illustrated at Lahore, a painting of arms and guns which have the characteristics of the *Fauj-i-khas*: muskets with bayonets, carbines for the light and heavy cavalry, field gun and mortar.

[81] The Triumphal Reception of the Sikh Guns
Victoria Memorial, Calcutta. Acc. N° C 1650
(detail)

The guns captured from the Punjab army or surrendered after the capitulation were transported to Calcutta and received by the Governor-General in front of the Governor's house. This impressive line of guns shows the degree of modernization of the Punjab army under Maharaja Ranjit Singh

[82] Fauj-i-khas
Two bombs for mortar and Honigberger's instrument for testing powder
Sikh Gallery. Lahore Fort. Lahore
Director of Archaeology. Government of Pakistan

With the availability of European military technology in India in the fields of fortification and artillery, many Indian powers got as advanced a technology as they could afford. The mortars for throwing bombs were among the most sophisticated weapons for siege of strongly fortified cities and forts, and for war in the hilly countries. General Court developed the mortars for the Punjab army, and they were the decisive factor in throwing the Afghans back to the Khyber Pass after the affair of Jamrud in 1837. Here are two bombs, about 75 kg each, which could be fired at 2.7 km by a 13" mortar. In between can be seen an instrument for testing the powder on which is inscribed the name of Dr. John Martin Honigberger (cf N° 61).

[83] Miniature French gun
Faqir Jalaluddin Collection.
Ref. 666 / List n° 38
Lahore Museum. Lahore, Pakistan

Models of artillery were made for the education of princes and to be used as a means of disseminating knowledge of gun-casting and military strategy. When he returned to Lahore in 1836, General Allard brought back from France a complete set of models of artillery.
Faqir Jalaluddin's collection also includes a curious mortar that is fired by sunlight through a magnifying glass. It might be one of the models brought by Allard to Lahore, or a gift of General Ventura to little Prince Dalip Singh.

[84] Diderot and d'Alembert : Encyclopédie
Art Militaire, Fortification. Plate VII
Mortar. Mortar in firing position. Bomb
Private collection.

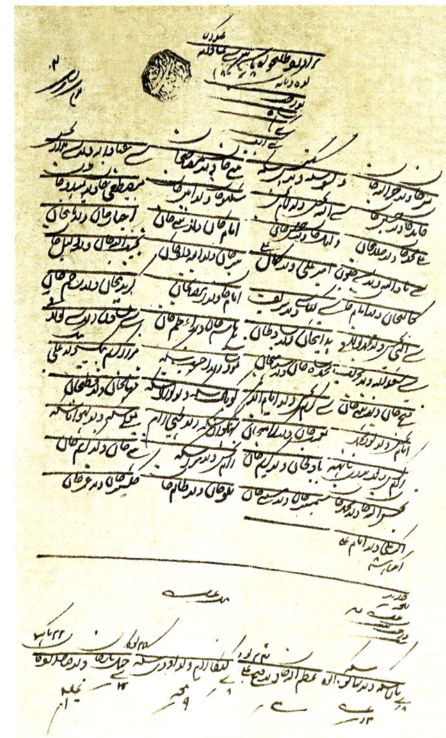

[87]

The *Grande Encyclopédie* by d'Alembert and Diderot has a full section on artillery, with detailed plates and explanations. This is a plate describing the function and the firing of a mortar, with a cross section of a bomb. Knowledge of European military technology travelled all around the world through prints, books and encyclopaedias. We know that this Encyclopaedia was in Claude Martin's personal library at Lucknow when he died in 1800.

[85] Fauj-i-khas. Musique
Sikh Gallery. Lahore Fort. Lahore.
Director of Archaeology. Govt of Pakistan

Music was an integral part of all European armies. Generals Allard and Ventura introduced a military band in the *Fauj-i-khas* and the other French brigades of the Punjab army. We see them on the regiment on parade, and some of the original instruments are still preserved in the Sikh Museum of the Lahore Fort. We have no information concerning the tunes they played. When Begum Sumro died at Sardhana in 1836, the musicians of her military band, which was directed by Mr. Antoine, asked for permission to join the *Fauj-i-khas*.

[86] Fauj-i-khas. Details of swords of General Allard
Private collection

Four swords of General Allard are preserved with their scabbard. The golden sword is the one Allard's has on the Darbar painting [N° 33]. Recently discovered, they deserve a full publication in which the Persian inscriptions will be translated.

[87] Manuscript volume of the Khalsa Darbar Records
Punjab State Archives. Chandigarh

Part of the archives of the Punjab kingdom have disappeared. Following the annexation of the country by the East India Company in 1849, a number of Persian documents were transfered from the *toshakhana* (Lahore fort) where they were kept, and put on the shelves of the Civil Secretariat. Rediscovered in the early 1900's, the 129 remaining bundles were catalogued by Sita Ram Kohli in two remarkable volumes published respectively in 1919 and 1927.

[88] Manuscript volume of the Khalsa Darbar Records
Punjab State Archives. Chandigarh

"Papers relating to several departments for one official year were arranged in a bundle, the two ends of which were protected by beautifully painted wooden case boards of Kashmir make and the whole tied tightly with cotton strings" . "Some of the bundles are as much as three feet in length, and contains as many as 3,000 sheets. The paper used is of the kind commonly known as Kashmiri or Sialkoti paper and, as a rule, the sheets measure 5" x 7 1/2 ". The language is Persian and the running *shikasta* by no means easy to decipher without considerable practice" (S.R. Kohli, 1927)

[89] Manuscript volumes of the Khalsa Darbar Records
Punjab State Archives. Chandigarh

"I have now after a thourough examination of these bundles grouped them in the following four main heads in reference to the subject matter :
(1) Daftar fauj -relating to the army
(2) Daftar mal -relating to the general revenue
(3) Daftar toshakhana - relating to royal wardrobe and the king's privy purse.
(4) Daftar jaghirat - relating to the jaghir accounts." (S.R. Kohli, 1927).

[90] Manuscript volumes of the Khalsa Darbar Records
Punjab State Archives. Chandigarh

In 1947, the Supreme Council of the Partition decided that the British records kept in the Punjab Record Office, Lahore, would stay in Pakistan, while the *Khalsa* Darbar Records would be given to India. The tranfer of the documents took two years (1947-49). They were first kept in Simla, then transferred to Patiala in 1959. Now kept at Chandigarh, they are certainly a most precious legacy of the kingdom of the Punjab and Maharaja Ranjit Singh.

[91] Medal of the Order of Guru Govind Singh
Gold and enamelled work
8 x 4.4 cm
Sheesh Mahal Museum, Patiala.
Acc. N° P 121 XLIX-19

In 1822 the French Generals started building new military units on the pattern of Napoleon's army. The French Military Code had a complex system of awards and punishments. Maharaja Ranjit Singh refused to introduce the death penalty, even for desertion and treason, in his regular troops. But he accepted to create an award for military fait d'armes and dashing courage on the pattern of the French Légion d'honneur.
This order was officially called Order of Guru Govind Singh, but was commonly referred to as Maharaja Ranjit Singh's order.

[92] General Allard's medal of Commander of the Order of Guru Govind Singh
Private collection

General Allard's medal of the Order of Guru Govind Singh. In the centre, portrait of Maharaja Ranjit Singh, gold medal done in France. The trefoil design has the French tricolour (blue, white, red, the colour of the *Fauj-i-khas* flag). On the arms, Persian inscriptions giving the names of the five major Punjabi victories on the Afghans. From top clockwise : Kashmir, Attock, Peshawar, Mankera and Multan. The two bulls symbolise the Punjab (Majha and Malva?), while the eagle resting on a sword is a symbol of imperial power.

[93] Medal of the Kaukab-i-Iqbal-i-Panjab , or Auspicious Star of the Punjab
Gold and enamelled, set with diamonds and emeralds
Sheesh Mahal Museum, Patiala. Acc. N° P 73-111-1

This order was created in 1837, in the year of Prince Nau Nihal Singh's marriage to which Maharaja Ranjit Singh had invited the governor-general (Lord Auckland), who deputed the commander-in-chief (General Fane) go to Lahore. The rules for the granting of the award were prepared by Captain Wade, the political agent posted at Ludhiana and in charge of Anglo-Sikh relations.
In the centre, an enamelled portrait of Maharaja Ranjit Singh. The arms are set with diamonds and emeralds, which characterized the second class of that order.
According to Emily Eden, two howitzers made for Ranjit Singh by order of Auckland and presented to him at Ferozepur had "the bright star of the Punjab with Runjeet's profile on the gun" (*Up the Country*, p. 189). One of them is kept in England, by the Board of trustees of the Armouries (XIX 247).

[94] Khilat awarded by Maharaja Ranjit Singh to General Allard
Gold embroidery on pashmina
Private collection

The traditional way of rewarding a high ranking dignitary in India was to offer him a *khilat*, or dress of honour, conferred in the *darbar*. The *khilat* consisted of several items: dress, shawls, turban, arms, jewels, bangles, aigrette, horse, elephant etc... A eleven-piece *khilat* was considered a first class award, although there are some instances of fifteen and even twenty-two-piece *khilat*.
This *khilat*, given by Maharaja Ranjit Singh to General Allard, is in red pashmina with gold embroidery. There is no information concerning the number and nature of items which accompanied the dress.

[95] Khilat awarded by Maharaja Ranjit Singh to General Allard
Gold emboidery on pashmina
Private collection

The *Umdat-ut-Tawarikh* gives several instances of the French generals receiving *khilat*. Only two of them have survived. This one is in pashmina with gold embroidery. It is strikingly similar to the *sozni* of Maharaja Ranjit Singh preserved in the Lahore Museum [N° 34]

[96] The Fauj-i-khas Headquarters at Anarkali, Lahore
From a photograph in a private collection.

The tomb of Anarkali, outside the ramparts of Lahore, was used by Maharaja Ranjit Singh as his headquarters during his siege of Lahore in 1799. Later on, he gave the premises and the garden to his son, Prince Kharak Singh, till 1822 when he transferred the whole area to Generals Allard and Ventura as their residence and headquarter for the *Fauj-i-khas*. At that time, two buildings existed inside the garden : the tomb of Anarkali, and a Mughal palace. Allard and Ventura built their own house between the two existing buildings. One can see on this sketch the three structures as they stood

[91]

in 1846, before the first occupation of Lahore by British troops following the first Anglo-Sikh war. Henry Lawrence, appointed "Resident" in 1846, decided to settle in this house hence its present name "the Residence". After annexation, he razed the Mughal palace and developed the area in a way best suited for the new rulers of the Punjab.

[97] Maharaja Ranjit Singh with generals Allard and Ventura
Watercolour on paper. Unfinished
Artist unknown. Lahore. c. 1837
22.5 x 17 cm
Chandigarh Museum. Acc. N D-3

Not many paintings showing Maharaja Ranjit Singh with his French officers in a private darbar have survived. One can find them in the most unexpected places like in Philadelphia, USA (probably from Harlan's collection), or in Osborne's *Court and Camp of Runjeet Sing*. Following a familiar pattern in the subcontinent, the French disappeared from reproductions of the *darbars* done under the British Raj.
This unfinished painting shows Allard and Ventura standing among a few other figures in a traditional representation of a private darbar.

[98] General Tej Singh
From Honigberger's *Thirty Five Years in the East ...*, plate IV, p. 119
Probably from an original painting by Imam Bakhsh Lahori. Lahore, 1829-1849
Punjab State Archives. Patiala. Acc. N° 279

Tej Ram, a brahmin and a nephew of Jamadar Khushal Singh, came from Sardhana to Lahore in 1811. He grew in favour with the Maharaja and became Tej Singh after he took the *pahul*. He participated in several campaigns in Kashmir, Mankera and Peshawar, and took charge of the *Campu* after the death of Diwan Ganga Ram in 1826. After he was made a general in 1834, he commanded for a while at Peshawar in 1836, was sent to Hazara in 1838 and again to Peshawar during the First Anglo-Afghan War. In 1845 he was appointed commander-in-chief of the Punjab army for a military campaign in which he played a traitrous role and which ended at Sobraon on 10 February 1846. He died in 1862.

[99] Maharaja Ranjit Singh Bahadur, King of Lahore
"Maharajah Randjit Singh Bahdour Roi de Lahor (Inde)"
Gouache on paper
Signed by Imam Bakhsh Lahori, Hij. 1257 / BS 1898 / AD 1841
217 x 173 mm
Court collection, Musée Guimet. BG 39756

This sumptuous painting of the Lion of Punjab shows Maharaja Ranjit Singh with a nimbus reminiscent of the gold medal struck in Paris. Mounted on one of his favorite horses, he is escorted by three officers wearing aigrettes on their turbans. One of them, in saffron uniform with épaulettes, is perhaps from a "French" brigade. Ranjit Singh was fond of riding and as long as he could, he rode and galloped in the fields of his Punjab.

[100] General Sham Singh Attariwala
Oil on canvas
Detail from A. Schoefft's 'The Court of Lahore'
Lahore 1841-Vienna 1855
Princess Bamba Collection
Sikh gallery, Lahore Fort
Director of Archaeology. Govt of Pakistan

Sham Singh was the son of Nihal Singh, one of Ranjit Singh's celebrated generals. His first campaign was the capture of Multan in 1818, where he was one of the first to climb up the ramparts of the fort. He fought in Kashmir in 1819 and saw active service in the Yusufzai country and Bannu (1834). His daughter Nanki married Prince Nau Nihal Singh in 1837. Sham Singh marched with Allard to Peshawar to relieve the Punjabi troops trapped at Jamrud, and he remained there with his regiments till 1839. Although he was opposed to the war with the East India Company, he joined the army and died valiantly while charging the enemy at Sobraon. Colonel Mouton bears testimony to his splendid behaviour, and British generals who witnessed the battle praised his bravery.

[101] Maharaja Ranjit Singh's fortifications of Lahore

In 1799 the fortifications of Lahore were mainly the ones built by Akbar in the late 16th century. Maharaja Ranjit Singh decided to rebuilt and modernise the defensive network of the Fort and his capital. The work was entrusted to Fakir Nuruddin in 1812, and the walls, 30 feet high according to S.M. Latif, were completed in the early 1820's. A deep broad ditch surrounded the city.

[102] Maharaja Ranjit Singh's fortifications of Lahore
The outer defences of the city gates and some of the bastions were completed after the arrival of generals Allard and Ventura at Lahore in 1822, and we know that they worked with Fakir Nuruddin to complete them. They show the workmanship of European fortification of the Napoleonic period. Describing the fortifications of Amritsar in 1827, Captain Wade says that "their design is unlike that of native forts. It partakes a good deal of the European style, a knowledge of which has probably been imparted to the Maharaja by his French officers. The works are still being executed and when completed will form a formidable defence".

[103] Maharaja Ranjit Singh's fortifications of Lahore
The fortifications of Lahore and Amritsar were razed to the ground by the British in the 1850's, and not much remains to be seen today except the "Sikh" rampart north of the Lahore fort, with its powerful bastion protruding in the centre.

[104] The fort of Rohtas
"Forteresse de Rottas"
Watercolour on European paper
By Imam Bakhsh Lahori
Lahore, 1827-1843. 300 x 194 mm
Court collection, Musée Guimet. MG 78 III 39734

The fort of Rohtas, built by Sher Shah Suri in 1542

[104]

to subdue the heart of the Punjab between Peshawar and Lahore, was used by Maharaja Ranjit Singh as the main base for his operations in Kashmir. It was also one of the dépôts of the kingdom. The extensive ramparts of the fort are still impressive. It is at Rohtas that Maharaja Ranjit Singh learnt of the death of General Hari Singh Nalwa at Jamrud, and he wept.

[105] The fort of Attock with boat bridge
"Forteresse d'Attok sur l'Indus"
Watercolour on European paper
By Imam Bakhsh Lahori. Lahore, 1827-1843
291 x 183 mm. Court collection
Musée Guimet. MG 78 III 39731

Built by Akbar in 1581, captured by Ranjit Singh in 1812, the fort of Attock was one of the main dépôts of the Punjab Army. When Dost Mohammed Khan of Kabul attacked Peshawar in 1837, the *Fauj-i-khas*, which was with the Maharaja on a leisure tour at Sheikupura, was ordered to rush to the north-west frontier without returning to Lahore. The French Legion took the equipment necessary to repeal the *ghazis* at Rohtas and Attock. On this miniature painting, there is an old *caravansarai* on the left bank, a boat-bridge on the Indus, and the fortress of Kaikora on the right bank. Not much of them remains today.

[106] The fort of Jamrud
"Dgémrod à l'entrée du Kheïber" / Forteresse construite par les Sikhs. Attaque du Kheïber"
Watercolour on European paper
By Imam Bakhsh Lahori.
Lahore, 1827-1843. 285 x 193 mm
Court collection. Musée Guimet. MG 78 III 39733

After the annexation of Peshawar (1834) to the Punjab Kingdom, the Punjabis and Afghans were eyeball to eyeball between Jamrud and the Khyber Pass until Dost Mohammed Khan decided to retire to Jalalabad and Kabul. The fort of Jamrud was built by Hari Singh Nalwa in 1836 to mark the frontier between Punjab and Afghanistan and keep the Khyberi tribes as far as possible at bay. In 1837, when the Afghans launched their massive attack in order to reconquer the territories between the Khyber Pass and the Indus, the heroic defense of Jamrud by Hari Singh Nalwa and his 900 men stalled the Afghan offensive, saved Peshawar and gave the *Fauj-i-khas* and other regular brigades the time to march from Sheikhupura to Jamrud.

[107] The fort of Govindgarh
Watercolour on paper
Artist unknown. Middle 19th century
20.5 x 34.5 cm
National Museum. New Delhi. Acc. n 85.26

The fort of Govindgarh was started by Maharaja Ranjit Singh in 1807 in order to protect Amritsar. Baron Hügel spoke of its tiers of guns, one over the other, commanding the plain. The fort was under the authority of Fakir Syed Imamuddin, the youngest of the three Fakir brothers, during practically the whole of Maharaja Ranjit Singh's reign. But it was garrisoned by elite units of the

[112]

Punjab, including the *Fauj-i-khas* as attested by the *Umdat-ut-Tawarikh* : in 1947 inscriptions in French (like "Ronde de l'Est") were still visible on the ramparts. Govindgarh Fort also served as a kind of reserve bank where part of the metallic reserve of the kingdom were kept.

[108] "Maharaja Ranjit Singh listening to the Granth being recited near the Golden Temple, Amritsar"
Oil on canvas
by A. Schoefft
Amritsar 1841-Vienna 1855
4' 8" 1/2 x 3' 7"
Princess Bamba Collection.
Sikh gallery. Lahore Fort
Director of Archaeology. Govt of Pakistan

As often as he could, Maharaja Ranjit Singh went to Amritsar, and stayed in his *bunga* in the Harmandir complex to listen to the *granthis* reading the *Granth Sahib*.
When A. Schoefft came to Amritsar in 1841, he visited the Harmandir and Maharaja Sher Singh asked for a painting of the Golden Temple illuminated at night. Schoefft suggested it would be more impressive in daylight. The story about how this painting was done at Amritsar is given at length in Honigberger's *Thirty-Five Years in the East*.

This is the painting commissioned by Sher Singh. Maharaja Ranjit Singh is sitting on a cushion under a dais, listening attentively to the *granthis* reading the *Granth*. Next to him are Princes Kharak Singh and Sher Singh.
This painting was done in *situ*, from a place overlooking the Harmandir complex in Ranjit Singh's building. It gives a fairly precise idea of the Golden Temple compound two years after the death of Maharaja Ranjit Singh.

[109] Granth Sahib used during the time of Maharaja Ranjit Singh

According to H.R. Gupta who quotes different sources, essentially Macauliffe and more recent scholars, the *Adi Granth*, or Sacred Book, compiled by Guru Arjun from 1599 to 1604, contains 3,384 hymns in 15,575 stanzas out of which 976 hymns are from Guru Nanak, 61 by Guru Angad, 907 by Guru Amar Das, 679 by Guru Ram Das and 2216 hymns and 116 *shabads* by Guru Arjun. There are also some later additions like 116 *shabads* and 2 *shlokas* by Guru Tegh Bahadur. The *Adi Granth* also contains 1,917 stanzas composed by saints, bards and sufis like Baba Farid of Pakpatan (116 verses), Kabir of Benares (122), Nam Dev of Maharashtra (245), Ravi Das of Benares (41 verses) etc. The *Adi Granth* was completed in July 1604 and entrusted by Guru Arjun to Bhai Bannu who made a first copy of it and had the two volumes bound in

Lahore in a beautiful hard cover. The original manuscript was installed in the Hari Mandir on Bhadon Sudi 1 Sambat 1661 [16 August 1604]. A huge congregation attended the ceremony. Bhai Budha was appointed the first *Head Granthi* and the recitations from the *Adi Granth* started from that time. Sikhism soon attracted the attention of European visitors in India, and one finds some mid-18th century miniature paintings showing a Sikh, with sometimes his wife. Colonel Polier, a Franco-Swiss officer who was in north India from 1757 to 1787, learnt a lot about Hinduism (Baghawat Gita and Ramayana) through a Sikh scholar from Sultanpur. Polier's personal library included a copy of the *Adi Granth* in 970 pages, which is now in the National Library in Paris. His friend Colonel Gentil, in the service of Shuja-ud-Daula of Avadh, had an Urdu manuscript entitled *History of Nanak, the Patriarch of the Sikhs* , also in the National Library of Paris.

[110] Guru Nanak
from the *Military Manual of Maharaja Ranjit Singh*
Probably the workshop of Imam Bakhsh Lahori
Lahore, 1822-1830
Maharaja Ranjit Singh Museum. Amritsar
Acc. N° 1035

The *Military Manual of Maharaja Ranjit Singh* contains in the beginning the portraits of the ten Gurus, painted against a rich background reminiscent of Imam Bakhsh Lahori's preference for the golden skies of sunset. The original manuscript, compiled from the notes taken by the

[113]

munshi of Sheikh Basawan at Lahore in March 1822, has not been traced. Other copies of the *Manual* certainly existed. This one is dated 1830 by R.P. Srivastava. Guru Nanak (1469-1539) was born in Nankana Sahib (Pakistan today). In 1485 he came to Sultanpur Lodi and in 1496 he had an enlightenment. For three years he prepared for his mission, and from 1499 to 1517 he made a series of long journeys in India, while from 1517 to 1522 he travelled in west-Asia. The last part of his life (1522-1539) was spent in Punjab, with his family and followers, cultivating his lands and preaching his doctrine. The Guru's hymns were sung in the evening, and the *Japji* in the morning. The last years of his life saw Babur's invasion of Punjab and the early years of Mughal rule. He died in 1539, after having nominated his disciple Lehna as his successor.

[111] Guru Angad
from the *Military Manual of Maharaja Ranjit Singh*
Probably the workshop of Imam Bakhsh Lahori
Lahore, 1822-1830
Maharaja Ranjit Singh Museum. Amritsar
Acc. N° 1035

Guru Angad (1539-1552) collected the hymns of Guru Nanak, either written in Lande Mahajni script or memorised by his disciples, and he transcribed them into Gurmukhi which he had systematised at the request of Guru Nanak. He also composed several hymns and he sent disciples to spread Sikhism in the neigbourhood. Tradition says that he met at Khadur the emperor Humayun who was fleeing to Persia (1540) and he gave him his blessing.

[112] Guru Amar Das
from the *Military Manual of Maharaja Ranjit Singh*
Probably the workshop of Imam Bakhsh Lahori
Lahore, 1822-1830
Maharaja Ranjit Singh Museum. Amritsar
Acc. N° 1035

Guru Amar Das (1552-1574) developed the *langar* system (community mess) initiated by Guru Nanak in order to reinforce unity between the members of the community and reduce caste distinctions among the Sikh brotherhood. He established the two Sikh festivals of Baisakhi and Diwali, and organised the *manjis*, or territorial divisions headed by a *sangatia* (preacher). Three out of the fifteen *sangatia* appointed by Guru Amar Das were women. He also encouraged his disciples to discard some of the darkest habits of the age : *sati, purdah*, and he encouraged the remarriage of the widows. Tradition speaks of emperor Akbar's visit to the Guru at Goindwal, where he dined in the *langar*.

[113] Guru Ram Das
from the *Military Manual of Maharaja Ranjit Singh*
Probably the workshop of Imam Bakhsh Lahori
Lahore, 1822-1830
Maharaja Ranjit Singh Museum. Amritsar
Acc. N° 1035

Guru Ram Das (1574-1581), when asked by Guru Amar Das to find a place for himself, selected a site with a sacred pool of water in the jungle. He started digging a tank there in 1577, which he called Amritsar. This is the established date for the foundation of the city.
Guru Ram Das insisted on the service or assistance every Sikh had to give to another Sikh.

[114] Guru Arjun
from the *Military Manual of Maharaja Ranjit Singh*
Probably the workshop of Imam Bakhsh Lahori
Lahore, 1822-1830
Maharaja Ranjit Singh Museum. Amritsar
Acc. N° 1035

Guru Arjun (1581-1606) institutionalised the financial contribution of the community (*daswandh*) through the *sangatia*, who now were called *masands* [nobles]. He started the building of the Hari Mandir in 1588, whose foundation stone was laid (according to certain traditions) by the famous sufi saint Mian Mir of Lahore. He dug many tanks (Taran Taran) and 'baolis' (at Lahore). He compiled the *Adi Granth*, popularly known as *Granth Sahib* or *Guru Granth*. The original manuscript was installed in the Harmandir in 1604. Emperor Akbar visited Guru Arjun in 1598. After Akbar's death, when the succession was disputed between Princes Khusrau and Salim (the future Jahangir), Khusrau paid a visit to Guru Arjun who applied a saffron mark on his head. That was construed by Jahangir as an act of rebellion, for which Guru Arjun was called to Lahore. His properties were confiscated and he was executed on 30 May 1606.

[115] Guru Har Gobind
from the *Military Manual of Maharaja Ranjit Singh*
Probably the workshop of Imam Bakhsh Lahori
Lahore, 1822-1830
Maharaja Ranjit Singh Museum. Amritsar
Acc. N° 1035

Guru Har Gobind (1606-1644), son of Guru Arjun, received from his jailed father the message to fight for the protection of the faith. After the ceremony of succession to guruship was performed, he put two swords (right and left) and declared that they were symbols of *miri* and *piri, shakti* and *bhakti*, *deg* and *teg*, temporal power and spiritual power. He raised troops (cavalry) and in 1606 built the Akal Takht, opposite the Harmandir. His activities aroused Jahangir's suspicion, who had him imprisoned at Gwalior (1609-1620?), although tradition says that their relations improved from 1621 to 1628. Under Shah Jahan, conflicts with the Mughal authorities of Lahore often ended in military fighting. When Guru Har Gobind died in 1644, he left a martial legacy in the Sikh community to fight for their faith, their rights and their survival.

[116] Guru Har Rai
from the *Military Manual of Maharaja Ranjit Singh*
Probably the workshop of Imam Bakhsh Lahori
Lahore, 1822-1830
Maharaja Ranjit Singh Museum. Amritsar
Acc. N° 1035

Guru Har Rai (1644-1661), grandson of Guru Har Govind, had a peaceful life, though he maintained a 2200 strong contingent fully armed around him, preaching the Sikh religion and going on short trips to meet the community. He had met Prince Dara Shikoh before 1657, and he joined him with his contingent during the war of succession in 1658.

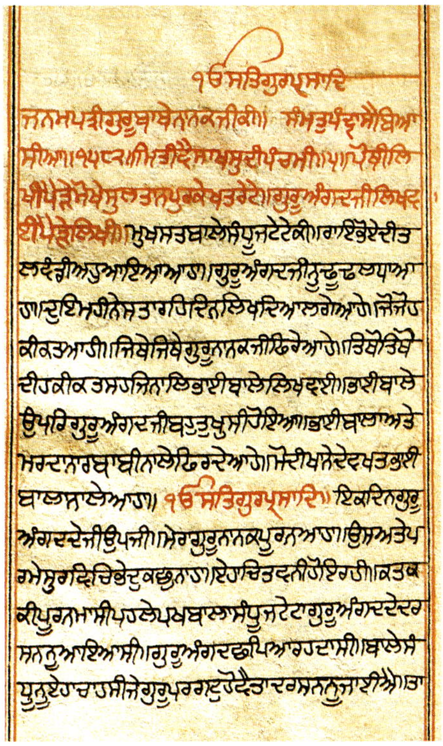

[120]

Aurangzeb kept Ram Rai, the Guru's eldest son, as hostage at Delhi. Guru Har Rai could not bear it, and he died heart broken in 1661 at the age of 32. He was a kind hearted man with a great love for nature.

[117] Guru Har Krishan
from the *Military Manual of Maharaja Ranjit Singh*
Probably the workshop of Imam Bakhsh Lahori
Lahore, 1822-1830
Maharaja Ranjit Singh Museum. Amritsar
Acc. N° 1035

Guru Har Krishan (1661-1664), younger son of Guru Har Rai, was five years old at the death of his father. Plotting to destroy the Sikh community by an interplay of contradictory forces amongst them, in 1664 Aurangzeb asked the young Guru to come to Delhi. He stayed at the haveli of Raja Jai Singh, where he suffered from an attack of smallpox and died at the age of eight. He is called the "child saint".
Note on this miniature painting the building in the background, with floral decorations similar to those of La Fontaine's *Fables* illustrated by Imam Bakhsh Lahori and to the ones done on the external walls of General and Fezli Azam Joo Court's residence at Naulakha, Lahore.

[118] Guru Tegh Bahadur
from the *Military Manual of Maharaja Ranjit Singh*
Probably the workshop of Imam Bakhsh Lahori
Lahore, 1822-1830
Maharaja Ranjit Singh Museum. Amritsar
Acc. N° 1035

Guru Tegh Bahadur (1664-1675), grand-uncle of Guru Har Krishan who appointed him as his successor, was fifteen years old when he distinguished himself in 1635 in a battle against the troops of Lahore. After the installation ceremony, Guru Tegh Bahadur went to Malwa, preaching Sikhism. Aurangzeb ordered his arrest, then his execution. Saved by Ram Singh of Jodhpur, he accompanied him on his military expedition to Assam (1667-1670). Back in the Punjab the Guru resumed his preaching in Malwa, thus again alarming the Mughal authorities. Aurangzeb ordered the arrest of Tegh Bahadur, had him transferred to Delhi where he and his followers were offered the choice to either perform a miracle, embrace Islam or face execution. His refusal of the first two led to his execution at Chandni Chowk, Delhi, on 11 November 1675.

[119] Guru Govind Singh
from the *Military Manual of Maharaja Ranjit Singh*
Probably the workshop of Imam Bakhsh Lahori
Lahore, 1822-1830
Maharaja Ranjit Singh Museum. Amritsar
Acc. N° 1035

Guru Govind Singh (1675-1708), son of Guru Tegh Bahadur, was nine years old when his father was executed. In the next thirty years he fought many pitched battles, most of them in the hills, several of them at Anandpur which he fortified by erecting five forts around the place. On 30 March 1699 Guru Govind Singh created the *Khalsa*, a martial congregation destined to fight oppression, protect the weak and uphold justice. The first five Sikhs ready to sacrifice their life in joining the *Khalsa* are the *Panj Pyare*. The Guru then prescribed the Five principles, which were Five beliefs, Five symbols, Five vows, Five deliverances and Five rules of conduct.
Between 1699 annd 1705 the Guru had to fight many battles with the Mughals and the hill chiefs. On 27 December 1704 his two youngest sons, arrested by the Mughals, were executed at Sirhind. In 1704 and 1705 Guru Govind Singh had written two "letters" to Aurangzeb, respectively known as the *Fateh Nama* and the *Zafar Nama*. In 1706 he decided to go to Aurangabad to meet the Emperor, but at Baghaur he learnt of Aurangzeb's death (20 February 1707). He then went to Agra (July 1707) to meet Emperor Bahadur Shah. In September 1708 the Guru deputed Banda Bahadur to the Punjab in order to complete his mission. Guru Govind Singh was severely wounded on 20 September by a Pathan, and he died on 7 October after he had declared that the *Adi Granth* would now be the guru of the Sikhs.
Note on this painting the black heron's feather on the Guru's turban, and the river bank similar to those we find in Imam Bakhsh's paintings.

[120] Janam Sakhi of Bhai Bala
Gurmukhi script, early 19th century
486 folios
Punjab State Archives. Patiala. Acc. N° 342

The *Janamsakhis* are biograhphies cum hagiographies of Guru Nanak, the *Bala Janamsakhis* tracing their ancestry to *Bala*, the companion of Guru Nanak. Most of the manuscripts were illustrated with miniatures, some of them beautifully painted like the *B-40 Janamsakhi Guru Baba Nanak* dated 1733 A.D. Written in various dialects of Punjabi and copied in Gurmukhi script, they were widely used for the instruction and education of the youth.
Under Maharaja Ranjit Singh, the *Janamsakhi* stories were largely reproduced in painting in the public and private buildings of the Sikh community all over Punjab, and wherever the Sikhs established themselves with their gurudwaras outside Punjab right from 18th century.

[121] Sikh mural paintings from Wazirabad (Pakistan)
Private collection

Wazirabad was entirely renovated under the governorship of General Avitabile who built a small residence for the Maharaja inside the fort. Business thrived in the new city, with residences and gardens being built inside and outside the ramparts. Several visitors, Indians like Ganesh Das or Europeans like Hügel and Barr, noticed the prosperity of the city and mentioned or described the mural paintings of Hindu mythology on the gates and in the fort. But private houses were also gaily decorated outside, and richly painted inside with religious and profane paintings.
These are two such mural paintings preserved today in a building inside the fort of Wazirabad.

[122] The Harmandir Sahib today
Photograph from a private collection

Founded by Guru Arjun in 1588, twice blown up by the Afghans of Ahmad Shah Abdali (1757 and 1762), it was immediately rebuilt on the same plinth by the Sikh community. Maharaja Ranjit Singh had the whole complex developed and decorated by artists belonging to different schools of the area. The domes and the outer walls of the Harmandir were gold plated, a work completed by 1830 AD and mostly financed by Maharaja Ranjit Singh and Fateh Singh Ahluwalia. The Maharaja also raised the four upper storeys of the Akal Takht : they were adorned with paintings and the dome gilded by General Hari Singh Nalwa. Ranjit Singh also increased from four to nine storeys the building of Baba Attal Rai and he paid for the new paintings and the gold plating of the dome.

[123] The Sonahri Masjid, Lahore
Built in 1753. Domes regilded in c. 1827
General view

This lovely mosque was built by Nawab Bhikari Khan in 1753 in the Kashmiri bazar of Lahore just next to the *baoli* of Guru Arjun in commemoration of his father. The Akalis occupied it in 1799. The mosque was returned to the Muslim community in c. 1827 at the request of General Allard, who paid for the regilding of the domes.

[124] The Sonahri Masjid, Lahore
Detail

[125] The Sonahri Masjid, Lahore
Detail

[126] The Sonahri Masjid, Lahore
Gulgashat-i-Punjab
Lahore, 1860
Maharaja Ranjit Singh Museum. Amritsar
Acc. N° 38

An interesting view of the highly picturesque mosque as it was in the mid-1850's. This lovely building attracted the attention of some European artists, especially of William Carpenter in a beautiful painting he did of Kashmiri Bazar in 1855. A similar drawing is kept in the Chandigarh Museum (Acc. N° 4358(3)) on which the caption in Persian wrongly attributes the building of the mosque to the time of Shah Jahan.

[127] The Holy Koran
Copied in Lahore under Maharaja Ranjit Singh
offered by Maharaja Ranjit Singh to Fakir Nuruddin (sic)
47 x 69 cm
Lahore Museum. Lahore

The story of this copy of the *Holy Koran*, done in Lahore and for a long time lovingly preserved in the Fakir family collection, is told by Fakir Syed Waheed-ud-Din in his *Real Ranjit Singh* : unable to sell it at a proper price at Lahore, the calligraphist was taking the *Holy Koran* for sale to Hyderabad (Sindh). Maharaja Ranjit Singh met the man and purchased the copy without discussing the price (ten thousand rupees). Later he had a passage (the "Surat Yusuf") read and explained to him by Fakir Azizuddin. Struck by the beauty of the text, he offered the copy of the *Holy Koran* to the Fakir as a token of friendship.

[128] Ain-i-Akbari
by Abul Fazl
copied at Lahore in 1838
National Museum, New Delhi. Acc. N° 59.587

Many *Ain-i-Akbari* and several *Akbarnama* are identified as having been copied at Lahore under the reign of Maharaja Ranjit Singh. Several of them have illustrations showing Emperor Akbar and Maharaja Ranjit Singh in their respective courts, though this particular one has only Maharaja Ranjit Singh. This is both an acknowledgement of the secular policy of the Maharaja which reminded the Punjabis of a similar policy enacted from Lahore two centuries ago, and probably a conscious build up of some part of the establishment and the intelligensia to present Ranjit Singh as the real inheritor of Akbar's open-minded policy towards all his subjets irrespective of caste and creed.

[129] Maharaja Ranjit Singh
From an *Ain-i-Akbari* copied at Lahore in 1838
Artist unknown
National Museum. New Delhi
Acc. N° 59.587, fol. 540v -541r

[130] Ain-i-Akbari
by Abul Fazl
copied at Lahore in 1838
Illustrated. Artist unknown
Asiatic Society of Calcutta. Inv. N° P.128

This copy of the *Ain-i-Akbari* has a rich decoration typical of the Lahore workshops of Maharaja Ranjit Singh's time. It contains two illustrations which are found in the other *Ain-i-Akbari* of these workshops: a particularly detailed set of arms [N° 80] and an exhibition of Punjabi jewellery.

[131] Ain-i-Akbari
by Abul Fazl
copied at Lahore under Maharaja Ranjit Singh
Illustrated. Artist unknown
Punjab State Archives. Patiala. Acc. N° M 658

This manuscript shows Akbar on his throne, with some of his courtiers sitting in front of him. Some people are examining manuscripts. In the background, right and left of the main building with its impressive green dome, two light structures can be seen with coloured feather-like decorations which are often seen in the illustrations of La Fontaine's *Fables* by Imam Bakhsh Lahori.

[131a] Ain-i-Akbari
by Abul Fazl
copied at Lahore under Maharaja Ranjit Singh
Illustrated. Artist unknown
Punjab State Archives. Patiala. Acc. N° M 658

This interesting miniature of the *Ain-i-Akbari* shows, better than any of these manuscripts illustrated at Lahore, a painting of arms and guns which have the characteristics of the *Fauj-i-khas*: muskets with bayonets, carbines for the light and heavy cavalry, field guns and mortars.

[132] Ain-i-Akbari
by Abul Fazl
copied at Lahore under Maharaja Ranjit Singh
Illustrated. Artist unknown. Acc. N° Nil
Lahore Fort Museum Library, Lahore
Director of Archaeology. Government of Pakistan

This little known manuscript has two opening illustrations, one showing Akbar in court, the other Ranjit Singh in court, which present a clear political message. It also shows the level of education, historical knowledge and political consciousness among the educated class of the state. Many copies of the *Ain-i-Akbari* were done in the Punjab kingdom, most of them in the second part of the reign (c. 1820-1839).

[133] "OM" with Vishnu, Lakshmi, Brahma and Shiva
from the *Military Manual of Maharaja Ranjit Singh*
Probably from the workshop of
Imam Bakhsh Lahori
Lahore, 1822-1830
Maharaja Ranjit Singh Museum. Amritsar
Acc. N° 1035

This is the opening page of the beautifully illustrated *Military Manual*. B.N. Goswamy has underlined the open-minded outlook of Maharaja

[32]

Ranjit Singh concerning Hinduism, and we know as a fact that there was no tension at all between Sikhism and Hinduism under Maharaja Ranjit Singh. On the contrary, Ranjit Singh took special care of that community's welfare, and his powerful Hindu ministers built splendidly decorated temples in Lahore.
It is therefore no surprise to find the sacred evocation "OM" in the opening page of a manuscript having both the illustrations of the ten Gurus and the military exercises of the "French" units of Maharaja Ranjit Singh.

[134] Temple north of the Lahore Fort (present state)
This small Hindu temple in marble was built outside the remaining "Sikh" rampart, but inside the advanced fortifications (not existing any more) north of the Lahore fort. Its exquisite panels were inlaid with semi-precious stones, like the Naulakha pavilion in the fort.

[135] Detail of the same

[136] Detail of the same

[137] Jawalamukhi, with golden dome offered by Maharaja Ranjit Singh
From the *Gulgashat-i-Punjab*
Lahore, 1860

Maharaja Ranjit Singh Museum. Amritsar
Acc. N° 7

The site of Jawalamukhi, near Kangra, has been honoured since time immemorial because of the flames which come out of the rock. In 1816, one month after Kharak Singh's investiture as heir-apparent, Ranjit Singh was at Amritsar celebrating Diwali, when there was a severe earthquake followed by a terrible wind. In a religious awe, the Maharaja betook himself to the goddess of Jawalamukhi.
There are contradictory informations as to the modern building of the temple. Some sources say that the gilded roof was offered by Maharaja Ranjit Singh in 1815 (1816?), while the golden dome and the silver gates were given by his son Kharak Singh at an unspecified date. Other sources say that in 1825 (or 1826) Ranjit Singh gave a huge amount of money for the golden dome, or roof, of the temple and credit him for the silver gates as well.

[138] Silver gates of the temple of Jawalamukhi
Courtesy: Government of Punjab

[139] The Temple of Jawalamukhi today
Courtesy: Government of Punjab

[140] Maharaja Ranjit Singh worshipping Devi
Gouache and gold on paper
Artist unknown
1838 AD
26.5 x 21 cm
National Museum, New Delhi. Acc. N° 72.313

Maharaja Ranjit Singh with his grandson Nao Nihal Singh stand with folded hands before the Devi. The Maharaja's haloed head is bent in obeisance before the four-armed Devi carrying a straight sword (*khanda*) and a pasha-noose, nimbus behind the head. She is in the gesture of granting blessing to the royal visitors.

[141] Mahabharata
Copied at Lahore under Maharaja Ranjit Singh
Punjab State Archives. Patiala. Acc. N° M 431

The numerous temples built by the Hindu community in Lahore under Maharaja Ranjit Singh show an intense activity, which was accompanied by other artistic activity like painting and copying of manuscripts. Most of them were of everyday use and are not adorned with splendid illuminated miniatures as the ones coming from the great workshops of the capital, yet they show the religious fervor of modest but literate people.

[142] Shiv Puran
by Pandit Daya Ram
Sambat 1929, "under the auspices of the Punjab Kingdom" (colophon)
Central public library. Patiala. Acc. n 1683

This interesting manuscript illustrated in the Kashmiri style is a testimony to the Shivaite worship in the Punjab kingdom.

[143] Bhagavat Puran
Punjab. Early 19th century
Punjab State Archives. Patiala. Acc. N° M 1679

Many manuscripts of this kind, without illustrations, were copied in the workshops of Lahore and other cities of Punjab under Maharaja Ranjit Singh. But nor many of them survived since their only purpose was the personal devotion of their owners.

[144] Shrimad Bhagavat Gita
Punjab. Early 19 th century
265 folios
Punjab State Archives. Patiala. Acc. N° M 466

[145] Diwan Bhawani Das
"Peshoria Bhuni Dass" in Devanagari
First great administrator of Maharaja Ranjit Singh
15,1 x 11,6 cm
Chandigarh Museum. Acc. N° D-27

The Mughal revenue system had collapsed for a pretty long time when Ranjit Singh took Lahore in 1799. No sustained conquest nor political reforms could be carried out without an efficient tax collection established on the produce of the land and the economic activities within the state.
In 1803, when the government was bankrupt and its revenues mortgaged to Rama Nand, a rich banker of Amritsar, Ranjit Singh appointed Devi Das as head of the Finance *daftar* with an order to clean up the mess. In 1808, Ranjit Singh was lucky to engage Diwan Bhawani Das, brother of Devi Das, who up till then had been serving Shah Shuja-ul-Mulk in Kabul. Bhawani Das started his own *daftar*, and the two brothers managed to redress the financial situation of the state. Bhawani Das, however diminutive he looks on this painting, was also a military man, who fought in Jammu, Multan, Peshawar and the Yusufzai country. He died in 1834.

[146] Diwan Ganga Ram
Second great administrator of Maharaja Ranjit Singh
[Till the time of going to press we expected a reproduction of Diwan Ganga Ram's portrait. We retain the caption we had prepared. JML]

Ganga Ram, a brilliant descendant of a Kashmiri pandit family who migrated to Delhi after the capture of Kashmir by the Afghans in 1752, was trained as a young political agent by the French officers of Sindhia. In 1799 he was appointed *diwan* of Colonel Bourquien when the 3rd Brigade of Hindustan operated between Pinjore, Ludhiana and Hansi from 1799 to1803. Later the English appointed him political agent to Colonel Ochterlony during his diplomatico-military operations on the Sutlej from 1809 onwards. Nobody knew the political situation of the petty states between Lahore and Delhi better than Ganga Ram. Warmly recommanded to Maharaja Ranjit Singh, he entered his service in 1813. First in charge of the regular troops of Lahore (infantry and artillery), he introduced great improvement in the system of military accounts. He was then requested to assist Diwan Bhawani Das till 1817, when he created his own Daftar-i-Ganga Ram. He was one of the most able ministers of the Punjab.
Ganga Ram in 1814 called his son Ajudhya Prasad from Delhi to Lahore, who in 1822 became the *bakhshi* of the *Fauj-i-khas*. And in 1815 he called his nephew Dina Nath who succeeded him as *diwan* when Ganga Ram died in 1826.

[147] Jamadar Khushal Singh
First 'Deorhidar' [Prime Minister] of Maharaja Ranjit Singh
Detail from "The Darbar of Maharaja Ranjit Singh"
Gouache on paper, stuck on wood panel
Artist unknown. c. 1850
Maharaja Ranjit Singh Museum. Amritsar
Acc. N° 110

Born in a Brahmin family of Sardhana, near Meerut, Khushal came to Lahore in 1807 and served in the Donkhal Singh regiment. Ranjit Singh remarked him and appointed him *deorhidar* (chamberlain, prime minister) in 1811. He took the *pahul* in 1812 and changed his name to Khushal Singh. He participated in military operations in Kashmir and Multan. In 1817 he fell from favor and was replaced as *deorhidar* by Mian Dhyan Singh Dogra, the future Raja and Prime Minister of the Punjab.
Khushal Singh served again in Kashmir, Peshawar and in the Katoch country. In 1832 he was sent to assist Prince Sher Singh, then governor of Kashmir, but his assistance was a disaster for the population. In 1837 he was again at Peshawar. After the demise of Ranjit Singh, Khushal Singh was one of the eleven conspirators who killed Raja Chet Singh, Kharak Singh's prime minister. He died in 1844.
The Jamadar's residence at Amritsar, adorned with beautiful paintings and a *darbar* room shining with mirrors still existed in the 1980's. It apparently

[97]

[152]

disappeared during the "beautification" drive after 1985.

[148] Raja Dhyan Singh
Prime Minister of Maharaja Ranjit Singh
"Raja Dhyan Singh Ministre" / "Rajah Dhian Sing"
Watercolour on European paper
By Imam Bakhsh Lahori. Lahore, 1827-1843
176 x 263 mm
Court collection, Musée Guimet. MG 78 III 39751

One of the three Dogra brothers from Jammu who entered the Punjab army in 1811 and reached a dominant position under Ranjit Singh. While Gulab Singh usually remained at Jammu and Suchet Singh was a splendid cavalry officer, Dhyan Singh quickly rose to become *deorhidar* (prime minister) in 1817. He was made a Raja in 1818, received the exalted title of "Raja Kalan" and was one of the most trusted and powerful men in the Punjab of Maharaja Ranjit Singh. In 1837 General Allard delivered him a letter from the French prime minister, and in 1839 Osborne saw him "dressed in a magnificent helmet and cuirass of polished steel embossed with gold, a present from King Louis-Philippe of France". Contrary to what is widely believed, relations were cordial between the Dogra brothers and the French officers till at least 1842, when Ventura interceded with Sher Singh in favour of Dhyan Singh. Dhyan Singh was assassinated the same day as Maharaja Sher Singh, on 15 September 1845.
Note on this painting the two thumbs of the Prime Minister of the Punjab: a rare display of this difformity which was usually not shown on paintings.

[149] Raja Gulab Singh
"Rajah Goulab Singh"
"Maharaja Golab Sing Bhadoor. Now he is doing Khizab"
Watercolour on European paper
By Imam Bakhsh Lahori. Lahore, 1827-1843
198 x 272 mm
Court collection, Musée Guimet. MG 78 III 41835

Eldest of the three Dogra brothers, Gulab Singh first served in the cavalry and in 1820 (or 1822) was made Governor of Jammu by Ranjit Singh. He spent most of the time in the hills, although he occasionally came to Lahore. His personal friendship with General Court induced him to entrust Court with the education of his eldest son Udham Singh, a very close friend of Prince Nau Nihal Singh. In his unpublished *Mémoires* Court says that he raised a mountaineering division for Raja Gulab Singh. In 1834 the Raja ordered Zorawar Singh to conquer Ladakh. Restrained by Ranjit Singh in 1835, after the Maharaja's death he again ordered Zorawar Singh to resume his operations. In 1846, Gulab Singh purchased Kashmir from the East India Company for seventy-five lakhs of Nanakshahi rupees, or one million sterling pounds, becoming the first Maharaja of Jammu and Kashmir. He died in 1857.
The first inscription in French refers to him as raja and is anterior to 1846, whereas the second in English calls him maharaja and is posterior to 1846.

[150] Raja Dina Nath
"Daftri Dina Nath" in Devanagari
Finance Minister of Maharaja Ranjit Singh
Artist unknown. Early 19th century [post 1826?]
18,2 x 15,4 cm
Chandigarh Museum. Acc. N° D-28

Nephew of Ganga Ram who called him to Lahore in 1815, Dina Nath first attracted Maharaja Ranjit Singh's attention in 1818 while putting in order the accounts of Multan. In 1826 he succeeded his uncle at the head of his *daftar* and received the charge of the royal seal. In 1834, when Bhawani Das died, Dina Nath took over his ministry, becoming the finance minister of Maharaja Ranjit Singh. Having his own agents in each and every corner of the kingdom, he was always very well informed. The British, whom he tried to contain during the 1846-49 period, called him the "Talleyrand of the Punjab". Most of the time he is represented with his typical cap, taking notes in close proximity to Ranjit Singh. He died in 1857.

[151] Fakir Syed Nuruddin
Personal physician and governor of Lahore
Oil on canvas
Detail from A. Schoefft's The Court of Lahore
Lahore 1841-Vienna 1855
Princess Bamba Collection. Sikh gallery
Lahore Fort. Director of Archaeology
Government of Pakistan

Fakir Nuruddin, the second of the three Fakir brothers, was more interested in devotion than in politics. Impressed by the ability of Azizuddin, the eldest Fakir brother, Maharaja Ranjit Singh called Nuruddin in 1810 and gave him several administrative appointments at Jalandhar, Sialkot, Wazirabad etc. till 1818 when he was called back to Lahore. He was then put in charge of the fort and of the completion of the ramparts, the royal gardens and palaces. He was also in charge of dispensing Ranjit Singh's charity to poor and deserving people. Ranjit Singh gave him one of the three keys of the royal treasury kept in the Moti Masjid (pearl mosque) at Lahore. A member of the Council of Regency in 1846-1849, he died in 1852.

[152] Desa Singh Majithia
Administrator of Maharaja Ranjit Singh in the Punjab hills
Artist unknown. Middle of 19th century
16 x 10.5 cm
Chandigarh Museum. Acc. N° 3798

Desa Singh Majithia (c. 1768-1832) joined Maharaja Ranjit Singh in 1809 and participated in the capture of Kangra, of which he was appointed commandant as well as nazim (governor) of the Hill States. Governor of Amritsar where he was in charge of the Harmandir Sahib, he served with distinction during the siege of Multan, was again appointed governor of the Punjab Hills. His popularity was great, his attitude always conciliatory. Then for about ten years, Ranjit Singh kept him at Lahore. He died in 1832.

[153] Lehna Singh Majithia
Artist unknown. Middle 19th century
11.8 x 9 cm
Chandigarh Museum. Acc. N° D-35

Lehna Singh, son of Desa Singh, was a most cultured person and the best scientist in the Punjab kingdom. Trained in mathematics and astronomy by the famous Akhwand Ali Ahmad, he worked closely with the French officers for the modernization of the armed force, and especially with General Court at Idgah (Lahore) for casting the new artillery.
His military career started at Multan in 1818, and he was entrusted by Maharaja Ranjit Singh the unpleasant task to seize the possessions of Sada Kaur, chief of the Kanhaya *misl* and mother-in-law of the Maharaja. At the death of Desa Singh in 1832, Lehna Singh was appointed governor of the Hills, a task he performed till 1844. He also succeeded his father in the charge of the Harmandir Sahib. He was probably the most

[95]

[95]

benevolent and open-minded governor of the Punjab kingdom. After 1839 he went through difficult times, specially under the prime ministership of Hira Singh, and he left Punjab for a long pilgrimage trip. His last years were a mixture of official assignments and distancing from the power that be at Lahore. He died at Benares in 1854.

[154] Punjab countryside and folk
La Fontaine, "Les souhaits" ["The Wishes"]
Gouache and gold on paper
Imam Bakhsh Lahori. Attock, 1837-1841
Musée Jean de La Fontaine, Château-Thierry

A garden in the Punjab of Maharaja Ranjit Singh. Punjab flourished and prospered from 1799 to 1839 as attested by Ganesh Das' *Char bagh-i-Punjab* which describes the new gardens created inside and outside the ramparts of the cities. Maharaja Ranjit Singh repaired the Shalimar Gardens at Lahore, and many *sardars* built new gardens outside the cities. The French officers took great care of their gardens, and they created the Soldier's Garden along the Ravi river, close to the *Fauj-i-khas*' cantonments at Anarkali. The serenity emanating from this miniature painting, with its rich nuances and delightful colours, shows the excellence attained by Imam Bakhsh.

[155] Punjab fields and folk
La Fontaine, "Le loup et le chasseur" ["The Wolf and the Hunter"]
Gouache and gold on paper
Imam Bakhsh Lahori. Attock, 1837-1841
Musée Jean de La Fontaine, Château-Thierry

The story of a hunter who wanted to kill too many beasts, and was himself killed by a wild boar. In the background, well-cultivated fields.

[156] Tarikh -i-Kala Kashmir
By Mir Ahmed Jalalawad
Artists unknown
Maharaja Ranjit Singh Museum, Amritsar
Acc. N° M 829
858 pp on paper. 38 x 54 cm
Maps painted on 18 single-page
and 15 double-page
Text in Persian

Colonel Mian Singh succeeded Prince Sher Singh as Governor of Kashmir. He is remembered for his kind and lenient administration. He abolished the forced labour (*begar*) in the Valley, developed shawl production and tried to call back some of the workers settled elsewhere. He also resumed the silk industry, which had sharply declined under the Afghans.
Perhaps at Ranjit Singh's request, Mian Singh asked Mir Ahmad Jalalabad to write this voluminous report illustrated with maps of the *parganas* of the province. K.N. Maitra says that it was done on the pattern of the *Ain-i-Akbari*, of which several copies were done in Lahore at that time. Its compilation of statistics is exemplary indeed, but apparently no translation has been done nor any in-depth study undertaken of this extraordinary document.

[157] Map from the Tarikh -i-Kala Kashmir
Artists unknown
Maharaja Ranjit Singh Museum. Amritsar
Acc. N° M 829

[158] Shawl of Bannu Pan Dei, of Chamba, wife of General Allard
Detail
Kashmir. c. 1826-1841
Private collection

General Allard, with Maharaja Ranjit Singh's permission, took his wife Bannu Pan Deï [Pandey] and their children to France in 1834. He settled them in Saint-Tropez, his native town on the French Riviera before returning to Lahore as he had promised the Maharaja. His family never returned to Punjab.
Bannu Pan Deï took along with her bundles of shawls and cloth from Punjab and Kashmir. After General Allard's death in Peshawar, his half-brother Benjamin came to Lahore for the succession, and he brought back to his sister-in-law the general's possessions from India.

[159] Shawl of Bannu Pan Dei, wife of General Allard
Detail : parrots in a field of flowers
Kashmir. C. 1826-1841
Private collection

The high ranking civil and military officers in the state were paid their salaries partly in shawls coming from the annual tribute of Kashmir. Burnes in the early 1830's says that Ranjit Singh had a reserve of Rs. 50 lakhs in shawls, and in 1833 the Maharaja suggested that General Allard accept Rs. 30,000 in shawls as arrears of pay. These shawls were sold in the local market, at Calcutta and in France.

[160] Shawl of Bannu Pan Dei, wife of General Allard
Detail
Kashmir. c. 1826-1841
Private collection

General Allard had his own orders executed in Kashmir under the vigilance of his supervisors. A passage from Emily Eden's *Up the Country* (pp. 196-7) shows the excellence of the work : "We had a most interesting envoy from General A[llard] who is employed by Runjeet in Peshawar and who wrote to us his polite French regrets that he could not come here, but he sent 'un très petit paquet' [a very small packet] of the shawls we had commissioned him to get worked in Kashmir when we saw him in Calcutta, and also the Kashmir gowns he had promised. He declared that there were never such failure, that he had sent seven or eight 'surveillants' to Kashmir, but 'on m'a tout gâté' [Everything has been spoiled].
One hour after there arrived, instead of the 'petit paquet', a very large pillow or rather a small ottoman [...] We at last arrived at the treasures. Four shawl dresses, four magnificent square shawls, and four long scarfs to match the dresses -but the fineness and the brightness of the whole concern it is impossible to describe. One gets to value shawls only by their fineness at last, and we have seen nothing like these. They have been a year and a half in making"

[161] Dress of the son of General and Mrs Allard
Lahore. c. 1834
Private collection

This dress, in green *kimkhwab*, belonged to Jean-François, alias "Poulou", the eldest son of the general. In the family painting (No. 207), the Allard children are represented in rich oriental garb. This

[163]

[164]

dress is similar to the ones in the painting.

[162] Gown of Bannu Pan Dei, wife of General Allard
Kashmir. c. 1830-1836
Private collection

As we have said earlier, General Allard placed orders of pashmina gowns in Kashmir. Already in Lahore Bannu Pan Dei Allard sometimes wore dresses cut according to French designs and fashion, and General Allard's correspondence in 1837 says that his wife at Saint-Tropez was to have French dresses made for her from the cloth they had brought back from Lahore. This dress of Bannu Pan Dei's is made from pashmina with an intricate Kashmiri border. She is seen wearing this robe in the family portrait done in Paris in 1836 [N° 207], although the size on the border is bigger on the painting.

[163] Long shawl Pashmina
Kashmir. c 1820-25
314.6 x 129.6 cm
National Museum. New Delhi. Acc. N° 56.41/5

The National Museum, New Delhi, has a rich collection of Kashmiri shawls, some of them dated from the time of Maharaja Ranjit Singh. The real Kashmiri shawl had a fineness which the European imitation shawls could not even approach, though they had more intricate and convoluted designs since they were manufactured on jacquard looms. The long shawl was the one which can be seen on the oldest miniature paintings. Bernier gives the average size in the 1660's as "an eln and a half long and an eln broad" (114 x 170 cm), but Ames observes that shawls of that period usually measure 129 x 280 cm. Under Ranjit Singh's reign, the shawls underwent a considerable change in their design, what F. Ames calls the "modern Sikh shawl" with a considerable increase in border size, the floral motifs taking "a fanciful and fantastic nature".

[164] Long shawl Pashmina
Punjab. c.1830-35
343 x 143.3 cm
National Museum. New Delhi. Acc. N° 51.28/6

Maharaja Ranjit Singh received part of the tribute of Kashmir in shawls that he kept in his *toshakhana*. The growing prosperity of Kashmir, the increasing production at Amritsar and the import of European shawls in India by the East India Company resulted in a glut which Ranjit Singh acknowledged while discussing this point with Alexander Burnes in 1831. Burnes estimated at five million rupees (Rs. fifty lakhs) the value of Kashmiri shawls in the reserves of the Maharaja. The Marwari merchants also accumulated a large reserve of shawls in their stores at Bombay and Calcutta. Maharaja Ranjit Singh was very fond of shawls, but this particular situation explains the extraordinary number of shawls he distributed as gifts or tried to use as "salary" for his high ranking officers.

[165] Moon shawl
Pashmina
Kashmir. c. 1830-50
164 x 144 cm [Sr. n 3]
National Museum. New Delhi. Acc. N° 55.39/1

According to F. Ames, the square shawl, or rumal, developed in the mid-eighteenth century when Kashmir came under Afghan domination. Easier to produce and less expensive, it was mainly exported to the Near East. The circular central motif gave this kind of shawl its name, the "moon shawl". Each corner of the field was ornamented with a quarter circle coordinating with the central motif.

[166] Moon shawl Pashmina
Kashmir. c. 1830-35
166 x 166 cm
National Museum. New Delhi. Acc. N° 64.210

Moon shawls became fashionable in Europe in the 1810's, and when Kashmir was annexed to Lahore in 1819 the artists and craftmen developed what F. Ames calls "a new format"of the rumal : bigger (180 x 180 cm), and made with four separate panels joined together with a border fringe of multi-coloured strips of pashmina.

[167] Patka (sash)
Kashmir. c. 1820-40
316 x 50 cm
National Museum. New Delhi. Acc. N° 62.2351

The *patka*, or waistband, also called "turban" by F. Ames, could measure upto 70 x 460 cm. During Mughal time, it showed the military or social rank of the wearer. After the fall of the empire, some states like Awadh and Hyderabad continued the Mughal tradition of the *patka*, and they continued to be woven in Kashmir till the end of the Punjab kingdom.

[168] Twelve coins of Maharaja Ranjit Singh
Private collection
Courtesy : Mrs Jyoti Ray

Maharaja Ranjit Singh struck coins, gold mohur, silver rupee and copper paisa, in all provinces of his kingdom. Gold and silver denominations have legends in Persian, while the copper paisas have them in Gurmukhi. Here are eleven silver rupees and one copper coin from Maharaja Ranjit Singh's mints. Ranjit Sing's name does not appear on any of his coins: considering himself the servant of the Gurus, he continued the Sikh tradition to strike coins with their names, especially the Amritsari tradition in honour of Guru Nanak : hence the name "Nanakshahi" for the coinage of the Punjab kingdom.

[169] Silver rupee
Amritsar mint. BS 1859 (1802 AD)
Punja (hand) and doted leaf
Private collection
Courtesy : Mrs Jyoti Ray

One of the oldest silver rupees struck by Maharaja Ranjit Singh, it bears the leaf, the symbol appearing on most of his coins. The significance of the leaf, and indeed its botanical identification, are not even ascertained.

[170] Silver rupee
Kashmiri mint. BS 1879 (1822 AD)
Inscription "Har" for Hari Singh Nalwa
Private collection
Courtesy : Mrs Jyoti Ray

The coins sruck in the kingdom have no identifying inscriptions concerning the officials under whom they were struck, with the exception of Kashmir. Eleven governors hold charge of that province under the reign of Ranjit Singh. This coin was struck under the governorship of Hari Singh Nalwa, and till 1849 the rupees struck in Kashmir were known as Hari Singhji.

[171] A two paisa copper coin
Amritsar mint
Private collection
Courtesy: Mrs Jyoti Ray

The copper coins, just like the gold mohur and the silver paisa, had an inscription commemorating Guru Nanak. On the copper coins the inscription read "Akal Sahai Guru Nanakji".

[172] Tak Shal Mint
Artist unknown
27.5 x 21.5 cm
National Museum. New Delhi. Acc. N° 88.342

This interesting miniature painting shows a scene from one of Maharaja Ranjit Singh's mints. A worker is holding the seal while another one is striking it. A mint supervisor is seated on the left. Inscription in Gurmukhi.
The greatest benefit of Maharaja Ranjit Singh's economic policy was the monetarization of the society, with more money circulating between the

peasants and the state. Transactions, which included the pay of the army -most of the soldiers were of peasant stock – were increasingly conducted in cash. Consequently taxes were also levied in cash, instead of crops.This led to a development of monetary mints all over the country.

[173] A Punjabi provincial town
La Fontaine, "Le meunier, son fils et l'âne"
["The Miller, his Son and the Ass"]
Gouache and gold on paper
Imam Bakhsh Lahori. Attock, 1837-1839
Musée Jean de La Fontaine, Château-Thierry

A modern town in the Punjab, seen by Imam Bakhsh Lahori. The city probably represented here is Wazirabad, which had just been renovated by Avitabile : "It seems like a dream when I found myself seating in this carriage, and drawns by four horses to Wazirabad [...]. Avitabile, while he resided there, almost rebuilt the town in the European style, and pulled down the old bazar, making the streets wide enough to admit a carriage and four horses, to the astonishment of the natives, the streets being so excessively narrow in most Indian towns [...]. The people are enraptured with the present beauty of the bazar of Wazirabad, and its charms were boastingly represented to me long before I saw it" (Von Hügel, 1836).

[174] A Punjabi provincial town
La Fontaine, "Les deux aventuriers et le talisman"
["The two Adventurers and the Talisman"]
Gouache and gold on paper
Imam Bakhsh Lahori. Attock, 1837-1839
Musée Jean de La Fontaine, Château-Thierry

Another modern town by Imam Bakhsh Lahori. A crowd is looking at an "adventurer" carrying an elephant in stone. In the crowd, a European officer of Maharaja Ranjit Singh (no beard, but rouflaquettes –sidewhiskers- : General Avitabile?). A *najib* from Avitabile's regiment is on duty at the gate. A throne can be seen on a terrace in the city palace. Note the closed green doors of the building behind the throne, showing the characteristic persiennes of the French officers' residences.

[175] A Punjabi countryside
La Fontaine, "Le milan, le roi et le chasseur"
["The Hawk, the King and the Falcon"]
Gouache and gold on paper
Imam Bakhsh Lahori. Attock, 1837-1839
Musée Jean de La Fontaine, Château-Thierry

Another little town, this time with a wild countryside in the foreground. It is worth noting that this story, like many other stories of the *Fables*, was inspired by a *Pancatantra* brought back from India by the French physician Bernier in 1669.

[176] Gulgashat-i-Punjab
1860
Maharaja Ranjit Singh Museum. Amritsar
Acc. N° 7

This general history of the Punjab from 1469 to 1849 is illustrated by paintings showing monuments in Amritsar, Lahore and other cities in the kingdom of the Punjab. Written by Raja Ram Tota, it is sometimes dated 1849 and sometimes 1860 AD. It is illustrated with paintings of historical figures (including young Maharaja Ranjit Singh, Maharaja Sher Singh) and views of buildings all over the kingdom. Even if the miniature paintings are from unknown artists, details on some of the historical illustrations show a clear inspiration from Imam Bakhsh Lahori's workshop. Six paintings on leaves published by B.N. Goswamy in his *Piety and Splendour. Sikh Heritage in Art* (plates 164-169) are similar to the illustrations of the *Gulgashat-i-Punjab* we reproduce here. Although they are more richly decorated with gold and vivid colours, their captions and the historical explanations in Persian are often misleading. Still they show the interest given by some enlightened people to the architectural heritage of the Punjab and its capital, Lahore. It is from that kind of material that a Kanaya Lal and later on a Syed Muhammed Latif collected their preliminary information on the historical monuments of Lahore.
The fact that a similar drawing of the Govindgarh fort at Amritsar is found both in the *Gulgashat-i-Punjab* and in the National Museum, New Delhi (Acc. N° 85.26. See [N° 107] above) is another indication that these paintings were more widely circulated than we realise.

[177] Fort of Kamlagarh
Gulgashat-i-Punjab
Maharaja Ranjit Singh Museum. Amritsar
Acc. N° 38

The series of fortified strongholds in his territory were used by the Raja of Mandi as a last defensive resort against any invader from the plains. Mandi loosely depended on Lahore under Maharaja Ranjit Singh. The expansion of the Punjab Kingdom in the hills after 1839, and the rich iron deposits of the small hilly state, led to the annexation of Mandi by Ventura after a memorable siege of the fort of Kamlagarh (August-November 1840).
It was during that siege, according to Ventura (as reported by Feuillet de Conches) that two artists did (i.e. completed) the illustrations of the *Fables* of La Fontaine. After the capture of the fort, Ventura styled himself Count Ventura de Mandy, while his daughter in France, dropping "Ventura", became Victorine de Mandy, one of the most beautiful French women of the Second Empire.

[178] The Fort of Kangra
Gulgashat-i-Punjab
Maharaja Ranjit Singh Museum. Amritsar
Acc. N° 38

One of the most picturesque and powerful citadels of the Rajputs in the Himalaya foothills, it belonged for a very long time to the Chand dynasty who patronised the famous Kangra school of paintings. In 1809 Raja Sansar Chand, who for years had been dreaming to capture Lahore, became a vassal of Maharaja Ranjit Singh.The temples in the fort and city of Kangra were famous, and the city was

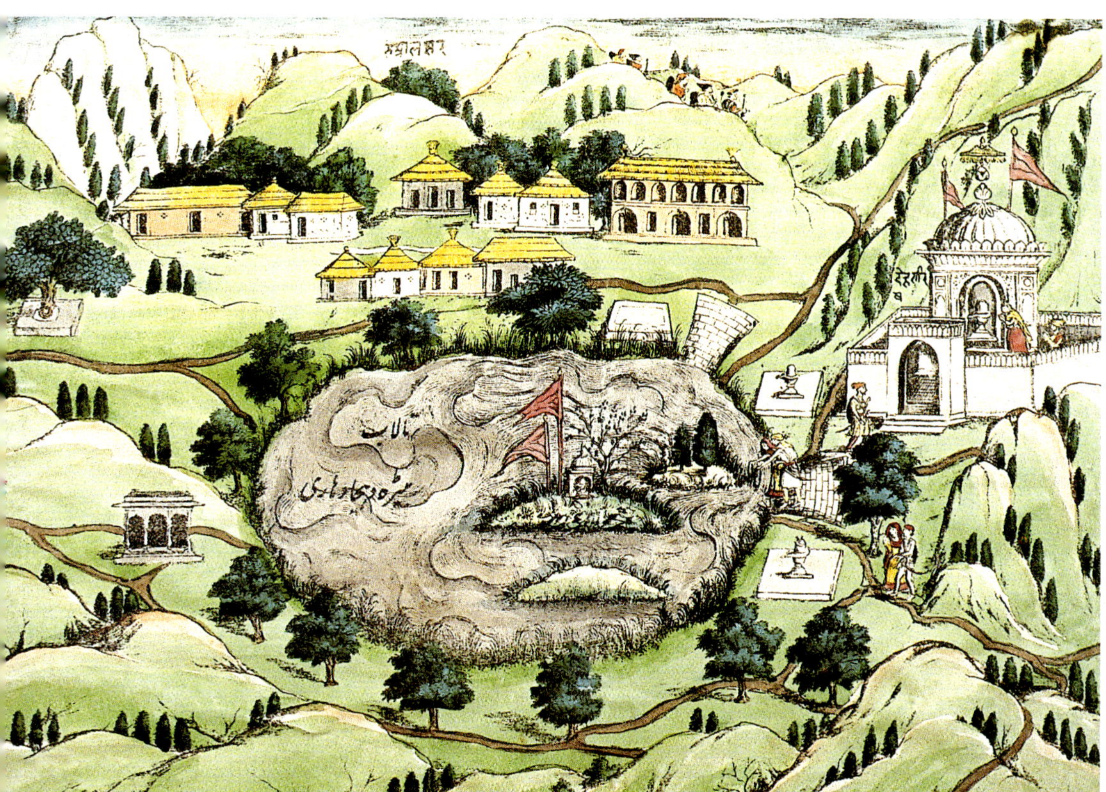

[179]

[191]

known for surgeons doing plastic surgery which surprised the Europeans physicians when they came to know about their methods and their success.

[179] The pool and temples of Kitas (tentatively)
Gulgashat-i-Punjab
Maharaja Ranjit Singh Museum. Amritsar
Acc. N° 38

This interesting painting showing a pool in a hilly setting with temples around it could well be the Khitas and Gandhala in the Salt Range, the famous Jaina and Hindu shrines in Punjab visited and described by Hiuen Tsang in the early 7th century AD The pool was 200 feet long and 150 broad. The "Sat Ghara" or seven temples were attributed to the Pandus, but Cunningham counted no less than twelve temples around the pond and described some of them as being in the Kashmiri style of the Karkota and the Varma dynasties. Not far from there is the fort of Nandana.

[180] Two complementary views of the fort and city of Lahore
Gulgashat-i-Punjab
Maharaja Ranjit Singh Museum. Amritsar
Acc. N° 38

A naïve picture of the capital of the Punjab kingdom, compared to the rigorous drawing attributed to Imam Bakhsh Lahori (N° 186). The most impressive building in the city (left) is identified by the inscription as being the Jamadar [Khushal Singh] haveli. What must be noticed in the walled city are the Shivaite and Vishnuite temples which can be seen next to the Mughal mosque of Wazir Khan.

[181] The Harmandir, or Golden Temple Amritsar
Gulgashat-i-Punjab
Maharaja Ranjit Singh Museum. Amritsar
Acc. N° 38

"The temple is of pure gold, really and truly covered completely with gold, most beautifully carved, till within eight feet from the ground, and then there are panels of marble inlaid with flowers and birds -very Solomonish altogether. There are four large folding-doors of gold. We walked around it, and then Runjeet took us in" (E. Eden, *Up the Country* , p. 216. December 1838)

[182] Rambagh Palace, Amritsar
Gulgashat-i-Punjab
Maharaja Ranjit Singh Museum. Amritsar
Acc. N° 38

The Rambagh was in construction when Jacquemont visited Amritsar in March 1831. In December 1838 Maharaja Ranjit Singh gave a sumptuous reception there in honour of Lord Auckland, Governor-General :
"In the evening we went to a garden half a mile off, where Runjeet is living and where he was going to give us an evening fête. The house was beautifully painted in an arabesque fashion, with small pieces of looking-glass let in, in various patterns. The walks of the garden were all lined with those splendid soldiers. [E. Eden expresses the wish to see the guards] The old Maharaja did not wait to have the question explained. He delights to show off his soldiers. He jumped up, and took hold of my hand, and ambled out into the garden, and then made all the guards march by, and commented on their dresses, and he looked so fond of the old grey-bearded officers. There is something rather touching in the affection his people have for him" (E. Eden, *Up the Country* , pp. 217-218. December 1838)

[183] Map of the Darbar Sahib and environs
Watercolour and gold on paper
c. 1840. Central Sikh Museum, Amritsar
Shiromani Gurudwara Parbandakh Committee

This view of the Harmandir concentrates on the temple itself and its new golden decoration, but it also gives a glimpse of the surrounding buildings and *bungas*, as well as the other sacred and historical places around the tank.

[184] Map of Lahore City and Fort
Kangra. Before 1818
193 x 132 cm
Maharaja Ranjit Singh Museum. Amritsar
Acc. N° 112

The date of this exceptional document, kept for a long time in the vice-regal lodge at Simla, is uncertain. V.S. Suri put it at c. 1830, while B.N. Goswamy at c. 1825 "from the family workshop of Purkhu". Its Kangra provenance is commonly accepted. Retracing the connection between Lahore and Kangra from 1809 onwards, Fakir Syed Aijazuddin rightly noticed the absence of Ranjit Singh's *baradari* in the Hazuri Bagh, built by the Maharaja in 1818.

[185] A three-dimensional model of Lahore city and fort with ramparts
Lahore, 1847. Destroyed 1949
From a photograph in a private collection

This three-dimensional model of the city of Lahore was done for Henry Lawrence in 1847 and sent to London in 1848. It was exhibited not far from the Koh-i-noor in the Great Exhibition in 1851. It fascinated many a layman interested in "oriental" architecture and drew enthusiastic comments from Théophile Gauthier. How it survived the Second World War to be destroyed in 1949 remains a mystery.
The ramparts of the city were rebuilt by Ranjit Singh at an uncertain date. The panoramic vista of the city of Lahore by Longcroft (c. 1808-1811) does not show to the north of the fort any addition to Jahangir's fortifications.. We know the new ramparts were almost complete in 1822, with two lines of fortifications erected north of the fort which can be seen also on various drawings done in 1846-1848.
These two new ramparts are clearly visible here, and the gates are fortified with the latest improvements of the time. The proportions are not exact concerning the height of the buildings -a visual distortion destined to give more relief to the structural perception of the plan. Some of the main features of the city, great havelis of Raja Dhyan Singh and Khushal Singh, Sonahri masjid and Wazir Khan Mosque, are easily discernible. The ramparts were demolished from 1851 onwards (Circular Road today).

[186] Panoramic view of Lahore in 1846
"Lahore during Sikh rule N° 1"
Lahore Museum, Lahore. Pakistan

We reproduce here one of the two similar drawings in the Lahore Museum, "Lahore under Sikh rule N° 1 and N° 2". The first line of fortification which is clearly visible in the painting is no longer there while the second one is still existing.
It is similar to plate XV in Dr. Martin Honigberger's *Thirty-Five Years in the East*. If we go by Honigberger's own acknowledgement and the other evidence we have, this panoramic view must be, like the other illustrations in his book, attributed to Imam Bakhsh Lahori or some artist from his workshop. Honigberger had already sold a copy of the sketch to Prince Soltykoff in 1842 before W. and N. Hanhart engraved the drawing for the publication of Honigberger's *Memoirs* in 1852.

[187] The Shalimar Gardens, Lahore
Gulgashat-i-Punjab
Maharaja Ranjit Singh Museum. Amritsar
Acc. N° 38

Several illustrations of the *Gulgashat-i-Punjab* show the monuments of Lahore as they stood in the 1850's. This naive view of the Shalimar Gardens makes an interesting contrast with other more "classical" drawings made by Indian / Punjabi artists showing the gardens in a more balanced "European" perspective and imperial grandeur.

[188] The Badshahi Masjid, or Imperial Mosque. Lahore
Gulgashat-i-Punjab
Maharaja Ranjit Singh Museum. Amritsar
Acc. N° 38

One of the most impressive monuments of Lahore, this superb edifice was built by Aurangzeb in 1673-74. Strategically situated close to the city as well as to the fort, which the towering minarets dominate, the Badshahi Masjid was attached to the state from 1764 to 1849 and used for military purposes. Before the building of his marble pavilion in the Hazuri Bagh in 1818 Maharaja Ranjit Singh sometimes held his *darbar* there.

[189] The Tomb of Anarkali. Lahore
Gulgashat-i-Punjab
Maharaja Ranjit Singh Museum. Amritsar
Acc. N° 38

The legend of Anarkali, a lovely young wife of Akbar buried alive in 1599 because the old Emperor saw her in a mirror responding to a smile of Prince Salim, the future Jahangir's smile, is still alive in popular imagination in Lahore. According to Latif the tomb was built in 1615, in the centre of a large garden where a Mughal palace was built later at an unspecified period.
Ranjit Singh fixed his headquarters there during the siege of Lahore in 1799. He then gave the place to Prince Kharak Singh, the heir-apparent. But in 1822 he gave it to generals Allard and Ventura and it became the headquarter of the *Fauj-i-khas* cum residence of the two generals.
Allard had only one wife, who lived with their children in a wing of the modern classical residence built by the two generals. But Ventura, who had a most replendent harem, lodged his beloved ones in the tomb of Anarkali. After annexation, the tomb was used as a church, and then turned into the Punjab Record Office which it still is.
A similar drawing is kept in the Chandigarh Museum (Acc. N° 4358(3)), on which an inscription wrongly attributes the repairs of the dome to General Avitabile (Abu Tabela) instead of Allard and Ventura. See above N° 96 and 176.

[193]

[190] Nau Nihal Singh Haveli
Lahore. c. 1835-1837

One of the best private buildings preserved in Punjab from the time of Maharaja Ranjit Singh. In 1837 the Maharaja celebrated the wedding of his grandson Prince Nau Nihal Singh. This haveli was built by the Prince as his personal residence. It had numerous spacious chambers, halls and balconies. The walls and ceilings were richly painted with flowers, cypress trees and scenes from Hindu mythology interspersed with mirrors, while the ceilings were gilded with mirrors and paintings. It is now the Victoria High School for Girls.

[191] Nau Nihal Singh Haveli
Lahore. c. 1835-1837
Details of the same

[192] Nau Nihal Singh Haveli
Lahore. c. 1835-1837
Details of the same

[193] Hazuri Bagh
Lahore. 1818

Built by Maharaja Ranjit Singh in 1818 in the open space (*serai* of Aurangzeb) between the Badshahi Masjid and the Alamgir Gate of the Lahore fort, this beautiful two storeyed marble pavilion was used as a quiet place for himself, a place where private *darbars* could also be held and visitors entertained on a more intimate and amiable way. It is one of the few marble constructions that is preserved from Maharaja Ranjt Singh's period. The upper storey of the pavilion collapsed in 1932.

[194] Hazuri Bagh
Lahore. 1818
Detail of the same

The chaste decoration of the pavilion is mainly flowers exquisitely carved in white marble, with one exception reproduced on each face of the *baradari* : peacocks, facing each other in the corner openings of the building. It might be fortuitous to remember that the symbol of the peacock is traditionally linked to Ranjit Singh's great love, the beautiful Moran whom he had to exile to Pathankot in 1811. There is a tradition of the so-called Moran Shahi coins, and the written testimony that she danced "like a peacock". Right to the end of his life, the Maharaja spoke with emotion and nostalgia of their love for each other.

[195] Hazuri Bagh
Lahore. 1818
Detail of the same

[196] Hazuri Bagh
Lahore. 1818
Detail of the same

[197] L'Ermitage. Residence of General Court at Lahore
"L'Ermitage. Habitation du général Court à Lahore"
Watercolour on European paper
By Imam Bakhsh Lahori. Lahore, 1827-1843
325 x 593 mm
Court collection, Musée Guimet. MG 64836

Maharaja Ranjit Singh gave General Court the tomb of Nusrat Khan to be used both as headquarters for his brigade and residence. When he married Fezli Azam Joo, Court kept the tomb as his headquarters and built a Punjabi-style residence for his family.
This bird's eye view painting is most probably by Imam Bakhsh Lahori. In the newly planted garden the tomb of Nusrat Khan can be seen in the foreground with sentries, while the residence is in the background. Called "L'Ermitage" ["The Ermit's dwelling"], it is built within a rectangular courtyard and decorated with floral paintings. The servants quarters and the stables can be seen on the right. Fezli Azam Joo's mosque can also be seen
Syed Mohammed Latif wrote in 1892 that General Court modified the structure of the tomb through additions on the ground floor ("many rooms") and on the terrace ("three arches on the upper storey to the west" still existing in 1892). One can see on this painting the three arches on the terrace, but no other drastic modifications in this painting nor in the portrait of Mrs Court dated 1841 (N° 209).
After the general left for France with his wife and children in 1843, the house was occupied by the Nawab of Mamdot, who certainly did not desecrate the tomb. After 1849 the Nawab was expelled and the house occupied by a British resident.

[198] Inside a Punjabi residence
La Fontaine, "Le vieillard et ses trois fils"
"The old Man and his children"
Gouache and gold on paper
Imam Bakhsh Lahori. Attock, 1837-1839
Musée Jean de La Fontaine, Château-Thierry

An old man, presumably on his death-bed in his residence, surrounded by his three sons. A man on the terrace is preparing some medicine. Note the impressive architectural landscape with the green shades of a garden in the background.

[199] Inside a Punjabi residence
La Fontaine, "Le mari, la femme et le voleur"
"The Husband, the Wife and the Robber"
Gouache and gold on paper
Imam Bakhsh Lahori. Attock, 1837-1839
Musée Jean de La Fontaine, Château-Thierry

This is a representation of the amusing story of a frigid woman who was terrified one night by a burglar and took refuge in the arms of her loving husband. Note the elaborate architecture of the house with a lovely balcony. On the upper storey, the persiennes are closed to keep the room cool.

[200] Shahnama of Firdausi
Scribe : Tawakal Beg
Copied in 1653 AD

[212]

400 folios
65 illustrations
Punjab State Archives. Acc. N° 363

This splendid *Shahnama* of Firdausi was copied in 1069 Hijra [1653 AD] for Shah Jahan by the scribe Tawakal Beg. It has 65 illustrations. More interesting for our purpose is that it carries the seal of "Ghulam Ali Sahib Bahadur Kitab Khana Sarkar Wala", i.e. the library of Maharaja Ranjit Singh, with the date 1244 Hijra [1828 AD] : testimony, rare at this moment - of the kind of illustrated manuscripts which were in the Lahore fort during Maharaja Ranjit Singh's reign.
The presence of that manuscript in the Royal Library explains the copying and illustration of a splendid *Shahnama* done at Lahore in c. 1830, and also some of the classical influence we have already noticed in the paintings of Imam Bakhsh Lahori.

[200 A] The Court of Sulaiman
Shahnama of Firdausi
Artist unknown. Lahore. c 1830
National Museum. New Delhi. Acc. N° L 532/8
43 x 28 cm

This *Shahnama*, most probably copied in Lahore under Maharaja Ranjit Singh, illustrates the place of classical Persian culture in the Punjab Kingdom. Ebba Koch has shown how the memory of Suleiman was alive and cherished under the Mughals, and particularly Shah Jahan. Suleiman, just like Sikandar, also belonged to the cultural tradition of the Sikh court. Under a canopy which is quite similar to the one offered by Maharaja Ranjit Singh to the Harmandir Sahib, Suleiman is in the midst of angels, *peris*, demons and wild beasts, all living peacefully under his wise government.

[201] Heer Ranja
Gurmukhi script
Early 19th century
Folio 112
Punjab State Archives. Patiala. Acc. N° 406

Probably the most famous love story in the Punjab, taking place around Gujranwala, the native place of Maharaja Ranjit Singh, and the Chenab. Here written in Gurmukhi.

[202] Shirin Farhad
Lahore, 1812 AD.
Punjab State Archives. Patiala. Acc. N° 486

The *Khusraw-u-Shirin* of Nizami tells the love story of Emperor Chosroes II of Persia and the Armenian princess Shirin. The story goes that Farhad, a stone cutter, fell in love with Shirin when things were not going well between the princess and the emperor, but this idyll was interrupted by a false message from Chosroes, and Farhad committed suicide. This love story has been copied and illustrated in all the confines of Iranian culture, including pre-Mughal and Mughal India. It is obvious that manuscripts of this story were copied in the Punjab of Maharaja Ranjit Singh too.

[203] Honigberger, Thirty Five Years in the East
Punjab State Archives. Patiala. Acc. N° 279

Dr. Martin Honigberger (1795-1865) was an Austro-Hungarian physician who came to Lahore and was introduced to Maharaja Ranjit Singh by his French officers. His fascinating *Memoirs* are illustrated with engravings from miniature paintings. It seems that with the one exception mentioned above, all of them were from the workshop of Imam Bakhsh Lahori.

[204] Barr, Journal of a March ...
Punjab State Archives. Patiala. Acc. N° 259

Young Lieutenant Barr commanded a section of artillery moving from Delhi to Kabul via Lahore and Peshawar in 1839. He left a detailed *Journal of a March* published in London in 1844. This Journal is particularly interesting since Barr took great interest in the paintings he saw in Lahore, Wazirabad and Peshawar. While at Lahore, he paid a visit to the body of General Allard lying in state in his *baradari*, waiting for burial, and he told Fakir Nuruddin about the Christian rites of funerals. At Peshawar he met Avitabile and, being an artilleryman, he has given us the best testimony on the remarkable work done by General Court in this field.

[205] Hügel, Travels in Kashmir ...
Punjab State Archives. Patiala. Acc. N° 273

Baron von Hügel (1796-1870) travelled in Punjab and Kashmir in 1835-1836. The original German edition of his travels in four volumes (1840-1844) was immediately translated into English (1845). Hügel has interesting descriptions of the cities and the bazars of the little towns which he visited on his way. The depiction of the most impressive monuments he saw with their mural paintings is a good addition to our knowledge of Maharaja Ranjit Singh's flourishing kingdom at that period.

[206] Vigne, A personal Narrative ...
Punjab State Archives. Patiala. Acc. N° 256

A British traveller who toured northern India from 1832 to 1839, Vigne left in his *Narrative* a vivid description on how he was allowed to make a famous sketch of Maharaja Ranjit Singh, much used afterwards by Punjabi artists. Vigne was present at the wedding of Prince Nau Nihal Singh in 1837 and described some of the events which took place on that occasion.

[207] General Allard and his family at Lahore
Oil on canvas
"Paris, 1836"
Author unknown
Size not recorded. c. 60 x 40 cm
Private collection. Stolen in 1977

This beautiful oil painting dated "Paris 1836" shows General Allard and his wife, Bannu Pan Deï, in their residence at Anarkali, Lahore, with their five children. The artist used miniature paintings of the Allard family members and probably a drawing done in Lahore in 1834 by Imam Bakhsh Lahori. He started working in Paris in October 1835 and had not yet completed the work in June 1836. General Allard is wearing a hussar uniform, braided on the chest, while Bannu Pan Dei Allard is dressed in a yellow gown with a Kashmiri border. The children are all in rich Punjabi attire, and two Punjabi servants are in attendance, the one on the right holding the youngest daughter, Felicie, in her arms. These two servants accompanied Madame Allard to France and settled there in 1835.
In June 1836 the original oil painting was still incomplete. General Allard brought to Lahore the sketch done by the French artist, which was seen at Anarkali and described by Barr in 1839. General Allard had a copy made of it, (probably) by Imam Bakhsh Lahori, in 1838. That copy has survived and

[253]

is now in the Harvard University Art Museums, Cambridge, Massachussets.

[208] Bannu Pan Deï, wife of General Allard
Oil on canvas
Artist unknown
No place, no date [Lahore, 1837-1839?]
72 x 58 cm
Private collection. Stolen in 1977

Bannu Pan Deï, born in 1812 in Chamba (now in Himachal Pradesh), married General Allard at Lahore in 1826, and gave him five living children. In 1834 she went with him and their children to France and settled at Saint-Tropez. Allard returned to Punjab and died in Peshawar in 1839. Bannu Pan Dei educated the children, built a *baradari* in Sainte-Maxime and purchased a beautiful country-house in Saint-Tropez where she lived till 1884, going every evening, as the family tradition goes, to the port of Saint-Tropez to wait for her husband. She is buried in the cimetière marin of Saint-Tropez.

[209] Fezli Azam Joo, wife of General Court
Oil on canvas
by August Schoefft
Signed "Schoefft 1841 Lahor"
114 x 95 cm (with frame)
89.5 x 70.5 cm (within frame)
Private collection
[Published for the first time]

Fezli Azam Joo, a beautiful Kashmiri girl born in 1821, married General Court at Lahore. They had four children and lived in the residence they built themselves at Naulakha, Lahore. She went to France with the general and their children in 1843, settled in Marseilles where she died in 1869. In her will dated 1868, she expressed her deep love for her husband, and thanked him for the respect he always showed to her and the freedom she enjoyed with him. She strongly recommended him to their three daughters.
Published here for the first time, this painting shows Fezli sitting for Schoefft in her residence at Naulaka with her two eldest children, Joséphine and Alexandre. In the background, the tomb of Nusrat Khan which was the headquarters of General Court's brigade, and the skyline of Lahore. This is one of the very rare interiors we have of a great Punjabi residence at Lahore before 1849. While in India, August Schoefft made several paintings on the spot. The painting of Fezli Azam Joo confirms that Schoefft accepted private commissions in Punjab. We can now safely presume that the portrait of General Court in uniform (not yet traced) which he bequeathed to his nephew Mazar in 1880, was also done by Schoefft in Lahore in 1841.

[210] Raja Hira Singh
"Rajah Hyra Singh" / "Rajah Heera Sing"
Gouache on European paper
By Imam Bakhsh Lahori. Lahore, 1827-1843
178 x 249 mm
Court collection, Musée Guimet. MG 78 III 41829

Raja Hira Singh, son of Raja Dhyan Singh, was one of the favourite courtiers of Maharaja Ranjit Singh, and one of the rare persons allowed to take a seat in presence of the Maharaja. "Enfant gâté" of the Prime Minister, as a child he enjoyed the paraphernalia of power. The *Umdat-ut-Tawarikh* records that whenever he was going to Jammu he asked General Allard for an escort of "French" cavalry, the most prestigious troops in the kingdom. He specifically got one *risalah* of *Francisi sowars* when he went there for his wedding in 1830. Hira Singh played an important role in the Punjab after the assassination of his father in 1843. Prime Minister in 1844, he fell under the spell of Pandit Jalla, his spiritual leader, and was killed in a revolution in December 1844.

[211] Raja Suchet Singh
"Rajah Sutcheyt Singh" / Rajah Semtcheyt Sing"
Gouache on European paper
By Imam Bakhsh Lahori. Lahore, 1827-1843
169 x 251 mm
Court collection, Musée Guimet. MG 78 III 41831

Suchet Singh, the youngest of the three Dogra brothers, was the most splendid commander of the *Gorcharas*, the irregular cavalry. He usually kept aloof from politics and enjoyed a great reputation as a courageous soldier and a great lover. His only attempt to power was in March 1844, when he thought he could appear in Lahore and wrest the power from his nephew Hira Singh. He reached Buddhu-ka-Ava with 45 cavaliers and sent an appeal to the troops. Not a man moved, while Hira Singh sent six regiments of elite infantry with 55 guns to extinguish this rebellion. The small Dogra unit fought to the last man and Suchet Singh was killed. Stories go that more than two hundred women in the Punjab, besides his thirteen wives and girl-slaves, committed sati when they learnt of his death.

[212] Sardar Jewaher Singh
"Sardar Djewaher Singh" / "Sirdar Jewahur Sing"
Gouache on European paper
By Imam Bakhsh Lahori. Lahore, 1827-1843
184 x 269 mm
Court collection, Musée Guimet. MG 78 III 39747

Brother of Rani Jindan and maternal uncle of little Maharaja Dalip Singh, Jewaher Singh played politics in 1843-1844 and was instrumental in the fall of Raja Hira Singh. Appointed prime minister by his sister in May 1845, he committed the fatal blunder to have Prince Peshora Singh, son of Maharaja Ranjit Singh, assassinated. He was asked to appear in front of the army and was executed in the presence of Rani Jindan and Maharaja Dalip Singh on 21 September 1845.

[213] Habitant of Bajaur
"Habitant de Badjore"
Watercolour on European paper
By Imam Bakhsh Lahori. Probably Peshawar, 1837-1843
108 x 196 mm
Court collection, Musée Guimet. MG 78 III 41824

The "Indian" miniature paintings of Court's collection - distinct from the "Afghan" drawings -

[217]

[233]

fall into two categories : the "Sikh" portraits, done in an oval shape with bright colors (gouache), and the more subtle drawings of the people of the Peshawar province, the Khyber Pass, the Himalayan foothills and the desertic regions of Bannu and Tank where Court and his brigade operated in 1840 (watercolours).
This man from Bajaur comes from a region north of Peshawar in the hills, whose chief Mir Alam Khan in 1838 was in close connection with the French commanders of Ranjit Singh at Peshawar. General Court was interested in Bajaur for its antiquities, and he sent some people there (Imam Bakhsh is not mentioned) to survey the country and copy the "Bactrian" [Kharoshthi] inscriptions.

[214] Habitant of Dir
"Habitant de Dhyr"
Watercolour on European paper
By Imam Bakhsh Lahori. Dir, 1837-1843
116 x 196 mm
Court collection, Musée Guimet. MG 78 III 41825

General Court sent two of his men to "Kafiristan": Haji Allah Dad Khan and Imam Bakhsh Lahori. The first was to collect intelligence while the second was to make drawings. Court recommanded them both to the chief of Dir, with whom he had friendly relations. Two of Haji Allah Dad Khan's reports in Persian are now in the National Library, Paris, and Imam Bakhsh's drawing is now a part of the Court collection.

[215] A Kafir Family
"Famille Kafférienne"
Watercolour on European paper
By Imam Bakhsh Lahori. Chitral / Peshawar
1837-1843. 194 x 298 mm
Court collection, Musée Guimet. MG 78 III 41832

The chief of Dir received the two emissaries sent by General Court cordially and recommanded them to the chief of the "Kamozi", or Kamoz, the Bashgul Katir of Chitral. Haji Allah Dad and Imam Bakhsh travelled to that area of Kafiristan, and in his *Memoirs* Court describes Imam Bakhsh's terror at the idea of being at the mercy of the *kafirs*. Imam Bakhsh made a painting of the Kamozi chief, his wife and their two sons (the painting we reproduce here). He then rushed back to Peshawar to the safety of the French brigades of the Punjab.
There are several copies of Imam Bakhsh's *kafir* family in various collections. They allow us to trace the link between these collections and the Imam Bakhsh workshop at Lahore. One collection is in the India Office, Add. Or. 1347-1396, consisting of fifty drawings probably from the same workshop and bound into one volume : the Kafir family is represented by the husband and wife only (Add. Or. 1355), and the same collection has *'Sawar-i-sher rajman'* correctly interpreted by "General Allard's Cavalry, Punjab. 1838".

[216] Habitant of the Khyber Pass : Shinvari, Afridi, Orakzais
"Habitants du Khéyber. Chinvari. Aféridi. Ouroukzeï"
Watercolour on European paper
By Imam Bakhsh Lahori. Peshawar, 1837-1843
171 x 249 mm
Court collection, Musée Guimet. MG 78 III 39736

Several miniature paintings done by Imam Bakhsh for General Court show the various tribes inhabitating the Khyber Pass. These tribes had ambiguous relations with the inhabitants of the plains : despising them for their agricultural occupations and acceptation of *kafir* rule, but envying them for the relative comfort of their life and proximity to Peshawar.
The governors of Peshawar had to settle terms with these Khyberi tribes for keeping the Khyber Pass open, assuring peace in the plains and securing water for the fort of Jamrud. In 1837 Maharaja Ranjit Singh entrusted this task to his French generals. These paintings are part of General Court's study of the populations he had to deal with, in peace and in war.

[217] Bronze mask of Lord Shiva
Bronze mask of an Indian deity discovered at Peshawar, now in the Cabinet of H.M. Louis-Philippe
"Masque en bronze d'une divinité indienne trouvé à Pichavor, Passé dans le cabinet de S. M. Louis-Philippe"
Watercolour on European paper
By Imam Bakhsh Lahori. Peshawar, 1834
132 x 170 mm
Court collection, Musée Guimet. MG 78 III 39752

An astonishing drawing of the bronze mask of Lord Shiva discovered by General Court at Banamari, near Peshawar, in 1834. Imam Bakhsh made this accurate drawing, taking great care of the inscription (undeciphered till 1990).Court sent the drawing to James Prinsep in Calcutta, who published it in the *Journal of the Asiatic Society of Bengal* in 1836. The bronze mask is today in the Cabinet des Médailles, Bibliothèque nationale, Paris. [Infra, N° 252-253]

[218] Frontispiece of the Fables of La Fontaine
Gouache and gold on paper
Imam Bakhsh Lahori. Attock/Peshawar, 1837
Musée Jean de La Fontaine, Château-Thierry

This brilliant composition is the frontispiece of La Fontaine's *Fables* illustrated by
Imam Bakhsh. Sitting on a *moorah*, Maharaja Ranjit Singh is flanked by Prince Nau Nihal Singh in yellow and Raja Hira Singh in pink, both seated on European chairs. On the carpet in front of the

[228]

Maharaja, we can easily identify Raja Dhyan Singh with the extra thumb on his right hand and Raja Gulab Singh. The third figure in green is probably Raja Suchet Singh. At the back are most probably Fakir Nuruddin with the green turban, and Raja Dina Nath with the white cap. The setting in a marble pavilion is drawn with a European perspective and not like traditional Indian miniatures.
When he penned his souvenirs for the review *L'Artiste*, the 83-year-old Feuillet de Conches said that the frontispiece showed General Ventura explaining the *Fables* to Maharaja Ranjit Singh and his Court. If the General told him so, it is one more case of deceit since Ventura was travelling in Europe in 1837-1839, when the *Fables* were illustrated. But it could also be a case of the author's confusion with the frontispiece of the *Military Manual of Maharaja Ranjit Singh* .

[219] La Fontaine, "La forêt et le bûcheron"
"The Forest and the Woodman"
Gouache and gold on paper

[234]

Imam Bakhsh Lahori. Attock/Peshawar, 1837-1839
Musée Jean de La Fontaine, Château-Thierry

In the *Fables*, Imam Bakhsh is representing various scenes of the Punjab countryside : here a woodcutter in the forest. The felling of trees, the main topic of the story, was of prime concern for La Fontaine, a nature-lover who used to spend a lot of time in the forests around Château-Thierry. But it might also have some connection with the deforestation of Punjab as well in that time, as also of Kashmir and Ladakh as observed by Jacquemont in 1831.

[220] La Fontaine, "Le petit poisson et le pêcheur"
"The Little Fish and the Fisherman"
Gouache and gold on paper
Imam Bakhsh Lahori. Attock/Peshawar, 1837-1839
Musée Jean de La Fontaine, Château-Thierry

On a riverside strikingly similar to some of the illustrations of the *Mémoires* of General Court, Imam Bakhsh represents a "French" officer of Maharaja Ranjit Singh fishing. With his beard just starting to grow, we can presume he is a fresh arrival. The Maharaja imposed two things on his foreign officers : grow beards and refrain from smoking.

[221] La Fontaine, 'Phébus et Borée"
"Phoebus and Boreas"
Gouache and gold on paper
Imam Bakhsh Lahori. Attock/Peshawar, 1837-1839
Musée Jean de La Fontaine, Château-Thierry

One of the most striking convergence of Greek mythology (Phoebus on his chariot carried by two winged-horses), Chinese clouds in the sky reminiscent of early central Asian and Mughal paintings, with a Punjabi landscape and figure in the style of Imam Bakhsh.

[222] La Fontaine, "La souris métamorphosée en fille"
"The Mouse metamorphosed into a Girl"
Gouache and gold on paper
Imam Bakhsh Lahori. Attock/Peshawar 1837-1839
Musée Jean de La Fontaine, Château-Thierry

A fable inspired by an Indian story on metamorphosis in which a mouse is transformed into a girl by a magician (dark blue man). In the background, the sun and the cloud, the two aspirants for the girl's hand. Note the flag in the garden and the delicately decorated buildings with typical Sikh columns.

[223] La Fontaine, "Le singe et le léopard"
"The Ape and the Leopard"
Gouache and gold on paper
Imam Bakhsh Lahori. Attock/Peshawar, 1837-1839

Outside the rampart of a city, in a meadow surrounded by trees, people have gathered to see an animal show, which takes place in front of the tent, on two elevated wooden platforms. The man exhibiting the monkey has a *dugdugi*, typical little drum, in his hand to rythm the show. Exquisite decoration of the border of the page.

[224] La Fontaine, "L'huître et les plaideurs"
"The Oyster and its Claimants"
Gouache and gold on paper
Imam Bakhsh Lahori.
Attock / Peshawar, 1837-1839
Musée Jean de La Fontaine, Château-Thierry

A rare depiction of the ocean, with two European ships which look more 17th than early 19th century. Punjabi artists often represented the great rivers of Punjab, including the Indus, as small rivulets with precise drawings of the riversides, but here the ocean takes up almost three quarters of the miniature.

[225] La Fontaine, "Le vieillard et les trois jeunes hommes"
"The old Man and the three young Men"
Gouache and gold on paper
Imam Bakhsh Lahori. Attock/Peshawar, 1837-1841
Musée Jean de La Fontaine, Château-Thierry

A rare mountainous landscape forms the setting for this philosophical story showing that death strikes at any age. The Muslim graveyard is in a peaceful green environment with a little town reminiscent of the ones described by von Hügel in the Himalayan piémont.

[226] Honigberger's Thirty Five Years ...
Plate I. "Maharajh, or Maharaja (King) Runjeet Singh
Maharajh (King) Kurruck Singh
Konwar (Heir-apparent) No-Nehal Singh
Maharajh (King) Shere, or Sheer Singh"
Probably from original paintings by Imam Bakhsh Lahori, 1829-1849
Punjab State Archives. Acc. N° 279

These accurate, refined and beautiful engravings, in contrast to the coarseness of most of the late series of the rulers of Lahore, come from a miniature paintings collection formed by Honigberger during his stay in Punjab. He took it with him to Europe and used engravings based on it for illustrating his *Memoirs*. The original miniatures are untraced uptil now.
It is interesting to observe the halo around Ranjit Singh's head, which is not the gold circle found on so many Mughal portraits, but a copy of the gold medal of the Maharaja struck in Paris and used in the centre of the order of Guru Govind Singh [N° 92].

[227] Honigberger's Thirty Five Years ...
Plate VI "Singh Sipahee (Sepoy)
Mooselman, or, Mussulman Sipahee (Mahommedan Sepoy)
Gorekhee Sipahee (Napaulese Sepoy)"
Probably from original paintings by Imam Bakhsh Lahori, 1829-1849
Punjab State Archives. Acc. N° 279

Honigberger states that "The lithographic engravings in this volume are faithful copies of portraits and sketches taken by a native at Lahore", except two portraits - one from Colonel Gardner's collection and the second from an unnamed collector.
The three soldiers represented here on one plate, all from the *Fauj-i-khas*, are copies of two miniature paintings done by Imam Bakhsh for General Court and now in Musée Guimet [N° 78], which is further proof that the collection of Honigberger also came from Imam Bakhsh's workshop.This is not surprising when we know of the close connection between Honigberger and General Allard : the physician operated upon the General's adopted son Syed Poor and saved his life just after he arrived at Lahore in 1829.

[228] Honigberger's Thirty Five Years ...
Plate VII "Haridas"
From an original painting belonging to Colonel Gardner
Punjab State Archives. Acc. N° 279

Fakir Haridas, the "Burying Faqueer", was one of the most famous and controversial figures in Lahore in the late 1830's, claiming he could be buried for several months. According to Osborne, even Ranjit Singh, Raja Dhyan Singh, Ventura and Wade were taken in by the clever *fakir*. After he was unmasked, Maharaja Ranjit Singh wanted to banish him from Lahore, but the man fled to the hills with a Hindu woman and died there some years later. According to Honigberger, this painting does not belong to the set of paintings done "by a native of Lahore", but was given to him by Colonel Gardner. The difference between this portrait and the other engravings of the books (most probably by Imam Bakhsh) is indeed glaring, while the similarity between this portrait of Haridas and the *fakir's* portrait in Schoefft's "The Court of Lahore" (Vienna, 1855) is amazing. Since Haridas left Lahore before the death of Ranjit Singh, it seems Schoefft copied "the Faqir" from Honigberger's painting in 1841-1842.

[235]

[122]

[229] **Honigberger's Thirty Five Years ...**
Plate IX "Attar, or Uttar (Druggist)"
Probably from an original painting by Imam Bakhsh Lahori, 1829-1849
Punjab State Archives. Acc. N° 279

"The Druggist is sitting outside his shop, serving a customer. A very small stand and simple distilling apparatus, with a refrigerator (cooling vessel) is before him. It is worthy of remark that not any name or labels are to be seen on any of the bottles or jars, probably to keep their contents a secret from others" (Honigberger)

[230] **Honigberger's Thirty Five Years ...**
Plate X "Bhangee (Hemp-plant drinker)"
Probably from an original painting by Imam Bakhsh Lahori, 1829-1849
Punjab State Archives. Acc. N° 279

"Chursee Bhistee, or Mushkee (a Mahommedan water-carrier) smoking churrus. In his hand he holds a hookah, which he is lighting with a coal taken from the fire before him. On his back is the goat skin in which he carries water.
Faqueer Postee (Poppy-head Drinker) smoking his hooka, while rubbing poppy-heads with his hands in a vessel with water, which he afterwards strains through a cloth and drinks. He is tattooed on the arm. Behind him may be seen the goat skin containing water". (Honigberger)

[231] **Honigberger's Thirty Five Years ...**
Plate XI "Kar-khana Abkaree (distillatory)"
Probably from an original painting by Imam Bakhsh Lahori, 1829-1849
Punjab State Archives. Acc. N° 279

"The Distiller, as well as the drinker, is a Mahommedan. This mode of distilling is however very imperfect" (Honigberger)

[232] **Maharaja Ranjit Singh in Darbar**
Signed by Imam Bakhsh Lahori
Gouache on paper
30.9 x 18.2 cm
Chandigarh Museum. Acc. N° 3722

Probably the first published painting of Imam Bakhsh : published by Mulk Raj Anand in 1981 and attributed by him to "Imam Bakhsh painter, Lahore, perhaps an apprentice of some Pahari artisan" who did it in a "Pahari-Mughal style". The difference with the Imam Bakhsh paintings we have seen is obvious. Still the signature is there and the painting, obviously done after 1843 if not after 1849, shows that the workshop was still active at that time.
Maharaja Ranjit Singh is seated on his golden throne, with his three sons and successors, Kharak Singh, Sher Singh and Dalip Singh, sitting in front, and the three Dogra brothers, Rajas Dhyan Singh, Gulab Singh and Suchet Singh, standing behind. Each figure is identified with a Persian inscription.

[233] **"A mason and a Labourer at work"**
Punjab State Archives, Chandigarh. Acc. N° 96

This painting and the following ones, describing everyday life in Punjab, comes from a set with watermarks "London" in the paper clearly showing the provenance of new masters and patrons. Their kind of hastiness indicates that they were produced quickly and probably sold at a cheap price. Nevertheless they show the tradition of Punjab popular paintings surviving under the Raj.

[234] **"Craftsman"**
Punjab State Archives, Chandigarh. Acc. N° 99

[235] **"Book Binder"**
Punjab State Archives, Chandigarh. Acc. N° 101

This miniature painting of a book binder reminds us of the remarkable activities of the Kashmiri and Lahori workshops reproducing both classical and modern literature in Persian, Sanskrit,Gurmukhi, as emphasized by Barbara Schmitz in her brilliant publications.

[236] **"Manufacturing Swords"**
Punjab State Archives, Chandigarh. Acc. N° 104

A flourishing activity in Lahore, according to many mediaeval sources, and still a noticeable item of export for the State in 1832 according to British intelligence.

[237] **"Hakim examining patient"**
Punjab State Archives, Chandigarh. Acc. N° 105

Different schools of medicine flourished in Punjab, including the Yunani school. During the reign of Maharaja Ranjit Singh, traditional medicine of high standard was dispensed by the Fakir brothers and several other *hakims* of repute. Sensing the pulse was, and still is, a major practice in traditional diagnostic in northern India. Ranjit Singh trusted his own physicians, but in 1826-27 he called Dr. Murray, a British physician, to Lahore. He is said to have treated the Maharaja's paralysis with an electrical apparatus recently imported from Europe. Dr. Honigberger, the Austro-Hungarian physician, had a long career in Punjab, first as an allopathic, and later as a homeopathic physician. Dr. Bianchi did not stay long, but Dr. Benet spent several years in the Punjab service under Maharajas Ranjit Singh, Kharak Singh and Sher Singh.

[238] **"Foundry"**
Punjab State Archives, Chandigarh. Acc. N° 116

Some of the commercial reports penned by British agents in Punjab, Afghanistan and Central Asia carefully described the metalworks sold in the bazars and commonly used by the local people. These reports were printed and distributed in Calcutta for the benefit of various commercial houses in British India.
Local foundries are very old in Punjab and northern India, with some remarkable achievements like the iron pillar in Delhi (5th century AD) and the bronze mask of Shiva (5th or 6th century AD) [N° 252-253]. The kind of foundry we see reproduced here was very common right from the Mughal period.

[239] **"Matchlock Manufacturer"**
Punjab State Archives, Chandigarh. Acc. N° 117

In the subcontinent, gunpowder was introduced by the Muslim armies, which were the first to use hand-grenades in the Sindh. Babur won at Panipat with the guns which he himself called *faranghia*. The Europeans introduced their own modernization of firearms and artillery. In 18th and early 19th century the French took a prominent part in sharing with the Indian states their know-how in military technology and organization.
Modern matchlock factories were established by enlightened rulers like the Nawabs of Awadh, the Sultans of Mysore, the Nizams of Hyderabad, the

Marathas at Pune and in northern India (Sindhia, Holkar), each one with the help of French technicians, officers or engineers.
In 1832 British intelligence observed that the matchlocks manufactured in Lahore were one of the main exports of the Punjab kingdom.

[240] "Tin Polisher"
Punjab State Archives, Chandigarh. Acc. N° 111

Copper vessels have to be tinned before they can be used safely for cooking and eating. This simple miniature shows an artisan carrying out the tinning process.

[241] "Brewer"
Punjab State Archives, Chandigarh. Acc. N° 122

There is a long tradition in Punjab, attested by discoveries on the site of Taxila, of brewing liquor. The techniques of infusion, boiling and fermentation are used to prepare alcoholic drinks as well as medicines. Here a brewer is stoking the fire while a client waits, empty bottle in hand.

[242] "Fuel Merchant"
Punjab State Archives, Chandigarh. Acc. N° 125

The deforestation of Europe from 17th to 19th century was partly due to consumption of wood as fuel in cooking, heating, forges, foundries and partly for carpentry, including the building and maintenance of blue navies. Punjab did not have any navy, but highly populated as it was, the problem of fuel was often acute.

[243] Great Stupa of Manikyala
"Coupole Manekyala"
Watercolour on European paper
By Imam Bakhsh Lahori
Manikyala. 1830-1843. 190 x 297 mm
Court collection, Musée Guimet. MG 78 III 41830

Ventura excavated the site in 1830, trying first from the side, and then from the top till he discovered the relics in a square room, 10.6 m below. Court excavated the monastery and smaller stupas in the area around, finding among other things the Kharoshthi inscription he sent to France.

[244] The Stupa of Manikyala today.

One of the greatest surviving stupas in northern India (100 feet high, 127 feet in diameter), its main structure dates back from the Kushana period. The stupas excavated by General Court, 3 km north of that one, have been identified respectively as the "Stupa of the blood-offering" and the "Stupa of the body-offering" mentioned by Hiuen Tsang (629-645 A.D). The Kharoshthi inscription, along with caskets of copper, silver and gold, was discovered by Court in the second one.

[245] Buddhist reliquaries and coins from the great stupa of Manikyala
British Museum. OA 1848.6-2, 1-4 and 5

Discovered by General Ventura in 1830, these reliquaries were first kept in Lahore and shown to many visitors. They were then sent by Ventura to James Prinsep, who published drawings of them in the *Journal of the Asiatic Society of Bengal*, 1836. Prinsep then took them to England where he died in 1840. They were deposited in the British Museum in 1848 where they are today in the "Prinsep Collection".

[246] Stupa of Bhallar, near Taxila
"Coupole Pahller dans le canton d'Osman Katter"
Watercolour on European paper
By Imam Bakhsh Lahori.
Taxila? 1830-1843. 195 x 291 mm
Court collection, Musée Guimet.. MG 78 III 39735

The French Academy did not believe the specialists who said that Manikyala was ancient Taxila. In the meantime, the French generals were advised to complete their excavations at Manikyala before starting work elsewhere. In his *Mémoires* Court says that the stupa of Bhallar was excavated by natives, who then discovered the real site of Taxila. Court unfortunately does not say who they were nor what they discovered.

[247] Kharoshthi inscription discovered by General Court at Manikyala
From H.T. Prinsep, *Note on … Discoveries in Afghanistan*, London, 1844
"Facsimile of a Aryan inscription from Manikyala Tope taken by James Prinsep from a wax impression received from General Court"

As soon as General Court discovered this inscription on stone in the "Stupa of the Body-offering", he sent a drawing and an impression to James Prinsep who reproduced it in his publications. The inscription proved useful in deciphering the Kharoshthi script in the late 1836-1838. As for the original stone, it was dispatched to France by General Court and fixed on the wall of the reading room in the Bibliothèque nationale, Paris. It is now in the Louvre Museum.

[248] Veira Ottar, a Hindu Deity. Discovered at Peshawar
"Veïra Ottar des Indous. Trouvaille faite à Pichavor"
Watercolour on European paper
By Imam Bakhsh Lahori. Peshawar, 1834-1843
167 x 168 mm
Court collection, Musée Guimet. MG 78 III 41823

"The Hindu who had this sculpture never agreed to sell it, maintaining that it was carved from an aerolite which fell from the moon. He keeps it carefully as a talisman for his family. In Europe some competent people also contend that aerolites are volcanic stones coming from the moon. One can see some of these bolides in the Museum [of Natural History] in France. An aerolite fell long time ago in Manja (Punjab) with so much strength that while penetrating into the earth it created a little lake, that people today show out of the tradition" (Court).

[249] Gold coin discovered in Punjab
Bibliothèque nationale. Cabinet des médailles.
Acc. N° L 547

Kushana coin of emperor Huvishka. Gold stater (equivalent to twenty drachmas)
c. 146-184 AD

[250] Gold coin discovered by generals Allard and Ventura in Punjab
Bibliothèque nationale. Cabinet des médailles.
Acc. N° AF (don Allard)

Kushana coin of emperor Kanishka II. Gold stater (equivalent to twenty drachmas)
c. 220-242 AD

[251] Silver coin discovered by generals Allard and Ventura in Punjab
Bibliothèque nationale. Cabinet des médailles
Acc. N° OB 36 (don Allard)

Indo-Greek coin (Indian weightage) of King Antialcidas of Taxila. Silver drachma.
Antialcidas (r. 125-95 BC) sent an ambassador, Heliodoros, to King Bhagabhadra in Vidisa (near Sanchi, Bhopal).This ambassador was a devotee of Vasudeva (Krishna) and erected a column there which is still standing in a bucolic surrounding.

[252] Bronze mask of Lord Shiva discovered by General Court at Peshawar
Front
"Tête antique découverte à Peshawer entre Caboul et Attock Près du haut Indus, par Mr le Général Court"
5th / 6th century AD.
H. 46 cm. W. 25,5 cm
Weight 4730 g.
Bibliothèque nationale. Cabinet des Médailles.
Paris

This extraordinary bronze was discovered by General Court at Peshawar in 1834. General Allard brought it to France in 1835 and offered it to King

[248]

Louis-Philippe: it is now in the Cabinet des médailles, Bibliothèque nationale, Paris.
The mask was studied and the inscription, a dedicace to Lord Haradawa, partly deciphered by Gérard Fussman in 1990. His conclusion : "There is no other mask of Shiva which is as big, as beautiful or as ancient as the Court mask, in any case none in metal that is so well dated and whose provenance is certain. For all these reasons the Court mask is an exceptional piece".

[253] Bronze mask of Lord Shiva discovered by General Court at Peshawar
Back
"Tête antique découverte à Peshawer entre Caboul et Attock Près du haut Indus, par Mr le Général Court"
5th / 6th century AD.
H. 46 cm. W. 25,5 cm. Weight 4730 g.
Bibliothèque nationale. Cabinet des Médailles Paris

Nothing is more surprising than the contrast between the obverse of the mask and the reverse which is clearly a Gandhara model used as support. Inside also is kept the label mentioning the discovery of the mask at Peshawar, "between Attock and Kabul", by General Court and the gift of the mask by Court to King Louis-Philippe. Related to the present-day *mohra* in copper or silver still used in the Himalaya foothills, but much bigger and heavier, this mask is one of the oldest and most beautiful Indian bronzes, and an exceptional masterpiece of 5th/6th century Indian metallurgy.

[254] Portrait of Victor Jacquemont (1801-1832)
Lithograph by Lemercier, from a portrait by Mrs. Léonor Mérimée
Private collection

One of the most brilliant young scientists of the time, Jacquemont also had a remarkable literary sensitivity and had friendly relations with Stendhal and Mérimée. In 1826-1827 he travelled to the United States to study the geology and botany of the Hudson valley.
In 1828 he came to India for a geological survey of the Himalayas, and he extended his survey to the kingdom of Punjab. His discussions with Maharaja Ranjit Singh in Lahore are among the most vivid testimonies of the Maharaja's wit, curiosity of mind and kindness.
During his stay in India, Jacquemont penned a voluminous correspondence with his family and friends in Europe, and he wrote a detailed *Journal* . After his death in 1832 his friends published a selection of his *Correspondence* which was a bestseller of the time and made Maharaja Ranjit Singh and the Punjab kingdom widely known in Europe.

[255] View of Dhankar
Illustration "Vue de Dhankar"
Victor Jacquemont's *Voyage dans l'Inde* , tome 5, Atlas, plate 46
Bibliothèque centrale
Museum d'Histoire Naturelle, Paris

Dhankar was a small village, only twenty houses forming a kind of defense as the "chef-lieu", or capital, of Spiti, The country had no more than 40 villages and hamlets. Jacquemont was struck by the almost complete desertification of these areas : "Not a single tree as far as we can see". Placed as they were, the people of Spiti were paying symbolic tributes to all their neighbours : Bissahir, Kulu, Ladakh and the Chinese resident at Garo.

[256] The head of the Tibetan Church in Kanawar
"Le Chef de l'Eglise thibétaine en Kanawer"
Victor Jacquemont's *Voyage dans l'Inde* , tome 5, Atlas, plate 55
Bibliothèque centrale
Museum d'Histoire Naturelle, Paris

In July 1830 Jacquemont visited Kanawar and left an interesting description of the country and its inhabitants. He described the polyandry of the women, the organisation of the lamas and the prerogatives of their head. On several occasions he met Csoma Korosi, the modest Hungarian scholar today ackowledged as the founder of Tibetology, who had been living in a monastery at Kanam, in Kinaur (High Bissahir), for some years.

[257] Map of Kashmir
Given by General Court to Jacquemont. 1831
Lettres de Victor Jacquemont
Ref. 2532, document 347
Bibliothèque centrale
Museum d'Histoire Naturelle, Paris

This map, from the Jacquemont's papers in the Museum of Natural History in Paris, was part of General Court's collection of maps, drawn by him (probably with help from his staff) from 1827 onwards. British political agents like Wade and A. Burnes were amazed by the intelligence and commercial networks of the French officers of Ranjit Singh in Afghanistan, Iran and Central Asia. They knew that General Court had done precise geographical surveys and drawn detailed maps of these areas. Court's letter to Jacquemont says that he is copying this map quickly so that Jacquemont can take it with him while leaving Lahore for Kashmir.
Note on this map the place written "Tchambé", which is Chamba, the native place of Bannu Pan Deï, wife of General Allard.

[267]

[258] Shalimar Gardens at Srinagar
Illustration "Shalibagh"
Victor Jacquemont's *Voyage dans l'Inde*, tome 5, Atlas, plate 69
Bibliothèque centrale
Museum d'Histoire Naturelle, Paris

Jacquemont was struck by the beautiful scenery of the garden, the freshness of the grass, the running water and the water-falls, the "colossal size of the trees" and in the background the light blue mountains covered by snow.

[259] Botanical plate : "Allardia Tomentosa"
Victor Jacquemont's *Voyage dans l'Inde* , tome 6,
[260] Ornithological plate : "Heron brag".
"Héron br ag"
Victor Jacquemont's *Voyage dans l'Inde* ,tome 6, Atlas. Plate 8
Bibliothèque centrale
Museum d'Histoire Naturelle, Paris

"The Sikhs call it 'Lomtingue'... The price of one feather (for aigrette) is one rupee (2,50 F). Every year two to three thousands are collected. They are all sent to Ranjit Singh who distributes as a present the aigrettes in which they are mounted. There are forty feathers in the Sikh aigrette. The Pathans used to put more than five hundred"... "The Punjabi name of the aigrette done with these feathers is Colegui; the Persian name is Djirehs, and in

Kashmiri Gounde".

[261] Entomological Plate : Butterflies"
"Insectes. Papillons"
Victor Jacquemont's *Voyage dans l'Inde* ,tome 6, Atlas. Entomologie, Plate 1
Bibliothèque centrale
Museum d'Histoire Naturelle, Paris

Jacquemont also collected butterflies for the Museum, and two colour plates illustrate the ones he captured in Punjab and Kashmir. On plate 1, n° 1, 2, 5 and 6 come from Kashmir; 3 , 4 and 8 from the Himalayas (3 and 4 discovered by Jacquemont). No information concerning the provenance of n° 7. On Plate 2, one has been captured at Lahore.

[262] Honigberger's Thirty Five Years ...
Plate VIII "Hakim, or Hakeem (Mohammedan or Mahommedan Doctor)

"The Doctor is feeling the pulse of his patient, behind whom is a urinal bottle. A medicine chest, containing simply electuaries and pills (in wooden boxes) is besides him. Before him lies his notebook, and near it his inkstand, with a cane-pen sticking in it, together with penknife, scissors, recipes, and a couple of pomegranates". (Honigberger)

[263] Fakir Syed Aziz-ud-Din
Watercolour on paper
20.7 x 10.8 cm
Chandigarh Museum. Acc. N° D-29

Eldest of the three Fakir brothers, Azizuddin entered Ranjit Singh's service as a physician soon after 1799. In 1808-1809 he refrained the Maharaja from declaring war on the British and he then became his most trusted adviser on British and European affairs. In 1831 he headed the Punjabi delegation to Simla in order to prepare the meeting of the Field of cloth of gold at Ropar (October 1831). In 1835 he and the American Dr. Harlan were sent to Dost Mohammed Khan of Kabul to keep him amused while the Punjab army was silently surrounding the Afghan army at the entrance of the Khyber Pass. Both of them were taken hostage, and released only after the flight of the Afghans in the Khyber. In December 1838 he organised the reception of Lord Auckland and other British high dignitaries at Lahore since Ranjit Singh was already ill.
More than an adviser, Fakir Syed Azizuddin was one of the closest friends of the Maharaja and he assisted him till his last hour in June 1839, being the only one at court who could decipher Ranjit Singh's almost inaudible utterances. He still conducted important diplomatic misions in 1839-1842, and then retired from public life. He died in 1845 before the disasters of the First Sikh War.

[264] Letter of Louis-Philippe, King of the French, to Maharaja Ranjit Singh
appointing General Allard as Agent de France to the Punjab
Tuileries Palace, Paris, 27 October 1835
Seal in Gold "Charte de 1830"
Last place known : the *toshakhana* in the Lahore fort
British Museum, Mss. Eur. G 59

At the end of 1834 Maharaja Ranjit Singh granted General Allard two years leave, ostensibly to bring his family to France and settle them in Saint-Tropez. The General promised to come back, and he did return to Lahore in March 1837. While in Paris, Allard delivered a message from Maharaja Ranjit Singh to the King of France, explaining the position of Punjab to the French Government. For the reasons stated above, Allard was appointed Agent de France to Lahore. He returned to India on a frigate especially sent from Brest to Calcutta, since he brought a full cargo of arms. He also carried two letters : one from King Louis-Philippe to Maharaja Ranjit Singh, and one from Duke de Broglie, prime minister, to Raja Dhyan Singh, "Prime minister of Punjab".
This is the credential letter of General Allard, delivered to Maharaja Ranjit Singh in full *darbar* in March 1837. The Persian original has disappeared. The French original was taken from the *toshakhana* of Lahore in 1849, most probably by Dr. Login. The person who gave it to the India Office is not mentioned in the entry records.

[265] "Treaty of Alliance and Friendship between Maharaja Ranjit Singh and Shah Shuja-ul-Mulk, with the approbation of and in concert with the British Government"
(Done at Lahore. 26th June 1838, ratified at Simla, 23rd July 1838)
National Archives of India. Acc. N° 121

Lord Auckland quickly let MacNaghten, then secretary in the Secret and Political Departments (1833-1837), take over British policy on Punjab, Afghanistan and Central Asia. MacNaghten decided to send an army to Afghanistan to reinstate Shah Shuja-ul-Mulk on the "throne" of Kabul, and thus thwart any Russian design on British India. Original proposals considered a joint Anglo-Punjabi military operation. But MacNaghten, more and more confident in the might of his troops and willing to downgrade the Lahore alliance, reduced the Punjabi contribution to the 5,000 troops mentioned in paragraph 15 of the Treaty.

[266] Cremation of Maharaja Ranjit Singh
Central Sikh Museum, Amritsar
Courtesy: Shromani Gurudwara Parbandhak Committee

Maharaja Ranjit Singh died on 27 June 1839. His cremation took place the next day. Four ranis and seven maidservants decided to burn themselves on the pyre. "The Brahmins performed their prayers from the Shasters. The Gurus, or priests of the Sikhs, did the same from their holy scripture called *Granth Sahib*, and the Mussalmans accompanied them with their "Ya Allah ! Ya Allah !" (Honigberger). The drums were beating. The consuming of the pile took two days. On the third the ashes were collected and conveyed to the Ganges in five palanquins which traversed Lahore, the Maharaja's palanquin being open. The ministers and high ranking dignitaries accompanied them. When they reached Delhi Gate, "a profuse royal salute was given by the thundering of cannon from the fort and the ramparts of the city". Then everybody returned home, and the cortege continued towards the Ganges under the protection of the guard.

[267] The Late Maha Raja Runjeet Singh
From an original drawing of Emily Eden
Lahore, 1838. c 22 x 17.5 cm
Maharaja Ranjit Singh Museum. Amritsar

In Amritsar, Maharaja Ranjit Singh received Lord Auckland and Emily Eden at the Rambagh Palace, but on arriving in Lahore, he was already too ill. It is the last portrait of the Maharaja.

GLOSSARY

Adi Granth: "The First Book". The Sikh holy book compiled by Guru Arjun and including hymns of his predecessors, his own hymns and some compositions of bhagats and Sufi saints. Also called Granth Sahib and Guru Granth Sahib.

Akali: "Adorator of the intemporal" (or eternal). Also called "nihang". A mystic and militant sect of Sikhism tracing its history back to Guru Govind Singh, the tenth and last guru. Its avowed purpose was the protection of the Sikh shrines and community. Under Ranjit Singh, they were organised into elite irregular troops quite similar to the Muslim ghazi . In peaceful times, their unruly behaviour made them difficult to control for any government. Their headquarters was at Anandpur, and their mystical centre was the Akal Takht, opposite the Golden Temple within the Harmandir precincts in Amritsar.

Akhbar Nawis: A newswriter, a person charged to send news to the court.

Bakhshi: Paymaster of the troops, also invested with military responsibilities.

Baradari: Lit. "twelve doors". Building in a garden with three doors on each face, e.g. Allard's baradari at Lahore.

Bedi: Sikh section of the khatri (former kshatrya) to whom Guru Nanak, the first Guru, belonged. Hence the privileges they enjoyed in the Sikh states, especially fiscal privileges in customs and octrois.

Beema: The insurance at a fixed rate of any property, goods, commodity transported by road (caravan) and river to its destination.

Bhagat: Poets of Hindu as well as Sufi origins whose stances are included in the Adi Granth.

Bhai: "Brother", also in the meaning of spiritual sharing and brotherhood. Title given to a Sikh of renowned learning and piety.

Brigades of Hindustan: Regular corps raised, trained and commanded from 1784 onwards by Benoît de Boigne for Madhoji Sindhia in the doab.

Bunga: Building erected around the sacred pool at Amritsar by members of the different misls, used as a resting place by the pilgrims of that misl.

Campu-i-mualla: "The great camp". Name given to the regular units which did not belong to the Fauj-i-khas or to another French brigade. The commanding officer of the Campu from 1826 to 1846 was Raja Tej Singh.

Caracoli: "an alloy of gold, silver and copper" used for several items discovered by the French generals of Maharaja Ranjit Singh inside the stupas they excavated, particularly the Manikyala stupas excavated by Ventura and Court from 1830 onwards.

Chaudry: The hereditary chief of a tappa, the subdivision of a pargana.

Cuirassiers: Heavy cavalry. The French army had 14 regiments of cuirassiers under Napoleon. In 1837 Allard raised a regiment of cuirassiers for Ranjit Singh. This regiment was equipped with French helmets, breast and backplates, swords and pistols brought back from France by the general.

Daftar: Chapter of a book. Collection of texts. Ministries (secretariats) of a government

Darbar: Government (Ranjit Singh's darbar). Royal court. Place where the Government meets (Ranjit Singh in the darbar)

Dar ul-Islam: "House of Islam". A Muslim concept that comprises of all states under a Muslim government (with or without a numeric majority of Muslims), or acknowledging the supremacy of another Islamic state. Legally speaking, the Sharia is enforced in the Dar ul-Islam, and two kinds of populations live there: the Muslims, and the Dhimmis ("protected ones") who accepted the pact of Dhimma . Any political unit which does not belong to the Dar ul-Islam falls under the category of Dar ul-Harb ("House of War"). The political relations between the two are regulated by two concepts : aman (truce) and jihad (Legal war).

Deoridar: "In charge of the door", the chamberlain, another name for the prime minister of the Lahore kingdom.

Dera, derah: The camp, or the place. Also the name of an artillery unit

Dhimmi: Religious and political minorities (though they can be the numerical majority, like in Mughal India or in Muslim Spain and Ottoman Europe) who belong to the Ahl-ul-Kitab ("People of the Book") and accept the pact of Dhimma (protection). The Dhimmis acknowledge the supremacy of Islam and accept an inferior status with many obligations derived from the Sharia and codified in the "Pact of Umar"

Diwan: under a Muslim government, the finance minister. Also the head of a ministry.

Doab: The land between the Ganges and the Jamuna rivers. That territory was entrusted to de Boigne by Sindhia, with the gift of 52 parganas in jaghir.

Dogra: A native from the Dugar Desh, in the foothills of Jammu.

Dragoons: Light European cavalry also trained to fight as infantry. Napoleon's cavalry of the line comprised of 20 to 30 regiments of dragoons . General Allard, a hussar officer, raised and commanded two regiments of dragoons (daragoon) for Maharaja Ranjit Singh. They were attached to the Fauj-i-khas .

Ducats: see Venetian ducats.

Fakir: From Arabic, meaning a poor man. A mendicant. A Muslim devoted to meditation. Also applied to Hindu devotees and naked ascetics. The surname was given by Maharaja Ranjit Singh to the Fakir family at Lahore, whose three brothers held important positions in the Darbar.

Farenghi: see Ferenghi.

Fauj-i-khas: "Special (or royal, 'King's own') army", "the French Legion" of British intelligence reports. A special military brigade raised and commanded from 1822 onwards by Generals Allard and Ventura for Maharaja Ranjit Singh. "Khas ", as for the Mughal Diwan-i-khas , had the dual meaning of "special" and "royal". This brigade, consisting of five regiments, was 5,000 strong and was organised on the pattern of Napoleon' Old Imperial Guard. The Fauj-i-khas, backed by Allard's cavalry (dragoons, lancers, cuirassiers) and Ilahi Bakhsh's topkhana (artillery corps), was the elite unit of the Sikh army of the Punjab.

Feringhi, Farenghi: The Franks, or the French, meaning the Westerners or Europeans. The military connotation was widely spread in the Dar ul-Islam, since Babur, in his Memoirs (written in Chaghatai Turk) called "Farangiha" the artillery he used at Panipat (1526). The name was attached to the Portuguese right from the early 16th century. When the East India Company established its sway in the subcontinent, "Ferenghi" was more or less replaced by "Angrezi".

Gaddi, Gadi: A cushion, a throne

Ghazi: A Muslim performing the ghazia , the "expedition", a compulsory duty for every male of the nomadic tribes of Arabia to go once a year on war against the sedentary populations settled all around the desert of Arabia. Ghazia was replaced by the word and the concept of jihad from the time of Prophet Muhammad, while the title of ghazi lasted till the early 20th century, when the ghazis became the mujahideens.

Gorchara: A horse-rider. The elite units of the irregular cavalry of Lahore formed from the rich sons of the land.

Granthi: The reciter of the Adi Granth.

Guru: A teacher, a preceptor, a mentor. The Sikh community acknowledges a hierarchy of ten Gurus, from Guru Nanak to Guru Govind Singh.

Gurudwara: "The Guru's door". A Sikh temple in which is kept a Granth Sahib. A place of worship for the Sikhs.

Gurmukhi: "From the mouth of the Guru". Script in which the Granth Sahib is written, and subsequently the Punjabi language written by the Sikhs.

Haj: The Pilgrimage to Mecca which every Muslim must undertake at least once in his life. He can then add the honorific title of Haji before his name.

Hukumnama: From hukum, an order. A command by a Guru or another Sikh authority.

Huri: Plural of Arabic haura, the women of Paradise described in the Koran, surate LV, 56-78 ; "Therein shall be the damsels with retiring glances, whom no man nor djinn hath touched before them...' (translation : Th. P. Hughes, Dictionary of Islam , s.v. hur).

Hussars: European light cavalry of Hungarian origin, hence their particularly flamboyant uniform all over Europe. French hussars served Hyder Ali and Tipu Sultan in Mysore from 1761 to 1785. Napoleon had 10 to 13 regiments of hussars. General Allard, who served Maharaja Ranjit Singh in the Punjab, was a former officer of the 7th Hussar, the élite de l'élite of Napoleon's Old Imperial Guard.

Indo-Greek: The composite culture(s) which evolved in the Greek state(s) of Gandhara (the territories south of the Hindukush in Afghanistan, down to the NWFP and part of Punjab in Pakistan).

Jaghir, jagir: a "place-holding", an assignment of land and its rent in exchange for serving the state. For the military officers, the revenue was used for the maintenance of a fixed number of troops (salary, equipment) and for their own remuneration as well. The jaghirs were not supposed to be hereditary.

Japji: A prayer composed by Guru Nanak and recited every day.

Jihad: "legal war" : One of the two possible relations (with aman ,"truce") between the Dar ul-Islam and the Dar ul-Harb. Originally, every able Muslim male had to do it physically, and rich handicapped Muslims had to sustain it financially. Jihad is waged not only for adding new territories to the Dar ul-Islam, but also when part of the Dar ul-Islam is threatened by an element of the Dar ul-Harb. Another instance of automatic jihad is when the dhimmis break the pact of dhimma and assume political independence, as was the case of the Greeks in Europe (1822-30) and the Sikhs in the Punjab.

Kafir: legally speaking an idolater. According to the Sharia, the non-Muslim population is divided between the Ahlu'l-Kitab, "People of the books", who can become dhimmis if they come under Muslim domination (Dar ul-Islam), and the kafirs, who do not have a book and worship idols.

Kafiristan: an area of the Himalayas (today divided between Afghanistan and Pakistan) where non-Muslim, non-Hindu populations live. The Afghan part of Kafiristan has been rebaptized "Nuristan" (land of light).

Kashi art: art of decorating buildings with enamelled or glazed tiles.

Khalsa: The order created in 1699 by Guru Govind Singh, the "community of the pure".

Khan: A Mongol, Turkish, then Persian title of nobility meaning lord, prince. In India under Muslim rule it became the traditional affix to any person claiming a Pathan or Afghan descent.

Khilat: A dress of honour given by a sovereign or a prince to a high ranking officer or distinguished visitor.

Kotwal: Head of the police in a town.

Kumedan: from the French "commandant". Highest grade given to Indian officers commanding native troops attached to the French army right from the 1740's. These troops were trained and equipped according to the French system of warfare. The English used the same title for their first sepoy units (Yusuf Khan for example, "commandant of all the sepoys" in 1760). This prestigious title was used in the "French" units created by Sindhia, the Nizam, and later Maharaja Ranjit Singh in the Punjab.

Kut, koot: Saussurea. A plant growing in the Himalayas. Used in pharmacology and perfumes, it is also used for the protection of Kashmiri shawls against moths and other insects. The presence of its smell was one of the ways to differentiate between an original shawl and its imitation.

Lancers: Light cavalry units (of Polish origin) introduced by Napoleon in the French army. Allard raised and commanded two regiments of lancers (Lansia) for Maharaja Ranjit Singh.

Langar: The community kitchen attached to each gurudwara where Sikhs and non-Sikhs alike are served food freely.

Lohani: see Shikarpuri.

Majha: The middle country, meaning the area in central Punjab between the Beas and the Ravi rivers.

Malwa: The area south of the Sutlej river, around Ludhiana and Patiala.

Manh: see Maund.

Marwari: inhabitant of Marwar. In a restricted sense, a merchant belonging to the ten Pothidar families originating from four villages in Shekawati and Bikaner. The Marwaris set up an extensive trading network in India in the 1770's. Their correspondents in Iran, Afghanistan and central Asia were the Lohanis, also called Shikarpuri.

Maund: unit of weight containing 40 seer, and weighing from 36 to 40 kg according to the area. Burnes however wrote in 1831 that the maund of Lahore corresponded to 100 English pound (46,56 kg).

Miri: The temporal power. Linked to Piri, the spiritual one, by Guru Hargovind who had two swords as the dual symbol of his authority.

Misl: from Arabic "misal" meaning "equal", term given to the Sikh confederacies which evolved in the 18th century and named after the village of the head (sardar) of each of them. At least twelve misls are recorded in the late 18th century.

Mooza, Mauza: A village, a hamlet.

Mufti: "An expounder of the Mahommedan Law, the utterer of the fatwa. Properly the mufti is above the qazi who carries out the judgement" (Hobson-Jobson, s.v. Mufty").

Mullah: a Persian abbreviation for maulvi, a pious Muslim in charge of the mosque in a village, and in charge of the attached school as well.

Nihang: See akali

Pahari: Lit. "from the mountain'. Name given to an original school of painting which developed in the Punjab hills from the late 17th century upto the 1850's.

Pahul: Rites of the Sikh baptism.

Pari, Peri: A supernatural winged creature, angel-like, sometimes riding a horse or an elephant. Well represented on the mosaic tiles of the Lahore fort done under Jahangir.

Platoon: From French "peloton" ; a unit of regular infantry.

Pothidar: "Homme d'affaires", treasurer. Bugatee Ram, founder of the Marwari House, was Pothidar of the Nawab of Fatehpur (Shekawati). Hence the name "Ten Pothidars " given to his grandsons and great-grandsons who managed the Marwari house in the 1830's.

Qazi: A judge administering civil and criminal justice according the Islamic Law.

Qissa: A compilation of legends or stories.

Rajman: "regiment", a unit of regular horse as opposed to the following term risala.

Risala: A unit of irregular cavalry, usually opposed to "rajman".

Ryot: From Arabic ra'iyat meaning a herd at pasture, and consequently the "subject" in India. Therefore the "tenant of the soil", farmer or cultivator.

Samadh: A commemoration building erected on the place of cremation of a prominent person.

Sardar: The head, the chief. Particuarly applied to the chief of a misl, and thereafter to every Sikh male.

Sawaran i-Frances: Lit. "French cavalry". Name given by the Punjabis to General Allard's cavalry : dragoons, lancers and cuirassiers.

Shalok, schlok, schloka : A stanza from a religious text.

Sharia: The Islamic legislation as it is enshrined in the Koran, developed in the Hadith (traditions) and interpreted by the various Islamic schools of jurisprudence. The best authority for its explanation and implementation is the body of Ulemas (sg. Alim, "savant"). They usually meet under the chairmanship of the Sheikh ul-Islam.

Shikarpuri: Lit. inhabitants of Shikarpur (Sindh). Name given to the families from Shikarpur (Sindh) who played a leading role in trading between India and Iran, Afghanistan, central Asia. Also called Lohani. Their "Indian" counterparts were the Marwari.

Shikesta: A quick "broken" way of writing Persian, difficult to read without a considerable training. Most of the existing records from the Punjab kingdom are written in shikesta.

Sheesh Mahal: Lit. "Palace of Mirrors". Rooms of Mughal palaces with thousands of small convex mirrors fixed in the ceiling. This technique was also used in Rajasthan (Amber palace), and by some rich Europeans living in pre-British India (e.g. Allard at Lahore).

Sikh: A disciple. A term applied to the disciples of Guru Nanak and his nine successors.

Singh: A lion. A name given to the male member of the Khalsa.

Suba: A province of the Mughal empire.

Taqawi: Money advanced to the peasant for developing his land.

Taziah: Lit. a consolation. A representation or model of the tomb of Hasan and Husain at Karbala, carried in procession during the Muharram festival by the Shi'ahs.

Timbol, Tembool Tambool: The betel-leaf. A gift offered on special occasions.

Tope: Lit. a mound. Name given to the hills under which archaeological remains lie. By extension, the stupa, big or small, discovered under the mound.

Toshakhana: The store-room, the treasury room.

Vakeel, Vakil : An authorised representative of a chief or a government. An ambassador or a chargé d'affaires.

Venetian ducats or sequins: gold coins struck in Venice, "long current on the shores of India" (Hobson-Jobson). They were still in use in early 19th century India, since E. Pottinger had some of them stitched in his garments when he set forth on his exploration of Sindh.

Zamindar: The owner of the land, the holder of a right on a land.

Zenana: a Persian word from zan , "woman" : literally the gynecee, or the section of the house reserved for the women.

SELECT BIBLIOGRAPHY

Ahluwalia, M.L.,

Select Documents. Ranjit Singh-Metcalfe Negociations, New Delhi, 1982.

Ahmed, K.A.,

Intercultural Encounter in Mughal Miniatures (Mughal-Christian Miniatures), Lahore, 1995.

——, and Nusrat Ali, "*Mirat-ul-Quds (The Mirror of Holiness) or Dastan-i-Masih*", *ibid.*

Aijazuddin, Fakir Syed,

Pahari Paintings and Sikh Portraits in the Lahore Museum, London, 1977.

——. *Sikh Portraits by European Artists,* London, 1979.

——. *Lahore. Illustrated Views of the 19th Century,* Lahore, 1991

——. *Historical Images of Pakistan,* Lahore, 1992

Aitchinson, C.U.,

India Foreign and Political Department. A Collection of Treaties, Engagements and Sanads Relating to India and Neighbouring Countries, vol. I, Calcutta, 1931.

A la cour du Grand Moghol, Paris, 1986, Exhibition Année de l'Inde en France.

Ames, F.,

The Kashmiri Shawl and its Indo-French Influence, Woodbridge, UK, 1988.

Anand, M.R., ed.,

Maharaja Ranjit Singh as Patron of the Arts, Marg Publications, Bombay, 1981.

Anonymous,

"Histoire du Royaume de Lahore", *in Le Magasin pittoresque,* Tome IV, 1836, pp. 1-15.

Apuzzo, Aniello,

Agerola. La Svizzera Napoletana, Naples, 1964.

Archer, M.,

Company Drawings in the India Office Library, London, 1972.

——, *Between Battles: the Album of Colonel James Skinner (a Portfolio),* London, 1984.

——, *Company Paintings. Indian Paintings of the British Period,* V & A, London, 1992.

Archer, M. and Falk, T.,

Indian Miniatures in the India office Library, London, 1981.

————, *India revealed: the art and adventures of James and William Fraser, 1801 - 1835,* London, 1989.

Archer, Mildred and William,

Indian Painting for the British. 1770-1880. An Essay, OUP, London, 1955.

Archer, W,

Paintings of the Sikhs, HMSO, London, 1966.

——. *Indian Paintings from the Punjab Hills, 2 vol.,* London, 1973

Arora, Faquir Chand,

Commerce by Rivers in the Punjab, Lahore, 1930.

Aryan, K.C.,

Punjab Paintings, Patiala, 1975.

B-40 Janamsakhi Guru Baba Nanak Paintings, Guru Nanak Dev University, Amritsar, 1987.

Baden-Powell,

Handbook of the Manufactures and Arts of the Punjab, Lahore, 1872.

Balboni, Maria Pia,

Ventura. Dal Ghetto del Finale alla Corte di Lahore, Modena, 1993.

Ballhatchet, K.,

Race, Sex and Class under the Raj, Imperial Attitudes and Politics and their Critics. 1793-1905, London, 1980.

Baluchistan. Imperial Gazetteer of India. Provincial series. Calcutta, 1908 [Lahore, 1976]

Bamzai, P.N.K.,

A History of Kashmir, New Delhi, *2nd edition, 1973.*

Banga, Indu,

Agrarian System of the Sikhs, New Delhi, 1978.

——, "The Social Mobility in the Punjab under Maharaja Ranjit Singh", *in Maharaja Ranjit Singh and his Times,* Amritsar, 1980, pp. 125-37.

——. see under Grewal, J.S.

Banerjee, A.C.,

The Khalsa Raj, New Delhi, 1985.

Bannerjee, B.N.,

Life of Begam Samru, Calcutta, 1925 [New Delhi, 1989].

Barr, William,

Journal of a March from New Delhi to Peshawur and from thence to Cabul, including travels in the Punjab, London, 1844 .

Barthoux, Jules,

Les Fouilles de Hadda. I. Stupas et Sites. Textes et Dessins, Mémoires DAFA, IV, Paris, 1933, and *Les Fouilles de Hadda. III. Figures et Figurines. Album photographique,* Mémoires DAFA, VI, Paris, 1930 (volume II was never published).

Bayer, T.S.,

Historia Regni Graecorum Bactriani, Saint Petersburg, 1738.

Bayly, C,A. (ed.),

The Raj. India and the British 1600-1947, London, 1990.

Bernard, Paul,

Fouilles d'Aï Khanoum. I. (Campagnes 1965, 1966, 1967, 1968). Mémoires D.A.F.A. XXI, Paris, 1973, 2 volumes.

Bidwell, S.,

Swords for Hire, European Mercenaries in Eighteen-Century India, London, 1971.

Blochet, E.,

Bibliothèque Nationale, Catalogue des Manuscrits persans, 4 volumes, Paris, 1905 to 1934.

Bopearachchi, Osmund,

Monnaies gréco-bactriennes et indo-grecques, Catalogue raisonné, Paris, Bibliothèque nationale, 1991.

Bouchot, H.,

Le Cabinet des Estampes de la Bibliothèque Nationale. Catalogue général et raisonné des collections qui y sont conservées, Paris, [s.d.].

Buckland, C.E.,

Dictionary of Indian Biography, London, 1906 [Lahore, 1985].

Burgess, J.,

The Chronology of Modern India. 1494 to 1894, Edinburgh, 1913.

Burnouf, Eugène,

Introduction à l'histoire du Bouddhisme indien, Paris, 1844.

Burnes, A.,

"On the Commerce of Central Asia", *Calcutta Monthly Journal*, 1833, pp. 306-66

——, *Travels into Bokhara and a Voyage on the Indus,* London, 1834 [Karachi, 1973], 3 volumes.

Cambon, P.,

Paris-Tokyo-Begram Exhibition. Hommage à Joseph Hackin (1886-1941), Musée Guimet, Paris, 1986.

Caroe, O.,

The Pathans, London, 1958.

Cary, G.,

The Medieval Alexander, Cambridge, 1956 [1967].

Catalogues

L'extraordinaire aventure de Benoît de Boigne aux Indes, Paris, 1996.

Guide-Catalogue du Musée Guimet. Les collections bouddhiques, Paris, 1923.

Nîmes et le châle, Musée du vieux Nîmes, Nimes, 1988.

Les canons de Valmy. Exposition de 20 juillet au 20 août 1989. Modèles réduits d'étude d'artillerie de la fin du XVIIIème siècle. Système Gribeauval. Hôtel National des Invalides, Musée de l'Armée, Paris, 1989. By Michel Decker.

Chaghatai, A.,

Le Tadj Mahal d'Agra, Bruxelles, 1938.

——, *The Badshahi Masjid,* Lahore, 1972.

Chandler, D.G.,

The Campaigns of Napoleon, London, 1966.

Chaudhry, N.A.,

Calendar of Persian Correspondence ..., 2 vol., Lahore, 1972-1985.

C.H.E.A.M., *Trois siècles de présence française en Inde,* Paris,1994.

Chopra, G.L.,

The Punjab as a Sovereign State, Lahore, 1929. Reed. Lahore, 1977.

Compton, Herbert,

A Particular Account of the European Military Adventurers of Hindustan from 1784 to 1803, London, 1892.

Cousens, H.,

The Antiquities of Sindh with historical Outlines , Calcutta, 1929 [Karachi, 1975].

Court, Claude-Auguste,

'Further information on the Topes of Manikyala, being a translation of an extract from a Manuscript Memoir by C.A. Court', *JASB* , III, 1834, p. 558-9.

——, 'Extracts translated from a Memoir on a Map of Peshawar and the Countries comprised between the Indus and the Hydaspes', *JASB* , 1836, p. 468-82.

——, 'Extrait d'un manuscrit sur le Taxile et sur le Manikyala par A. Court', *JA,* 1836, I, p. 561-72.

——, 'Conjectures on the March of Alexander, by Mr Court' in *JASB* , V (1836), p. 387-95.

——, 'Conjectures sur les marches d'Alexandre dans la Bactriane', *JA,* October 1837, p. 359-396.

——, 'Collection of Facts which may be useful for the Comprehension of Alexander the Great's Exploits on the Western Bank of the Indus', in *JASB* , VIII (1839), pp. 304 sqq.

—— : see Longpérier, Adrien de ; Prinsep, James.

——, *Mémoires,* 5 manuscript volumes. Volume IV et V on the Punjab, to be published by J.-M. Lafont.

Court, Henry,

History of the Sikhs, Lahore, 1888.

Culture et Développement (ed.),

L'extraordinaire aventure de Benoît de Boigne aux Inde , Paris, 1996.

Cunningham, J.D.,

A History of the Sikhs from the Origin of the Nation to the Battles of the Sutleje, London, 1849 [New Delhi, 1972].

Cuvillier-Fleury,

Notes historiques sur le général Allard et sur le Royaume de Lahore , Paris, 1836. Reprint of three articles published anonymously in the *Journal des Débats ,* 15 October and 16 November 1835, 19 June 1836.

Damamme, J.Cl.,

Les soldats de la Grande Armée, Paris, 1998.

Dar, Saifur Rahman,

'Excavations at Manikyala-1968', *Pakistan Archaeology,* 7, 1970-1971, pp. 6-22.

——, 'The Question of Roman Influence in Gandhara Art : Numismatic Evidence', *in Rivista Italiana di Numismatica,* LXXIX (1977), pp. 61-89.

Decker, M.,

Les canons de Valmy. Exposition de 20 juillet au 20 août 1989. Modèles réduits d'étude d'artillerie de la fin du XVIIIème siècle. Système Gribeauval. Hôtel National des Invalides, Musée de l'Armée, Paris, 1989.

Dewey, Clive J., (ed.),

Arrested Development in India. The Historical Dimension, Maryland (USA)-Manohar (New Delhi), 1988.

Deydier, H.,

Contribution à l'étude de l'Art du Gandhara. Essai de bibliographie analytique et critique d'articles parus de 1922 à 1949, Paris, 1950.

Dictionary of National Biography, London.

D'rozario,

The History of the Sikhs together with a Concise Account of Cashmere, Calcutta, 1846.

Duprée, L.,

Afghanistan, Princeton, 1973 [1980].

Durate, A.,

A History of British Relations with Sindh, Karachi, 1976.

Dussaud, R.,

La nouvelle Académie des Inscriptions et Belles-Lettres, Paris, 2 vol., 1846-7.

Eden, E.,

Portraits of the Princes and the People of India, London, 1844.

——. *Up the Country, 2nd ed.,* London, 1978.

Elphinstone, Montstuart,

An Account of the Kingdom of Caubul , 2 vol., London, 1815, 3rd edition by R. Bentley with corrections and additional notes,1839 [Karachi, 1972].

Errington, Elisabeth,

The Western Discovery of the Art of Gandhara and the Finds of Jamalgarhi , Ph.D. thesis, London University (SOAS), 1987.

——, 'Rediscovering the Coin Collection of Claude-Auguste Court. A Preliminary Report', *Topoi . Orient-Occident ,* 5/2, 1995, pp. 409-24, 4 plates.

——, 'The British East India Company Collection', *in* P. Callieri ed., *Seals and Sealings from the North-West of the Indian Subcontinent and Afghanistan (4th Century BC-11th Century AD). Local, Indian, Sasanian, Graeco-Persian, Sogdian, Roman .* Istituto Universitario Orientale, Naples, 1997, pp.20-27, plates 2-3, 9, 15, 22-3, 30-7.

——, Cribb, J., Claringbull, M.,

The Crossroads of Asia. Transformation in Image and Symbol. An Exhibition at the Fitzwilliam Museum, Cambridge. 6th October -13th December 1992, Cambridge, 1992.

Events at the Court of Ranjit Singh. 1810-1817, Lahore, reed. Patiala, 1970. [From the Maratha Records].

Extracts from the District and State Gazetteers of the Punjab. Vol. I and II (Pakistan), vol. III and IV (India), Lahore, 1976-1979.

Fane, H.E.,

Five Years in India. 1835-1839, London, 2 vol., 1842.

Fattal, A.,

Le statut légal des non-Musulmans en pays d'Islam, Beirut, 1958.

Fauja Singh Bajwa,

The Military System of the Sikhs during the period 1799-1849, New Delhi, 1964.

——, *Some Aspects of State and Society under Ranjit Singh,* New Delhi, 1982.

——, *After Ranjit Singh,* New Delhi, 1982.

——. *(Ed.) The City of Amritsar,* New Delhi, 1978.

Forster, G.,

A Journey from Bengal to England, London, 1798 [Patiala, 1970], 2 volumes.

Foucher, A.,

'Les bas-reliefs du stupa de Sikri', *in Journal Asiatique,* September-October 1903, pp. 185-330.

——, *La Vieille Route de l'Inde de Bactres à Taxila,* Mémoires DAFA, II, 1947.

——, *La Vie du Bouddha,* Paris, 1949.

——, *L'art gréco-bouddhique du Gandhara,* 2 vol., Paris, 1905-51.

——, *Les vies antérieures du Bouddha,* Paris, 1955.

Franklin, W.,

Military Memoirs of Mr Georges Thomas ... compiled and arranged from Mr Thomas's original documents, Calcutta, 1803.

Fussman, G.,

'Un masque de Siva provenant du Gandhara' *in Revue de la Bibliothèque nationale,* 37 (automne 1990), pp. 42-7.

——, 'Le 'Masque Court' : une effigie en laiton de Siva au Gandhara', *in Journal Asiatique*, 1991, pp. 137-74, 5 photographs, 1 reproduction of the drawing of the mask from the collection of Court's miniatures (Guimet Museum).

Ganda Singh,

Bibliography of the Punjab, Patiala, 1966.

Gardner, A.,

Memoirs of Alexander Gardner, Edinburgh and London, 1898.

General report upon the Administration of the Punjab Proper for the Years 1849-50 and 1850-51. Calcutta, 1853.

Ghulam Hussein Khan Tabataba,

The History of the later Mughals, Seir Mutaqherin, or Review of Modern Times : being an History of India, as far down as the year 1783, the whole written in Persian by Seid-Gholam-Hossein-Khan. Translated by Nota Manus, 3 volumes, Calcutta, 1789. Reprinted at Lahore, 1975.

Gole, S.,

Indian Maps and Plans from the earliest times to the advent of the European surveys, New Delhi, 1989.

Gommans, J.J.L.,

The Rise of the Indo-Afghan Empire, c. 1710-1780, New Delhi, 1999.

Goswamy, B.N.,

Painters at the Sikh Court ,Weisbaden, 1975.

——. "A Matter of Taste: some Notes on the Context of Paintings in Sikh Punjab" [25 illustrations], *in Journal of Regional History,* GNDU, Amritsar, 1981

——. "Painting in the Punjab", in S. Stronge ed., *The Arts of the Sikh Kingdoms,* London, 1999.

——. *Piety and Splendour. Sikh Art Heritage,* New Delhi, 2000

——, and Dallapicola, A.L.,

Krishna. The Divine Lover, Lausanne, 1982

——, and E. Fisher,

Pahari Masters. Court Painters of Northern India, Artibus Asiae, Zurich, 1992.

——. and Grewal, J.S.,

The Mughal and Sikh Rulers and the Vaishnavas of Pindari, Simla, 1969.

Goswamy, K.,

Kashmiri Painting: Assimilation and Diffusion; Production and Patronage, Simla, 1998.

Grewal, J.S.,

From Guru Nanak to Maharaja Ranjit Singh, Amritsar, 1982.

——. *The Sikhs of the Punjab,* Cambridge (UK), 1990.

Grewal, J.S. and Banga, Indu,

Early Nineteenth Century Punjab. From Ganesh Das's Char Bagh-i-Panjab, GNDU, Amritsar, 1975.

——. *(Ed.), Maharaja Ranjit Singh and his Times,* GNDU, Amritsar, 1980

——. *(Ed.), The Khalsa over 300 Years,* New Delhi, 1999.

Grey, C.,

European Adventurers of Northern India. 1785 to 1849, Lahore, 1929.

Griffin, L.,

The Panjab Chiefs. Historical and Biographical Notices of the Principal Families in the Territories under the Panjab Government ..., Lahore, 1865.

——. *The History of the Principal States of the Punjab and their Political Relations with the British Governments (The Rajas of the Punjab),* 2nd Ed. London, 1873.

——. *Ranjit Singh,* London, 1892.

Gros, François (ed.),

Passeurs d'Orient . Encounters between India and France, Paris, 1990.

Guimet Museum,

Guide Catalogue du Musée Guimet. Les Collections bouddhiques, Paris, 1923.

Gupta, H. R.,

Life and Work of Mohan Lal Kashmiri, Lahore, 1943.

——. [Same book revised and reprinted in 1987 as *Panjab, Central Asia and the First Afghan War,* Chandigarh, 1987]

——, *Later Moghul History of the Punjab,* Lahore, 1976 (reprint of his *History of the Sikhs,* vol. 2, Lahore, 1944).

——, *History of the Sikhs,* vol. 1 to 4 and volume 5, *"The Sikh Lion of Lahore. (Maharaja Ranjit Singh, 1799-1839)",* New Delhi, 1984-1991.

Gupta, S.N.,

Catalogue of Paintings in the Central Museum, Lahore. Lahore, 1922.

Guy, J. and Swallow, D., ed.,

Arts of India, London, 1990.

Hackin, Joseph,

L'oeuvre de la Délégation Archéologique Française en Afghanistan. 1922-1932. Les Antiquités bouddhiques, Tokyo, 1933.

—— : see Cambon, P.

Hans, S. (ed.),

see *Janamsakhi B-40.*

Harlan, J.,

A Memoir of India and Avghanistaun, Philadelphia, 1842.

——. See Ross, F.E.

Hasrat, B.J.,

Anglo-Sikh Relations. 1799-1849, Hoshiarpur, 1968.

——, *The Punjab Papers... 1836-1849 on the Sikhs,* Hoshiarpur, 1970.

——. *Life and Times of Ranjit Singh,* Hoshiarpur (India), 1977.

Heber, Reginald,

Narrative of a Journey through the Upper Provinces of India from Calcutta to Bombay. 1824/1825, London, 1827 [New Delhi, 1993], 3 volumes.

Hennessy, Maurice,

The Rajah from Tipperary, London, 1971.

Hoey, William,

A Monograph of Trade and Manufactures in Northern India, Lucknow, 1880.

Honigberger, Martin,

Thirty-Five Years in the East : Adventures, Discoveries, Experiments and Historical Sketches relating to the Punjab and Cashmere, in Connection with Medicine ... together with an original Materia Medica, and a medical Vocabulary in Four European and five Eastern Languages, London, 1852, 2 volumes in one.

Hügel, baron von,

Travels in Kashmir and the Panjab, containing a Particular Account of the Government and Character of the Sikhs, London, 1845.

Hughes, T.P.,

Dictionary of Islam, being a Cyclopaedia of the doctrines, rites, ceremonies and customs ... of the Muhammadan Religion...
Reprint Lahore, no date.

Hutchinson, L.,

European Freebooters in Moghul India, Bombay, 1964.

Hutchinson, J. and Vogel, J.P.,

History of the Punjab Hill States, Lahore, 1933, 2 volumes.

Ibbetson, D.C.,

Report on the Census of the Punjab of 1881, Lahore, 1882.

——, *Punjab Castes,* reprint of the chapter "The Races, Castes and Tribes of the People" in the above publication, Lahore, 1916.

Ikram, S.M.,

History of Muslim Civilisation in India and Pakistan, 3e. ed., Lahore, 1982.

Imperial Gazetteer of India. Baluchistan. Calcutta, 1908.

Imperial Gazetteer of India. North-West Frontier Province. Reprint Lahore, 1979.

Indo-French Relations : History and Perspectives, MSH-Embassy of France, New Delhi, 1990.

Ingram, E.,

The Beginning of the Great Game in Asia, 1828-1834, Oxford, 1979.

——, *Commitment to Empire : Prophecies of the Great Game in Asia, 1797-1800,* Oxford, 1981.

Irving, M.

List of Inscriptions on Christian Tombs or Monuments in the Punjab, North West Frontier Province, Kashmir and Afghanistan, possessing historical or archaeological Interest, 1910-12, 2 volumes.

Irvine, W.,

The Army of the Indian Moghuls, republished New Delhi 1962.

Irwin, J.,

The Kashmir Shawl, London, 1973.

Jacquemont, V.,

Voyage dans l'Inde par Victor Jacquemont pendant les années 1828 à 1832, 6 volumes (3 of texts, 3 of plates), Paris, 1836-41.

——, *Etat politique et social de l'Inde du Nord en 1830, ed. A.Martineau,* Paris, 1933 [Extracts from the *Voyage dans l'Inde. ..].*

——, *Correspondance de Victor Jacquemont,* 2 volumes, Paris, 2nd edition 1841.

——, *Correspondance inédite de Victor Jacquemont,* edited by P. Mérimée, Paris, 1861, 2 volumes. Reed. Paris, 1877.

Johar, S.S.,

Hari Singh Nalwa, New Delhi, 1982.

JA,

Journal Asiatique, published by the Société Asiatique, Paris.

JASB,

Journal of the Asiatic Society of Bengal, Calcutta.

JS,

Journal des Savants , published by the Académie des Sciences, Paris.

JSS,

Journal of Sikh Studies, published by the Guru Nanak Dev University, Amritsar, Punjab (India).

Kang, Kanwarjit,

'Maharaja Ranjit Singh's interest in the Art of Painting', *in Journal of Sikh Studies,* GNDU, Amritsar, IV-2, 1977, pp. 87-92.

Kapur, P.S., and Singh, D.

Maharaja Ranjit Singh Commemoration Volume, Patiala, 2001.

Kaye, M.M. (ed.),

The Golden Calm. An English Lady's life in Moghul India. Reminiscences by Emily, Lady Clive Bayley and her father, Sir Thomas Metcalfe, Exeter, 1980.

Keene, H.G.,

Hindustan under Freelances, 1770-1820 , London, 1907.

Kejarival, O.P.,

The Asiatic Society of Bengal and the Discovery of India's Past, New Delhi, 1988.

Khan, Ahmed Nabi,

A History of the Saddozai Afghans of Multan, Lahore, 1977.

——. *Multan. History and Architecture,* Islamabad, 1983.

Khan, F.A.,

The Princess Bamba Collection, Department of Archaeology, Lahore, 1961.

Khan, Ghulam Hussain : see Ghulam Hussain Khan.

Khullar, K.K.,

Maharaja Ranjit Singh, New Delhi, 1980.

Khushwant Singh,

Ranjit Singh, Maharaja of the Punjab, London, 1962.

——, *History of the Sikhs,* New Delhi, 2 vol., 1978.

Koch, E.,

"Jahangir and the Angels. Recently Discovered Wall Paintings under European Influence in the Fort of Lahore", *in* J. Deppert (ed.), *India and the West,* New Delhi, 1983.

——, *Shah Jahan and Orpheus. The Pietre Dure Decoration and the Programme of Shah Jahan's Throne in the Hall of Public Audience at the Red Fort of New Delhi,* Graz, 1988

——, *Mughal Architecture,* Munich, 1991

——, *Mughal Art and Imperial Ideology: Collected Essays,* Delhi, 2001

Kohli, S.R.,

Catalogue of the Khalsa Darbar Records, vol. I Lahore, 1919. Vol. 2 Lahore, 1927.

Kulbir Singh,

Trade and Industries in the Kingdom of Lahore, 1799-1849 , M.Phil. dissertation, Amritsar University, 1981 (unpublished).

Lafeuillade, Jean (Lt. Col.),

L'évolution Militaire Organique, Paris, 1937.

Laflotte, Commandant,

'Le Général Allard', *in Bulletin de la Société des Amis du Vieux Toulon,* 1927, pp. 107-32.

Lafont, J. M.,

French Administrators of Maharaja Ranjit Singh, 2nd edition, New Delhi, 1986. 19 illustrations.

——, *Le Penjab sous domination musulmane. 999-1799,* 1987 (Unpublished).

——, *La présence française dans le royaume sikh du Penjab. 1822-1849,* Paris, EFEO, 1992. 557 p., 1 frontispiece in colour, 15 maps. [Prix Giles 1995 of the French Academy].

——, [Editor], *Reminiscences. The French in India,* French Embassy-INTACH, New Delhi, 1997, 132 colour illustrations.

——, *INDIKA. Essays in Indo-French Relations 1630-1976,* New Delhi, Manohar-CSH. A Publication of the French Research Institutes in India, 2000. 72 B&W illustrations.

——, *CHITRA. Cities and Monuments of Eighteenth-Century India from French Archives,* New Delhi, 2001

——, "Colonel François-Henri Mouton : his unpublished Letter to the Minister of War, France, 1844", *in Journal of Sikh Studies* , IV-1, 1977, Guru Nanak Dev University [GNDU], Amritsar, pp. 55-72, 1 illustration.

——, "Bannou Pan Deï Allard and the Family of General Allard", *in Journal of Sikh Studies* , V-2, 1978, GNDU, Université d'Amritsar, p. 104-134, planches I à V. [Reprinted in *Punjab Past and Present,* XV-1, 1981, Punjabi University, Patiala, India, pp. 28-63, without illustrations]

——, 'Maharaja Dalip Singh and France', *in Journal of Sikh Studies* , VIII-1, 1981, GNDU, Amritsar, pp. 88-101.

——, 'Military Activities of the French Officers of Maharaja Ranjit Singh', *in Journal of Sikh Studies,* IX-1, 1983, GNDU, Amritsar, pp. 118-50.

——, 'Political and Administrative Activities of the French Officers of Maharaja Ranjit Singh', *in Journal of Sikh Studies,* IX-2, 1982, GNDU, Amritsar, pp. 29-73

——, 'Private Business and Cultural Activities of the French Officers of Maharaja Ranjit Singh', *in Journal of Sikh Studies,* X-1, 1983, GNDU, Amritsar, pp. 74-104.

——, 'French Excavations at Ai khanum (Afghanistan) and the Origin of Gandhara Art', *Oriental College Magazine, Centenary Volume,* LVIII, 1982, University of the Punjab, Lahore (Pakistan), pp. 25-62, 1 map.

——, 'Observations sur le commerce du Penjab et

du Cachemire, d'après un rapport de C.-M. Wade, 1832', *in Bulletin de l'Ecole Française d'Extrême-Orient,* LXXIV, Paris, 1985, pp. 58-78, 3 maps.

——, 'La présence française dans le royaume sikh du Penjab. 1822-1849', *in Journal Asiatique,* Paris, 1987, pp. 131-42, 1 carte, 3 illustrations.

——, 'Sur l'Inde et sur la France. Nouveaux regards', *in Rencontre avec l'Inde,* XVII, 1988, ICCR (Ministry of Foreign Affairs, India), pp. 13-22. Special issue published for the International Congress of AUPELF at New Delhi, December 1988. [Reprinted *ibid.,* 26/1, 1997, pp. 49-60].

——, 'Notes sur une collection particulière de peintures indiennes sur mica', *in Indologica Taurinensia,* XVI, Turin, 1987-1988 (published 1989), pp. 251-63, 16 colour illustrations. [Felicitation volume of Professor Colette Caillat].

——, 'Le mécénat français dans le royaume sikh du Penjab', being a historical introduction to Jean de La Fontaine, *Le Songe d'un habitant du Mogol,* Paris, 1989, pp. 177-81 [Ouvrage de prestige of the Festival of France in India].

——, 'Les Indes des Lumières. Regards français sur l'Inde de 1610 à 1849', *in Passeurs d'Orient. Encounters between India and France,* Paris, Ministère des Affaires Etrangères, 1991, pp. 12-33.

——, 'Les Français au service des Etats indiens indépendants', *ibid.,* pp. 34-40, 19 illustrations B and W, 9 colour plates.

——, 'European Curiosi in North-Western India during the Time of Csöma de Korös. 1822-1842', *in* National Seminar on Csöma de Korös , University of New Delhi and Academy of Sciences of Hungary, New Delhi, 21April 1992, published in *Alexander Csöma de Korös (1784-1842) Pioneer of Oriental Studies in Hungary,* New Delhi, 1992, pp. 67-87.

——, 'Les Indo-grecs : recherches archéologiques françaises dans le royaume sikh du Penjab. 1822-1843', *in Topoi . Orient-Occident,* 4/1, 1994, pp. 9-68, 1 map.

——, 'Tableau de l'Hindoustan à la fin du XVIIIème siècle', *in L'extraordinaire aventure de Benoît de Boigne aux Indes,* Paris, C and D, 1996, pp. 8-21, 9 illustrations, 1 map.

——, 'Benoît de Boigne. Essai de chronologie', *ibid.,* pp. 149-50.

——, 'Benoît de Boigne en Hindoustan. L'homme et son impact sur le Doab Gange-Jamouna. 1784-1795', *in L'Inde, la France, la Savoie. Le général de Boigne,* University of Savoye, Chambéry, 1996, pp. 157-91, 7 illustrations.

——, 'Observations sur la présence militaire française dans les Etats indiens. 1750-1849', *in International Seminar on History of Indo-French Relations and Indian Independence,* University of Pondicherry, 22-27 September 1997.

——, 'Politics and Architecture in the French Settlements', *in Reminiscences. The French in India,* INTACH, New Delhi, December 1997, pp. 15-49, numerous colour illustrations.

——, "Vive le Punjab! The French Role in the Building of Maharaja Ranjit Singh's Army", *NISHAAN,* IV / 2000, pp. 4-23

——. and Schmitz, B.,

"The Painter Imam Bakhsh of Lahore", Marg Publications, (forthcoming).

La Fontaine, Jean de,

Le songe d'un habitant du Mogol et autres Fables illustrées par Imam Bakhsh Lahori , Paris, RMN et Imprimerie Nationale, 1989.[Reprinted 1994]

Laissus, Yves (ed.),

Jacquemont, Museum d'Histoire Naturelle, Paris, 1959.

——. see Michel, F.

Latif, Syed Mohammed,

History of the Punjab from the Remotest Antiquities to the Present Time, Lahore, 1891.

——, *Lahore. Its History, Architectural Remains and Antiquities,* Lahore, 1892.

Lawrence, H.,

Adventures of an Officer in the Punjab in the Service of Maharaja Ranjit Singh, London, 1846, 2 volumes. Reed. Karachi, 1975

Leech, R.,

'Report on the Commerce of Multan', *in Reports and Papers... ,* pp. 79-88.

Leitner, G.W.,

History of Indigenous Education in the Panjab Since Annexation and in 1882, Calcutta, 1883.

Le Livre du Centenaire, Société Asiatique,

Paris, 1922.

Le Prieur, C.,

'Les miniatures d'Imam Bakhsh Lahori et la collection Feuillet de Conches', *in* La Fontaine, Jean de, *Songe d'un habitant du Mogol,* Paris, 1989, pp. 184-7.

Lévi-Strauss, M.,

La Mode du Cachemire en France, Paris, 1982.

Longpérier, A. de,

'Rapport de Mr Adrien de Longpérier de la Bibliothèque de France sur la Collection Numismatique du Général Court' (unpublished. No date).

——, 'Rapport sur la collection numismatique du Général Court', *in Revue Numismatique,* 73, 1839, pp. 81-8, with the table of this coin collection on p. 88.

Losty, J.P.,

The Art of the Book in India, London, 1982.

Louvat, capitaine,

Historique du 7e Hussar, Paris, n.d.

Macauliffe, M.A.,

The Sikh Religion, its Gurus, Sacred Writings and Authors, 6 vol., Oxford, 1909.

Madanjit Kaur,

The Golden Temple Past and Present, Amritsar, 1983.

Marg Publications,

Maharaja Ranjit Singh as Patron of the Arts , Marg Publications, 1981.

Marshall, J.,

Guide to Taxila, Oxford, 1936, reed. Cambridge, edition 1960.

Martineau, A.,

Le Général Perron , Paris, 1931.

McClenaghan, A.N.,

Indian Princely Medals. A Record of the Orders, decorations and medals of the Indian Princely States, New Delhi, 1996.

M'Gregor, W.L.,

The History of the Sikhs, London, 2 vol., 1846.

Marshall, J.,

Guide to Taxila, Oxford, 1936, reed. Cambridge

Mehra, P.,

North-Western Frontier and British India, 1839-42, Chandigarh, 2 vol., 1978.

Michel, F. and Laissus, Y.,

'Jacquemont et Stendhal', *in* Laissus, (ed.), *Jacquemont,* Paris, 1959, pp. 29-76.

Mohan Lal,

Life of the Amir Dost Mohammed Khan of Kabul, 2 volumes, London, 1846 [Oxford, 1978].

——, *Travels in the Punjab, Afghanistan, and Turkistan to Balkh, Bokhara and Herat and a visit to Great Britain and Germany,* London, 1846, reed. Patiala, 1970.

Moorcroft, William, and Trebeck, George,

Travels in the Himalayan Provinces of Hindustan and the Panjab, in Ladakh and Kashmir, in Peshawar, Kabul, Kunduz and Bokhara... from 1819 to 1825 ..., 2 volumes, London, 1837 [Lahore, 1976].

Murray, John,

Handbook of the Panjab..., London, 1883.

Nîmes et le châle, Musée du vieux Nîmes, Nîmes, 1988.

Norris, J.A.,

The First Afghan War. 1838-1842, Cambridge, UK, 1967

Okada, A.,

Imperial Mughal Painting, London, 1972.

——, see *A la cour du Grand Moghol,* Paris, 1986.

——, *Miniatures de l'Inde impériale,* Paris, 1989.

——, *L'Inde du XIXe siècle. Voyage aux sources de l'imaginaire* , Paris, 1991.

Orlich, L. von,

Travels in India including Sinde and the Punjab , London, 2 vol., 1845.

Osborne, W.G.,

The Court and Camp of Runjeet Singh, London, 1840.

Palluel-Gaillard, A.,

'Napoléon et les Indes', *in L'Inde, la France, la Savoie. Le Général de Boigne,* Université de Savoie, Chambéry, 1996, pp. 87-107.

Panigrahi, P.N.,

Charles Metcalfe in India. Ideas and Administration 1806-1835. New Delhi, 1968.

Parker, G.,

La révolution militaire. La guerre et l'essor de l'Occident. 1500-1800. , Paris, 1993 (Original edition, Cambridge, 1988).

Parks, F.,

Wanderings of a Pilgrim in Search of the Picturesque, London, 1850 [Oxford, 1975], 2 volumes.

Patwant Singh,

The Golden Temple, New Delhi, 1988.

Paul, S.,

"A Dated Sikandarnama Shawl in the Chandigarh Museum", *Lalit Kala,* 20.

——, *Sikh Miniatures in the Chandigarh Museum,* Chandigarh, 1985.

Philips, C.H.,

The Correspondence of Lord William Bentinck, Governor-General of India 1828-1835, London, 2 vol., 1977.

Pottinger, H.,

Travels in Beloochistan and Sinde, London, 1816 [Farnborough, 1972].

PPP : Punjab Past and Present , Journal published by the Punjabi University, Patiala, Punjab (India).

Press Lists of the Punjab Records , vol. III, Lahore, 1915.

Prinsep, H. T.,

Origin of the Sikh Power in the Punjab and Political Life of Maha-raja Ranjit Singh, Calcutta, 1834 [Patiala, 1970].

——, *idem.* French translation by Xavier Raymond under the title *Origine et Progrès de la Puissance des Sikhs dans le Penjab,* Paris, 1836.

——, *Note on the Historical Results deducible from Recent Discoveries in Afghanistan,* London, 1844.

Prinsep, J.,

Essays on Indian Antiquities, Historic, Numismatic and Palaeographic, of the late James Prinsep ..., edited by E. Thomas, London, 1858, [New Delhi, 1971], 2 volumes.

——, 'Discovery of an ancient Town near Behat, in the Doab of the Jam'na and Ganges by Capt. P. T. Cautley, Superintendent, Doab Canal', *in* J. Prinsep, *Essays on Indian Antiquities,* vol. I, pp. 73-89, reprinted from *JASB,* III, January and April 1834.

——, 'Note on the Coins discovered by M. Court', *in JASB* , III, 1834, pp. 562-7, plate XXXIV.

——, 'Further Information on Manikyala by Gen. Court', *in* J. Prinsep, *Essays on Indian Antiquities ...,* vol. I, pp. 138-59.

——, 'Addition to Bactrian Numismatics and Discovery of the Bactrian Alphabet' (July 1838), *in* Prinsep, J., *Essays on Indian Antiquities...* , vol II, p. 125-44.

——, 'Review of the Bactrian Alphabet', *in* J. Prinsep, *Essays on Indian Antiquities,* vol. II, p. 144-68.

——, 'Further Information on the Topes of Manikyala. By Gen. Court', and plate IX, with the commentaries of Prinsep and Thomas in J. Prinsep, *Essays on Indian Antiquities* , vol I, p. 138-159.

——, 'On the Coins and Relics discovered by M. le Chevalier Ventura, General in the Service of Maha Raja (sic) Ranjit Singh, in the Tope of Manikyala. [July 1834]', *in* J. Prinsep, *Essays on Indian Antiquities,* vol. I., p. 90-109, plates V, VI and VII for their publication, with notes by Thomas.

Prost, Philippe,

Les forteresses de l'Empire. Fortifications, villes de guerre et arsenaux napoléoniens, Paris, 1991.

Punjab Gazetteers,

Punjab Gazetteers, see *Extracts from the Districts and States Gazetteers ...*

Quraeshi, S.,

Lahore, the City within, Lahore, 1988.

Qureshi, I.H.,

Ulema in Politics, Karachi, 2e ed. 1974.

——, *The Muslim Community of the Indo-Pakistan Subcontinent, 610-1947,* 2e ed., Karachi, 1977.

Rahmani, A.

Introduction to Manuscripts Gallery, Lahore Museum, Lahore, 1988.

——, *Masterpieces of Lahore Museum,* Lahore, 1999.

Ramakrishna, Lajwanti,

Les Sikhs. Origine et développement de la communauté jusqu'à nos jours (1469-1930), Paris, 1933.

——. *Panjabi Sufi Poets* , Oxford, 1938 [reprint New Delhi, 1973]

Randhava, T.S.,

The Sikhs. Image of a Heritage , New Delhi, 2000

Reports and Papers,

Reports and Papers, Political, Geographical and Commercisal, submitted to Government by Sir Alexander Burnes, Lieutenant Leech, Doctor Lord and Lieutenant Wood employed on Missions in the Years 1835-36-37 in Scinde, Afghanistan and Adjacent Countries, Calcutta, 1839.

Roberts, P.E.,

History of British India under the Company and the Crown, completed by T.G.P. Spear, 3rd edition (with corrections), 1958, Oxford.

Robertson, G.S.,

The Kafirs of the Hindu-Kush, London, 1896.

Rochette, Raoul,

Notice sur quelques médailles grecques inédites appartenant à des rois inconnus de la Bactriane et de l'Inde, 28 p., 1 pl. (off-print of *Journal des Savants,* 1834).

——, *Supplément à la notice sur quelques médailles etc...,* 35 p., 2 pl. (off-print of *Journal des Savants,* 1835).

——, *Deuxième supplément à la notice etc...,* 62 p., 1 pl. (off-print of *Journal des Savants,* 1836).

——, 'Troisième supplément à la notice ... Deuxième article', *in Journal des Savants,* Feb. 1839, pp. 89-108.

Rose, H.A.,

A Glossary of the Tribes and Castes of the Punjab and the North-Western Provinces, 3 vol., Lahore, 1919.

Ross, F.E.,

Central Asia. Personal Narrative of General Josiah Harlan 1823-1841, London, 1939.

Rosselli, J.,

Lord William Bentinck. The Making of a Liberal Imperialist 1774-1839, London, Indian edition New Delhi, 1974.

Roux A., de Fauchère N., Monsaingeon G,

Les plans en relief des places du Roy , Paris, 1989.

Saint-Genis, Victor de,

Le général de Boigne. 1751-1830, Poitiers, 1873.

Saint Venant, Marie-Gabrielle de,

Benoît de Boigne (1751-1830). Du général au particulier, Chambéry, 1996.

Sandhu, A.S.,

General Hari Singh Nalwa, Lahore, 1935.

Sarkar, Sir Jadunath,

Fall of the Mughal Empire, 4 volumes, New Delhi,

1972 [First Edition 1950].

Schmitz, B.,

Islamic Manuscripts in the New York Public Library, New York and Oxford, 1992.

——, *Islamic and Indian Manuscripts and Paintings in the Pierpont Morgan Library,* New York, 1997.

——, *Illustrated Manuscripts and Albums in the Raza Library, Rampur,* New Delhi (forthcoming).

——, and Lafont J.M., "*The Painter Imam Bakhsh of Lahore*", Marg Publications, (forthcoming).

Schwab, Raymond,

La Renaissance orientale, Paris, 1950.

Selections from the Records of the Government of the Punjab, New Series, n° XVI, Lahore, 1880.

Sethi, R.R.,

The Lahore Darbar (in the light of the Correspondence of Sir C.M. Wade, 1823-1840), New Delhi, 1950.

——. *The Mighty and Shrewd Maharaja [Ranjit Singh's Relations with other Powers],* New Delhi, 1960. [practically the same as above]

Shahamat Ali,

Sikhs and Afghans in Connection with India and Persia, London, 1847.

Sharif, Jaffar,

Islam in India or the Qanun-i-Islam. The Customs of the Musalmans of India..., 1832, reed. Oxford, 1921.

Sharma, D.C.,

Kashmir under the Sikhs, New Delhi, 1983.

Siddiqi, Jamal Moh.,

'Aligarh (1791-1803). Quartier général administratif des genéraux de Boigne et Perron', *in* C and D. (ed.), *L'extraordinaire aventure de Benoît de Boigne aux Indes,* pp. 61-6, 6 illustrations.

Sinha, N.K.,

Ranjit Singh , Calcutta, 1933.

——. *Rise of the Sikh Power* , Calcutta, 1936.

Sinha, N.K., and Dasgupta, A.K.,

Selections From Ochterlony Papers in the National Archives of India (1818-1825), Calcutta 1964.

Smyth, G.C.,

A History of the Reigning Family of Lahore ..., Calcutta, 1847.

Sohan Lal : see Suri

Soltykoff, Alexis,

Voyages dans l'Inde, Paris, 1851.

Spain, J.W.,

The Pathan Borderland, La Haye, 1963.

Srivastava, R.P.,

Punjab Paintings, New Delhi 1983.

Steinbach, Henry,

The Punjaub, being a Brief Account of the History of the Sikhs, 2nd edition London, 1846 [Karachi, 1976].

Stronge, Susan (Ed.),

The Arts of the Sikh Kingdoms, London, 1999.

Suri, Sohan Lal,

Umdat-ut-Tawarikh , Daftar II (unpublished: Manuscript of the translation kindly communicated by V.S. Suri), *and Daftar III, 1831-9,* translated and edited by V.S. Suri, Chandigarh, 1974.

Suri, V.S.,

Panjab Through the Ages, Chandigarh, 1971.

Temple, R.C.,

The Legends of the Panjab, 3 volumes, reprint Patiala, 1962-1963.

Thairani, A.K.,

British Political Missions to Sind, 2nd edition, Karachi, 1981.

Théroulde, Saint-Hubert,

Voyage dans l'Inde. Notes recueillies en 1838, 1839 et 1840..., Paris, 1843.

Thomas, E.,

Ancient Indian Weights, 1874 [Varanasi, 1970].

Thomas, R.H. (ed.),

Memoirs on Sindh, 2 vol., Bombay, 1855 [Karachi, 1979].

Thornton, E.,

A Gazetteer of the Countries adjacent to India on North-West, including Sindh, Afghanistan, Beluchistan, the Punjab and the Neighbouring States, London, 1844, 2 vol.

Tod, James,

Annals and Antiquities of Rajasthan, London, 1829-32 [New Delhi, 1978, 2 volumes].

Trevaskis, H.K.,

The Land of the Five Rivers, Oxford, 1928.

Tulard, J.,

Napoléon, 4th ed., Paris, 1987.

Vigne, G.T.,

A Personal Narrative of a Visit to Ghuzni, Kabul and Afghanistan and of a Residence at the Court of Dost Mohammed Khan…, London, 1840 [Lahore, 1982].

Villepin, D. de,

Les Cent-Jours ou l'esprit du sacrifice, Paris, 2001.

Vogel, Jean-Philippe,

The Tile-Mosaics of the Lahore Fort, ASI, 1920 [reprinted in Karachi, no date].

Wade, Claude-Martine,

Narrative of the Services ... of Lieut-Col. Sir C.M.Wade, C.B., no date [1847], Isle of Wight.

Waheed-ud-Din, Fakir Syed,

The Real Ranjit Singh, Lahore, 1965.

Walia, J.M.,

Parties and Politics at the Sikh Court, New Delhi, 1982.

Watt, G.,

Indian Art at Delhi, Calcutta, 1903.

——, *The Commercial Products of India,* London, 1908.

Welch, S.C.,

Room for Wonder, Indian Painting during the British Period, 1760-1880, New York, 1978.

——, *India: Art and Culture. 1300-1900,* New York, 1985.

Wendel, François-Xavier, s.j.,

Les Mémoires de Wendel sur les Jat, les Pathan et les Sikh, ed. by J. Deloche, Paris, EFEO, 1979.

Whitteridge, G.,

Charles Masson of Afghanistan . Explorer, Archaeologist, Numismatist and Intelligence Agent, Warminster [U.K.], 1986.

Wilson, H.H.,

Ariana Antiqua, London, 1841 [Dehli, 1971].

Yapp, M. E.,

Strategies of British India. Britain, Iran and Afghanistan. 1789-1850, Oxford, 1980.

Young, Desmond,

Fountain of the Elephants, London, 1959.

Yule,Sir Henry, and Burnell, A.C.,

Hobson-Jobson. A Glossary of colloquial Anglo-Indian Words and Phrases..., New edition by William Crooke, reprinted New Delhi, 1979.

Zaidi, Inayat A.,

'French Mercenaries in the Armies of South-Asian States, 1499-1803', *in Indo-French Relations. History and Perspectives,* MSH-Ambassade de France, New Delhi, 1990, pp. 51-78.

Zwalff, W.

A Catalogue of the Gandhara Sculpture in the British Museum, 2 vol., London, 1996.

INDEX

Please note that the index covers only the text and not the catalogue.